GLOBALIZATION
AND NGOs

GLOBALIZATION AND NGOs

Transforming Business, Government, and Society

Edited by Jonathan P. Doh
and Hildy Teegen

Foreword by Jone L. Pearce

Westport, Connecticut
London

Library of Congress Cataloging-in-Publication Data

Globalization and NGOs : transforming business, government, and society / edited by
   Jonathan P. Doh and Hildy Teegen ; foreword by Jone L. Pearce.
      p.   cm.
   Includes bibliographical references and index.
   ISBN 1–56720–499–6 (alk. paper)
   1. Non-governmental organizations.   2. Economic dvelopment.   3. Social change.   4.
   Globalization.   I. Doh, Jonathan P.   II. Teegen, Hildy.
   HC60.G537   2003
   338.8′7—dc21   2003042857

British Library Cataloguing in Publication Data is available.

Library of Congress Catalog Card Number: 2003042857
ISBN: 1–56720–499–6

First published in 2003

Praeger Publishers, 88 Post Road West, Westport, CT 06881
An imprint of Greenwood Publishing Group, Inc.
www.praeger.com

Printed in the United States of America

To David and Robin,
without whose support this book would not have been possible.

We would like to dedicate this book to the memory
of Marc Lindenberg,
a pioneer in communicating the importance
of the nongovernmental sector
and a leader in fostering collaborations
among public, private, and not-for-profit organizations.

Contents

Figures   ix

Foreword   xi
Jone L. Pearce

Preface: Globalization and NGOs—Why Should We Care?   xv
Jonathan P. Doh and Hildy Teegen

1   Nongovernmental Organizations, Corporate Strategy, and Public Policy: NGOs as Agents of Change   1
Jonathan P. Doh

2   Nongovernmental Organizations and Business–Government Relations: The Importance of Institutions   19
Gerald Keim

3   After Seattle: How NGOs Are Transforming the Global Trade and Finance Agenda   35
Jacqueline Deslauriers and Barbara Kotschwar

4   Cooperative Strategies in Environmental Nongovernmental Organizations   65
Jonathan P. Doh, William E. Newburry, and Hildy Teegen

5 Prospects for NGO Collaboration with Multinational
   Enterprises   81
   A. Rani Parker

6 Business–Government–NGO Bargaining in International,
   Multilateral Clean Development Mechanism Projects
   in the Wake of Kyoto   107
   Hildy Teegen

7 Corporate Strategy, Government Regulatory Policy, and
   NGO Activism: The Case of Genetically Modified Crops   129
   Edward Soule

8 From Boycotts to Global Partnership: NGOs, the Private
   Sector, and the Struggle to Protect the World's Forests   157
   Joseph Domask

9 Corporate Social Responsibility and NGOs:
   Observations from a Global Power Company   187
   Gregory Adams

10 Conclusion: Globalization and the Future of
   NGO Influence   203
   Hildy Teegen and Jonathan P. Doh

   Index   223

   About the Editors and Contributors   233

Figures

1.1 Corporate Strategy, Public Policy, and the
    Business–Government Interface:
    Direct Effects Model with NGOs as "Zs"   7

1.2 Corporate Strategy, Public Policy, and the
    Business–Government Interface:
    Interaction Effects Model with NGOs as Moderators   9

1.3 Corporate Strategy, Public Policy, and the
    Business–Government Interface:
    Interaction Effects Model with NGOs as Mediators   9

1.4 Corporate Strategy, Public Policy, and the
    Business–Government Interface: NGOs as
    Integrated, Multidimensional Network Participants   11

2.1 Issue Life Cycle   27

4.1 NGO Cooperative Ventures: Cooperative Goal Focus
    and Cooperative Connection Focus   68

4.2 Representatives' Cooperative Ventures of the World
    Wildlife Fund and Worldwide Fund for Nature   74

7.1 Taxonomy of NGOs   139

7.2 Relationships among Key Stakeholders   145

8.1 Broad Changes in Drivers of Deforestation and
     Responses over Time   167

8.2 FSC Institutional Structure and Related Key Actors   172

Foreword

Jone L. Pearce

Nongovernmental organizations (NGOs) are changing the way we all do business. For all but the smallest and most local of businesses, a new actor has appeared on the scene, one that is well organized, innovative, and powerful. *Nongovernmental organizations* is the term given to those nonprofit associations focused on social change via political influence, or to those providing social and humanitarian services in highly politicized cross-national contexts. Because these groups exist to press social changes, they had not been something that most businesses noticed or managed. Of course, all but the smallest businesses have attended to the governments in those settings where they operate; governments have sovereign coercive power and can tax, regulate, and even expropriate at will. The larger the business, the more likely it is to be important to its local government and so the more likely that business is to manage its governmental relationship—via governmental affairs departments, publicists, lobbyists, or by developing close personal relationships with important government officials. Businesses that had to worry about politics did so and developed sophisticated tools to manage those relationships.

All this changed about a decade ago. Suddenly businesses were attacked from a wholly unexpected quarter. Most prominently, Star-Kist found that the icon it had invested millions of dollars in creating and nurturing was flipped and used against it. Now their advertisements featuring Charlie Tuna were converted into a high-visibility advertising campaign against the use of nets that killed dolphins.

The company had little choice but to insist on dolphin-safe nets and to use its own formidable influence with government to press for legislation requiring dolphin-safe nets industrywide so that its competitors would not have a cost advantage over them. Now nationally and internationally known brands are not just marketing investments, they are potential political vulnerabilities.

But NGOs are not just a factor in the developed world. In developing countries, businesses that were used to managing governmental relationships personally now find that they have to contend with large and (comparatively) rich NGOs that can bring pressure to bear on their local governments via influence with donor-country governments that control substantial amounts of revenue coming into the country. Logging rights can no longer be secured over an amicable dinner at the club; now foreign NGOs are able to impinge on business dealings in ways that were unimaginable only a few years before.

So NGOs are formidable actors for many businesses, and they are also new and different for three reasons. First, many are international in scope. Traditionally, associations most often were built around existing social ties, and these were necessarily local. Even nationally based associations were often federations that were only as strong as the strength of their local chapters. And, of course, those intending social change would direct political influence to their local and national governmental policy makers. After all, the term NGO first came into common use with reference to associations seeking to exercise influence across national boundaries. Today's NGOs are a phenomenon of globalization, use information technology, and have the ability to organize internationally dispersed individuals with common interests to create an interest group with the size and resources to make a substantial impact. If one government is not congenial, they can work through other governments or businesses.

Second, the NGOs of today are developing creative, innovative tactics. In the rich developed countries, businesses are used to a political process permeated by interest groups of various kinds and descriptions. That NGOs would lobby their governments for stricter environmental laws and safety standards, for example, is an expected part of doing business in those countries. But the tactics of today are more sophisticated and more difficult to counter in the traditional ways. NGOs now understand the element of surprise in strategy, and are as able to hire MBAs who understand marketing and information technology as are businesses. Knowledge is notoriously mobile and no one can have a monopoly on knowledge for very long.

But as disconcerting as these fresh tactics are for businesses operating in societies used to open interest-group influence, imagine the shock to those who are used to a cozy cronyism. Now they find themselves the target of large politically sophisticated NGOs that can influence the direction of 10 or even 30 percent of the country's gross domestic product via relief donations and trade sanctions. This is a wholly different way of doing things, and their own tools—relationships and money—are swamped by deals done in other countries involving vastly more resources than they could hope to command. Few in these countries have any experience with interest-group politics, and NGOs are difficult to influence by these businesses' traditional means since they not only are often distant and well financed but also operate largely out of reach of the local secret police.

Third, NGOs used to be a phenomenon for governments alone. Amnesty International has operated for many decades. But NGOs now have discovered that they can achieve their purposes through businesses when governments are unwilling or unable to give them what they want. For example, many governments are unwilling, for deeply held ideological reasons, to interfere in certain business practices. If so, an alternative target is a large consumer-focused business that must be concerned with its public image. In other cases, some governments may be willing to enact legislation but are themselves too weak to ensure their local officials will reliably enforce their laws in the face of attractive (or frightful) local inducements. In these settings NGOs can induce publicity-sensitive purchasers in the developed world to establish codes of conduct and operate their own auditing systems that are not subject to the same local pressures. NGOs have discovered that in many cases businesses are important tools that can be more effectively harnessed for social change than governments are. And this puts businesses into the business of dealing with NGOs as adversaries, collaborators, and often both.

How did this happen? Where is it going? And how can it be managed? Just such questions are addressed in this book. It is among the first to explain and discuss the role and functioning of NGOs, with a focus on their direct and indirect effects on businesses. The developing scope and tactics of NGOs are a genuinely new phenomenon in business and we need this systematic and extensive analysis of them. In this book the authors discuss such practical questions as identifying the situations where businesses can expect NGOs to be influential, and the differing responses of businesses and governments to the growing influence of NGOs. Furthermore, they analyze what the rise of NGOs means for our existing theories of business strategy, public policy, and business–government relations. It is a timely, thoughtful treatment of a subject about which we know too little.

Preface: Globalization and NGOs— Why Should We Care?

Jonathan P. Doh and Hildy Teegen

THE RISE OF NGOs

The events surrounding the effort to launch a new round of multilateral trade negotiations in Seattle in December 1999, the protests at the World Bank meetings in the spring of 2000, and the ongoing demonstrations by nongovernmental organizations (NGOs) at the meetings of the World Economic Forum and elsewhere underscore the increasing activism and visibility of nongovernmental organizations. Among the many important areas of activity, NGOs have emerged as important stakeholders in discussions over the terms and conditions under which business, government, and multilateral institutions manage the process of globalization, one of the most vexing issues facing public policy makers, corporate executives, and broader societal interests around the world. At the same time, nongovernmental organizations are increasingly influencing both government and corporate policy directly by undertaking research, organizing boycotts, and often highlighting the shortcomings of both business and governmental actions in terms of social, ethical, and environmental responsibility. Yet these impressions are only the most public and, in some observers' views, negative images of NGO activism.

Behind the scenes, NGOs increasingly work cooperatively with companies and governments to positively influence government policy approaches and corporate social priorities. For example, NGOs are now often involved in efforts to develop innovative programs that reorient or redirect corporate and governmental activities in a manner that may achieve broader social or economic goals. In so doing, NGO activity may result in perceived or real performance improvement of the participating organizations and has certainly enhanced the public perception and reputation of many organizations.

In these various interrelated activities, NGOs have changed the way governments and corporations do business and have altered the traditional bilateral relationship between government and business. The terms and conditions under which public policy is made and the legal, political, and social conditions placed on business firms in their activities have traditionally been governed by a two-way business–government interface. What had been a primarily two-sided set of negotiating and bargaining relationships in which governments legislate, regulate, and otherwise influence the conduct of business and corporations lobby, advocate, and otherwise influence public policies from which they will benefit (or could be harmed) has evolved into a trilateral bargaining situation. NGOs now function as both a distinctive force influencing business and corporate policy directly, and as a moderator or intermediary through which the business–government dynamic is shaped, altered, and, at times, amplified or distorted.

Through governance mechanisms, political institutions set the boundaries within which firms operate, but governance also "include(s) the informal constraints of society and organizational culture and norms" (North, 1990). The primary activities of governmental institutions are related to establishing, monitoring, and enforcing rules, as well as resolving disputes. Yet with the emergence within this landscape of NGOs as legitimate and influential institutions in their own right, this traditional definition of government's role and responsibility is altered.

ORIGINS AND HISTORY OF THIS VOLUME

This book was born from the acknowledgment that NGOs are having an increasingly profound impact on corporations, governments, and the various interactions between these sectors, with dramatic and influential spillovers on broader societal groups. But where to begin?

First, a session organized by Jonathan Doh at the 2001 Academy of Management meeting in Washington, D.C., provided an initial opportunity to assemble a group of scholars and practitioners interested in the topic. This session titled on "Governments, Firms, and Nongovernmental Organizations: How the Rise of NGOs Matters to Corporate Strategy, Public Policy, and Business–Government Relations" constituted an interesting twist on the 2001 theme of the Academy of Management, which was "How *Governments* Matter." Doh

turned the question on its head, asking corporations and governments, "How Do NGOs Matter?" The session explored how the advent of NGOs has influenced the business–government bargaining
dynamic in general, and how the power of NGOs is being felt at a
number of levels of analysis, under a range of situations and conditions, and by a wide array of organizations and institutions. Present-
ers who had developed research related to various aspects of the
NGO–government–business relationship reported on that research,
and scholars and practitioners presented cases to illustrate how NGOs
are changing the business–government bargaining and negotiation
dynamic.

Once the session was organized, it became clear that a broader
volume examining the range of ways in which NGOs affect corporations, governments, and society was not only in order, but overdue.
Such a volume was particularly timely given the involvement of
NGOs in debates about globalization, one of the most pressing issues affecting public policy, corporate strategy, and business–government relations. Publishers were approached to gauge interest in
the volume. The response was overwhelming. Praeger was selected
because it promised the opportunity to reach both scholars and practitioners with a rich but parsimonious volume of contributions related to how NGOs are transforming companies, governments, and
society at large. Shortly after the volume was accepted for publication, Hildy Teegen joined the editorial team, bringing interest and
expertise in alliances and agreements between governments, environmental NGOs, and corporations. Once we began training our collective eyes toward the impact of NGOs, we found NGOs to be present
in some form or shape in nearly every corporate decision, public
policy initiative, and business–government bargaining or other exchange we came upon, globally, regionally, and locally.

GOALS, OBJECTIVES, AND DIRECTIONS: NGOs AS
AGENTS OF CHANGE

Although we sought to provide a broad, inclusive statement about
NGOs and their impact on government and business, we did identify some specific goals for each of our authors in order to ensure
that a common thread linked each contribution. The broad goals we
laid out for the volume were as follows:

- To trace the emergence of NGOs and the impact of globalization on the
  growth, development, and strategies of NGOs.
- To evaluate the relevance of existing models, theories, and frameworks
  of strategic management, public policy, or business–government relations
  in light of the growing influence of NGOs.

- To isolate the impact of NGOs on business and government and to investigate the influence of NGOs as a moderator or mediator of business–government relations.
- To examine situations and contexts in which NGOs have had or will have a disproportionate impact on corporate strategy, public policy, and business–government relations, and develop generalizations regarding how and when that impact is most pronounced.
- To describe how governments and business have responded to the emergence of NGO influence in general, and assess cases in which the insertion of NGO interests into corporate strategic planning, public policy, and business–government bargaining has been helpful or harmful to corporate effectiveness or government performance.
- To develop preliminary suggestions for theoretical, empirical, and practitioner research that could be used to further investigate the role of NGOs in shaping corporate strategy, public policy, and business–government bargaining, particularly research that focuses on how the introduction of NGOs may alter the nature and outcomes of business–government bargaining and negotiation.

We also wanted to ensure that the volume provided concrete, practical implications for practitioners and scholars. Specifically, we were eager to begin to provide preliminary answers to the following core questions:

- How has globalization affected the emergence of NGOs, and how have NGOs responded to the challenges of globalization in terms of their overall strategies and their specific operational approaches?
- How has the rise of NGOs affected corporate strategy and public policy? How have NGOs disrupted the traditional business–government negotiating dynamic? How has the rise of NGOs affected political and social policy expectations of multinational corporations?
- In which countries and in which industries has the impact of NGO participation been most acute? How does the role of NGOs vary depending upon the economic, political, and institutional setting?
- How have NGOs responded to the "collective action" problem in their efforts to mobilize viable organizations with influence and impact? How has globalization helped NGOs in developing complex, adaptive, and globally responsive networks?
- In which cases have NGO–business negotiations occurred with little or no government intervention? Have these negotiations succeeded?
- Does the threat of government regulation or penalty still provide an important deterrent to corporate opportunism, or are the public relations or other NGO-born threats at least as important in constraining corporate behavior? How do these two points of leverage interact?
- How can business use relationships with NGOs to build competitive advantage?

- What does the rise of NGOs say about existing models, theories, and frameworks of corporate strategy, public policy, and business–government bargaining? How must these models, theories, and frameworks be refined or revised?

While we were not successful in fulfilling all of the goals or in providing definitive answers to each of these questions, we believe that the volume provides a comprehensive treatment of the issues were hoped to address.

A RANGE OF CONTRIBUTIONS

Although "associations" have been part of the political and economic milieu for centuries, in the last decade there has been a proliferation of the number and range of nonstate, nonfirm organizations: NGOs. By some estimates, the United States alone is home to more than 1.2 million NGOs (Doh, this volume; Independent Sector, 2001).

The emergence of NGOs has had a direct impact on public policy, corporate strategy and operations, and the interactions between business and government. The contributions that emanated from our efforts are clearly concerned with how NGOs are increasingly influencing public policy, corporate strategy, and business–government relations. The rise of NGOs suggests that management scholars and practitioners must reevaluate the relevance of existing models, theories, and frameworks of strategic management, public policy, and business–government relations in light of the growing influence of NGOs. In addition, basic assumptions about who and what really counts in public policy and corporate strategy are now under revision. In this volume we are primarily concerned with NGOs that are organized to promote an agenda for social, environmental, or economic changes and reform, using a range of techniques directed at multilateral institutions, government, business, and society at large, including advocacy and operational activities. Each author, however, adopts his or her own scope in terms of the definitions used and delimitations imposed.

Collectively, the chapters in this volume all respond to questions surrounding the impact of NGOs on business and government. The authors investigate the influence of NGOs on public policy, corporate strategy, and the interface between business and government. In particular, the contributions attempt to develop new frameworks for understanding how the rise of NGOs is affecting public and private actors, and examine situations where NGOs have had or will have a disproportionate impact on these actors and the economic and political exchanges between them.

Each contribution offers an evaluation of how governments or business have responded to the emergence of the influence of NGOs broadly, and assesses cases in which the insertion of NGO interests into corporate strategic planning, public policy, and business–government bargaining has been helpful or harmful to corporate effectiveness or government performance.

Several authors offer suggestions for new directions in theoretical, empirical, and practitioner research that could be used to further investigate the role of NGOs in shaping corporate strategy, public policy, and business–government bargaining. In particular, authors propose new insights that focus on how the introduction of NGOs may alter the outcomes of business–government bargaining and negotiation.

The first four chapters provide some background and conceptual development on the rise of NGOs and their increasing influence on corporate strategy, public policy, and business–government relations. They focus particularly on the role of NGOs in broad national and international policy debates and discussions. Doh's contribution argues that NGOs have disrupted the traditional business–government bargaining framework. He proposes several conceptual and theoretical perspectives that can be used to incorporate NGOs into the business-government bargaining dynamic. Keim evaluates the influence of the institutional environment on the role NGOs have played and will play in the business–government interface. Deslauriers and Kotschwar address the profound impact of NGOs on the globalization debate. Specifically, they chart the dramatic rise in NGO influence on the global trade and finance agenda, describe how different institutions such as the IMF, World Bank, and WTO have responded to NGO pressure, and offer insightful and instructive lessons to government policy makers and business executives on how this process can be best managed to accommodate NGO perspectives.

Doh, Newburry, and Teegen explore the area of cooperation and collaboration among and within international environmental NGOs. They develop a typology to understand how and why NGOs use different types of cooperative ventures, using illustrations from one of the best-known environmental NGOs, the World Wide Fund for Nature/World Wildlife Fund (WWF). Parker describes and evaluates the prospects for collaboration between NGOs and multinational enterprise (MNCs), focusing particularly on the experiences of collaboration between MNCs and international poverty-relief agencies.

In the four chapters that follow, contributions transition from broader, macrolevel analyses to more specific micro applications and case analyses, particularly focusing on the impact of NGOs on corporate activities and executives. Teegen uses a bargaining and negotiation perspective to evaluate how both international and local NGOs have worked with governments and businesses on projects to implement prototype carbon-credit-based exchange opportunities created by the Kyoto treaty on global warming. Soule evaluates a specific case of NGO intervention, that of the NGO role in the U.S.–EU disputes over genetically modified organisms. He describes the roles of the various corporate, government, and nongovernmental stakeholders and how the different frames and approaches they brought to the dispute led to increasing tension and conflict. Domask provides an interesting account of the changes in NGO–business–government relations over forest issues over time and the cooperative and institutionalized relations between NGOs and business that have developed into a private governance system for forestry operations throughout the world. Adams of the AES Corporation describes the opportunities, challenges, benefits, and frustrations associated with NGO–corporate cooperation from the vantage point of one of the global leaders in socially responsible business practices.

Finally, we close with a synthesis of these contributions. We offer some further perspectives on NGOs, how they differ from each other and from the other organizations, and how they interact with other NGOs and other public and private organizations in an increasingly integrated global economy. More broadly, we respond to questions related to how NGOs fit within the operating milieu of societies, and how they influence others in their environments. We offer some projections regarding emerging roles and likely directions for NGO influence and impact in the future.

THE FUTURE

The emergence of NGOs presents direct challenges to public policy-making and business management, but it also offers great opportunity. Each contribution to *Globalization and NGOs* offers practical insights to public policy makers and business executives as they seek to manage their relationships with NGOs in an environment increasingly characterized by turbulence and change. We are very proud of this volume and hope that it leads to a rich and diverse dialogue among governments, firms, and NGOs about the future of their relationships and exchanges.

ACKNOWLEDGMENTS

We would like to thank all the contributors to this volume, our capable and supportive editor Hilary Claggett, Joseph Domask for helpful editorial assistance, Seth Reichgott for exemplary copy editing, and John Beck for production support.

REFERENCES

Independent Sector. (2001). *The new nonprofit almanac.*

North, D. (1990). *Institutions, institutional change, and economic perfor-mance.* New York: Cambridge University Press.

CHAPTER 1

Nongovernmental Organizations, Corporate Strategy, and Public Policy: NGOs as Agents of Change

Jonathan P. Doh

> Americans of all ages, all stations of life and all types of disposition are forever forming associations. . . . In democratic countries knowledge of how to combine is the mother of all other forms of knowledge; on its progress depends that of all the others. (Tocqueville, 2000)

When Tocqueville visited the United States in the early part of the nineteenth century, he was impressed by the freedom and ease with which U.S. citizens formed associations. These associations provided an avenue through which members espoused beliefs and positions and worked together toward the accomplishment of specific goals (Tocqueville, 2000). In the 17 decades since Tocqueville's famous visit, American democracy has advanced in a number of fascinating directions. One of the more interesting developments related to Tocqueville's observations is the dramatic acceleration in the growth and development of nongovernmental organizations (NGOs), both in the United States and around the world.

In this chapter I survey the rapid growth in the number, size, and impact of NGOs. I employ a simple modeling taxonomy to derive preliminary observations regarding the range of influences NGOs may have on business and governments. Drawing from agency, stakeholder, network, and alliance theories, I argue that NGOs may affect business and governments directly, may serve in a moderating or mediating capacity in defining or altering the business–government interface, or may become full participants in a complex web of business–government–societal relationships. I postulate that as NGOs become a more permanent fixture on the political and economic landscape, their role is transitioning from a simple bilateral stakeholder–agent relationship with business and government to a more participatory position within a complex web of relationships between and among government, business and the nongovernmental sector. I argue that NGOs are reshaping the business–government interface by transforming it from a two-way exchange into a trilateral system of relationships and entanglements. Such a role may require new theoretical perspectives, particularly those drawn from network and alliance theories, in order to fully capture how NGOs, business, and governments interact in a reflexive and networked system.

This new dynamic presents management challenges that may require a new set of tools and insights for businesses as they seek to accomplish strategic objectives and for governments as they strive to fulfill basic responsibilities while they both serve an increasingly diverse set of stakeholder interests. Although political institutions, through governance mechanisms, set the boundaries within which firms operate, such institutions also include the informal constraints imposed by society and organizational culture and norms (North, 1990). I aim to demonstrate how the growth and development of the third sector—nongovernments—has significant implications for governmental policies, corporate strategies, and the ways in which governments and corporations interact.

THE EMERGENCE OF
NONGOVERNMENTAL ORGANIZATIONS

Over the past several decades, nongovernmental organizations have grown in number, size, and stature and have been instrumental in shaping the resolution of many issues facing businesses and governments. NGOs may include environmental, labor and human rights, consumer, or church and religious groups, in addition to think tanks, trade and industry associations, grassroots not-for-profit organizations, and many others. In this discussion, I am primarily concerned with those NGOs that are organized to promote social, environmental, and economic change and reform, using a range of techniques directed at governments, business, other NGOs and individual citizens.

The Rise of NGOs

Estimates on the number of NGOs currently operating in the world vary widely, although almost all analysts agree that the number is growing dramatically. Some of the earliest reports by the Organization for Economic Cooperation and Development (OECD) declare an increase from 1,600 to 2,500 NGOs within the twenty-four member nations from 1980 to 1990 (van Tujil, 1999). Counts including non-OECD nations suggest as early as 1990 there were only 6,000 international NGOs. In 1993, the United Nations Development Program identified 50,000 NGOs worldwide (Kellow, 1999). The Union of International Associations (2001) identifies 52,000 such groups worldwide. The Internal Revenue Service counted 819,008 501(c)(3) corporations for fiscal year 2000, generally known as "not-for-profits," up from 692,524 in 1997 ("Tax Report," 2001). In 1998, the last year for which complete figures are available, the total size of the "independent sector," which includes 501(c)(3) corporations as well as civic leagues, social welfare organizations, and religious congregations was estimated at 1.2 million organizations, employing an estimated 10.9 million individuals with revenues of nearly $680 billion (Independent Sector, 2001). In addition to the growth in numbers, individual NGOs are growing in size with some international NGOs employing thousands of professional supported by annual budgets approaching $500 million.

Examples and Implications of the Rise of NGOs

There are a number of high-profile examples of broad NGO advocacy within the late 1990s alone. These include efforts to discourage the purchase of non-dolphin-safe tuna and textiles or clothing made in countries with inadequate health and safety conditions, to incorporate environment and labor provisions in the North American Free Trade Agreement and the World Trade Organization (WTO) negotiations, to compel the World Bank and International Monetary Fund (IMF) to forgive the debt of developing countries, and to encourage governments to allow the banning or restriction of the import of genetically modified (GM) organisms and other food products, such as shrimp caught using methods that may harm sea turtles (Deslauriers & Kotschwar, this volume; "After Seattle," 1999; "NGOs," 2000).

Although some analysts have suggested that the presence of interest groups may lead to "institutional sclerosis" (Olson, 1982, pp. 41–47), NGOs are nonetheless an increasingly potent force with which business and government must interact. The rapid growth in the power and visibility of NGOs appears to have caught some government leaders and corporate executives off guard and has radically transformed both the strategy and operation of public and private institutions while dramatically altering the historic relationships between these actors. The emergence of NGOs therefore commands attention by managerial researchers in order to guide scholars and practitioners in understanding how NGOs affect corporations, governments, and business–government relations.

The Business–Government Interface: How NGOs May Best Fit In

There have been some limited examinations of the emergence of NGOs and the potential implications of that trend for political economies and international relations (van Tujil, 1999). These include accounts of the influence of NGO pressure on trade policy and global finance ("After Seattle," 1999; "NGOs," 2000), exploration of issues such as the controversy over trade in genetically modified organisms (Aubert, 2000), and examinations of the role of NGOs in individual countries (Manzo, 2000). To date, there have not been any formal investigations of how the emergence of NGOs may affect the business–government interface. Although NGOs have not been explicitly incorporated into models of business–government bargaining, there are several models of state–firm interactions and of political strategy and stakeholder relations that may help to develop conceptual notions about how NGOs affect businesses and governments and their many interactions.

Recent research in corporate political strategy has suggested that because government policies can have a significant impact on business activities, corporations adopt various strategies to both affect government policy and respond to competitor efforts to influence that policy (Hillman & Hitt, 1999; Shaffer & Hillman, 2000; Hillman & Keim, 1995; Marcus, Kaufman, & Beam, 1987; Mitnick, 1993; Vogel, 1996; Weidenbaum, 1980). Researchers have suggested various approaches to political strategy (Hillman & Hitt, 1999; Meznar & Nigh, 1995), described various techniques to accomplish political goals (Kaufman, Englander, & Marcus, 1989), and proposed the integration of political and corporate strategies (Baron, 1995). A related research stream on business–government bargaining, especially in the international context, can also help to answer questions surrounding the introduction of nongovernmental actors into the business–government bargaining dynamic (Boddewyn & Brewer, 1995; Doh, 2000; Lenway & Murtha, 1994; Rugman & Verbeke, 1990; Hillman & Keim, 1995). To date, research on corporate political activities has not explicitly incorporated nongovernmental organizations into the business–government bargaining equation.

Although no theoretical perspective explicitly incorporates NGOs, a number of taxonomies drawn from corporate political strategy and stakeholder theory may be helpful in further delineating the role of NGOs in the business–government bargaining dynamic. Hillman and

Hitt's (1999) taxonomy includes two general approaches to political action (transactional and relational), two levels of participation (individual and collective), and three types of generic political strategies (information, financial incentive, and constituency building). This is one example of a business–government framework that could be adapted to incorporate the influence of nongovernmental organizations by identifying different types of NGOs according to their political strategies.

As developed here, stakeholder theory presents a rich theoretical base for exploring the role of NGOs in the business–government interface. Mitchell, Agle, and Wood's (1997) theory of stakeholder identification and salience is based on the degree to which stakeholders possess one or more of three relationship attributes: power, legitimacy, and urgency. Kaufman, Englander, and Marcus's (1995) analysis of public affairs management is based on transactions costs and agency perspectives, and Doh (1999) and Meznar and Nigh's (1995) approach to business–government relations divides corporate public policy actions into "buffers" and "bridges." These approaches, most notably, Doh's extension of Meznar and Nigh's framework and his integration of this approach with the strategy/structure dimension first proposed by Chandler (1962), may be particularly suitable to understanding how NGOs may influence corporate strategy, public policy, and business–government relations.

Despite these contributions, research on business–government relations lacks an explicit approach for integrating NGOs, representing an increasingly important set of organizational and institutional interests, within the business–government bargaining framework. In the next section I propose an initial approach to this problem using a series of theoretical perspectives to inform the evolving role of NGOs in corporate strategy, public policy, and business–government relations.

THE ROLE OF NGOs IN THE
BUSINESS–GOVERNMENT INTERFACE

The introduction of nongovernmental organizations as influential actors in corporate and political strategy processes and as important stakeholders in the business–government bargaining dynamic suggests that established theories relevant to business and public policy and business–government relations need to be revised. An initial step in understanding how NGOs may affect corporate political strategy and business–government relations is to use a simple statistical taxonomy that is implied by extant research on political strategy, business–government bargaining, and stakeholder and agency theories. Specifically, these perspectives suggest that power relationships govern the interaction between business and government and that governments and corporations act as agents in representing a given set of stakeholders.

The introduction of NGOs into this equation can have a number of different impacts on business, government, and the exchange relationships that characterize their interactions. NGOs may have direct effects on business strategy and government policy or they may serve as intermediaries in business–government exchanges, either influencing the direction and intensity of business–government exchanges indirectly or serving as the main agent through which such exchanges occur. Finally, they may act as full complements within a broad framework of business–government relationships.

NGOs, Business, and Governments: Direct Impacts

Traditionally, business and governments have had direct dealings in the range of political, economic, and social matters that concern both sectors. With the rise of nongovernmental organizations, NGOs may affect corporations and governments directly (Figure 1.1). NGOs are likely to bring their case directly to governments (1) when issues are typically resolved in a rules-based environment, (2) when issues are sufficiently complex as to render a negotiated agreement difficult, or (3) when there is a history of governmental activities. Examples include environmental legislation, such as the 1991 amendments to the Clean Water Act, or trade legislation, such as the recent battles over extension of so-called fast-track trade negotiating authority for negotiation of the Free Trade Agreement of the Americas. Similarly, when government policy has been relinquished, government has become inactive or ineffective, or NGOs are seeking corporate actions that go beyond that required from government, NGOs will interact directly with companies in order to change behavior.

There are increasing examples of direct NGO influence on corporations that can sometimes include aggressive advocacy designed to publicly disgrace corporate actions and in so doing force companies to change behavior. One of the first widespread examples of NGO pressure on corporations began with the move to force U.S. public and private institutions to divest from South Africa in the early 1980s. Other examples include boycotts, such as that of Nestlé in the 1980s by a number of groups to protest alleged exploitation of women in developing countries who were misled about the benefits and proper use of infant formula, and more recent boycotts of Nike, Walmart, and other retailers for allegedly manufacturing or purchasing goods produced under exploitative working conditions in developing countries.

Figure 1.1
Corporate Strategy, Public Policy, and the Business–Government Interface: Direct Effects Model with NGOs as "Zs"

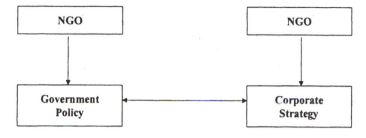

Direct action can also take a more cooperative or conciliatory form when NGOs work with companies to change production techniques or product characteristics in a manner that reflects greater social responsibility and/or a reduction in social or environmental externalities. Examples include NGO–corporate agreements on waste disposal, such as the one negotiated between the Sierra Club and McDonald's designed to reduce the amount and change the type of packaging materials used in McDonald's products, and agreements between power generators such as AES and environmental groups such as the World Resources Institute and the Nature Conservancy to offset carbon emissions through planting forests or protecting forested land (Adams, this volume; Teegen, this volume). One of the most significant agreements between NGOs and industry is in the area of forest products, where the Forest Stewardship Council (FSC), an independent organization that monitors forestry practices, developed a global program that combined public awareness, business collaboration, and green marketing. Through these means, the NGOs convinced Home Depot, Wicke's, Lowe's, and Ikea to commit to sell FSC-certified products (Carlton, 2000; Domask, this volume). This initiative, which had no direct government involvement, has paved the way for other campaigns, including the "paper campaign," a similar effort targeting Office Depot, Staples, and other large office supply firms, encouraging them to carry and promote greater shares of paper products with postconsumer content. In these instances, NGOs may replace or supplant the role of government or modify the way in which government and business have traditionally interacted.

Agency theory, or as it is sometimes known, principal–agent theory, has offered an approach to the financial organization and corporate governance of private business firms that focuses on why managers and owners do not necessarily behave in concert (Jensen & Meckling,

1976). An agency approach to organization has also identified tools and techniques to provide incentives for managers to act on behalf of shareholders (Demsetz, 1983; Jensen & Meckling, 1976). In particular, agency theory has helped scholars and practitioners of corporate finance and governance understand the need for vertical monitoring in order to enforce agency contracts (Hill & Jones, 1992) and also called attention to the costs of such monitoring (Eisenhardt, 1989).

Some researchers view traditional applications of agency as too narrow in their failure to incorporate nonshareholder stakeholder interests (Freeman, 1984). Stakeholder management is focused on those interests and actors who affect or, in turn, are affected by the corporation. Through identification, evaluation, and assessment of stakeholders and stakeholder relationships, firms can best navigate the public and private strategic environments in which they operate and in so doing account for the range of relationships, responsibilities, and interactions in their strategy formulation and implementation (Freeman, 1984; Mitchell, Agle, & Wood, 1997).

NGOs as Intermediaries: Interactive Stakeholder Roles

NGOs may also act as intermediaries in business–government relationships (Figures 1.2 and 1.3). In this capacity they may influence the direction and intensity of business–government exchanges indirectly (moderator; Figure 1.2), or serve as the main agent through which such exchanges occur (mediator; Figure 1.3); for example, when governments and businesses are engaged in a negotiation over the terms of a consent decree, such as when the American Cancer Society and the Tobacco Institute served in mediating roles between government agencies and private corporations over the landmark tobacco settlement (Figure 1.2). In addition, the chemical industry's "Responsible Care" Initiative involved various environmental NGOs acting as third parties to negotiations between the U.S. Environmental Protection Agency and chemical companies over a voluntary agreement to curb chemical emissions. NGOs may alter the nature of the interaction between business and government. In some instances NGOs may be the vehicle through which the business–government relationship operates, serving as mediators of this relationship, such as in their roles in the joint implementation projects on global warming described by Teegen (this volume) (Figure 1.3).

Recent trade disputes point to the very powerful and in some instances disproportionate role of NGOs in altering traditional business–government relations. NGOs such as the Earth Island Institute were very active in pressing the U.S. government to ban the import of tuna not deemed "dolphin safe." This advocacy contributed to

Figure 1.2
Corporate Strategy, Public Policy, and the Business–Government
Interface: Interaction Effects Model with NGOs as Moderators

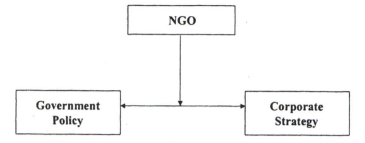

Figure 1.3
Corporate Strategy, Public Policy, and the Business–Government
Interface: Interaction Effects Model with NGOs as Mediators

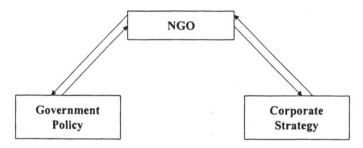

dramatic changes in U.S. legislation (the Marine Mammal Protection Act). A similar influence was recently felt when the United States banned imports of shrimp caught by harvesters in a manner deemed unsafe for sea turtles. This case was litigated in the WTO and the U.S. government maintained a consistently balanced position throughout this dispute, partly in response to NGO pressure.

One of the most visible and significant examples of NGO activism in influencing corporate–government relations came when many NGOs mobilized the European Community to ban imports of genetically modified material. This action not only had a direct impact on Monsanto's (the manufacturer of many GM products) plans for selling and distributing certain GM rice and other products in Europe but actually caused the company to substantially alter its entire GM product strategy. In this example, NGOs were not just moderators, but true mediators in the business–government dynamic, as discussed by Soule (this volume).

Through evaluation of relationships between organizations and stakeholders based on exchange transactions, power dependencies, legitimacy, or other claims, stakeholder theory seeks to systematically address the question of which stakeholders do and do not deserve or require management attention (Mitchell, Agle, & Wood, 1997). Limited efforts have been directed at the integration of agency and stakeholder theory (Hill & Jones, 1992; Jones, 1995). These efforts have attempted to broaden the range of stakeholders that would otherwise be examined from a purely agency-based view (a limited shareholder–manager principal–agent relationship) to include other stakeholder groups (Donaldson & Preston, 1995) and other forms of stakeholder relationships (Cummings & Doh, 2000). In theory, this research has opened the way for explicit recognition of nongovernmental actors as entities that may serve in multiple roles within the business–government bargaining framework. These perspectives may be useful pathways for understanding how NGOs can serve in a more integrated role within the business–government bargaining framework.

NGOs in Multiple Roles

Finally, NGOs may serve as full-fledged participants in the business–government interface, assuming a role on the same basis and with an equivalent (or even superior) status as business and government (Figure 1.4). While these instances are, to date, relatively rare, I anticipate that with the emergence of NGOs as legitimate players on the international economic landscape, they may increasingly occupy a status similar to that of business and government. Recent commitments by the World Bank to open nearly every aspect of Bank decision making to NGO input places NGOs on the same playing field as corporations and governments which have traditionally been the Bank's primary customers and advisors. Similar but not quite as ambitious moves by the WTO and the administrative apparatus of the Free Trade Agreement of the Americas also suggest a greater recognition of the legitimacy of NGOs in these fora and the likelihood of larger and more multidimensional roles for NGOs in their deliberations (Deslauriers & Kotschwar, this volume).

Network theory provides a useful framework for examining the multinodal nature of the NGO–business–government system. Moving beyond a focus on individual behaviors, attitudes, and beliefs (and the actions that result from them), social network analysis centers on the interactions themselves and the structures or frameworks that emerge as units of analysis in investigations (Galaskiewicz & Wasserman 1989; Nohria & Eccles, 1992). Network theory views organizations not as individual bounded entities but as a set of or-

Figure 1.4
Corporate Strategy, Public Policy, and the Business–Government
Interface: NGOs as Integrated, Multidimensional Network Participants

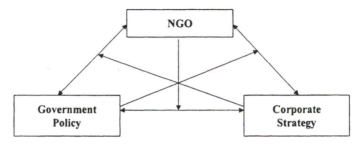

ganic relationships that are dynamic and fluid over time (Wasserman & Faust, 1994; Wasserman & Galaskiewicz, 1994). Unlike agency or stakeholder theory, which focus on specific actors and their activities, network theory centers on relationships and examines such relationships as systems that can be investigated and modeled. Within such networks, resources can be shared among network participants (Thorelli, 1986). Network theory is a particularly appropriate perspective for investigating the complex web that emerges when NGOs take on a more systemic role within a business–government–societal network. In Figure 1.4, such interactive nodes exist at multiple points in the system.

As a complement to network theory, research on cooperative strategy and strategic alliances provides an additional perspective on the emerging roles of NGOs (Brandenburger & Nalebuff, 1996; Inkpen, 1996; Inkpen & Beamish, 1997; Lado, Boyd, & Hanlon, 1997; Ring & Van de Ven, 1992). Dyer and Singh (1998) have identified four potential sources of interorganizational competitive advantage from alliances: relation-specific assets, knowledge-sharing routines, complementary resources and capabilities, and effective governance. They argue that resources acquired through extrafirm or intraorganizational contacts are critical to competitive success. Research on the importance of trust as a factor binding alliances together (Das & Teng, 1998; Ring & Van de Ven, 1992) is an appropriate theoretical reference point as NGOs gain more credibility and status and therefore are more likely to trust business and government partners and, in turn, to be trusted by them. Some researchers have suggested that governments may promote collaboration among firms through rules and norms (Ring, 2000). Examples relevant to this investigation include the U.S. government's relaxation of antitrust rules to allow automotive firms to work together (and with NGOs) in developing

alternative-fuel vehicles. Other researchers have suggested that collaboration between investing firms and local NGOs can increase
broader societal support in international infrastructure investment,
as in the case of AES and a number of other power companies that
include NGOs as part of their carbon offsets programs designed to
help mitigate the impact of CO_2 on global warming (Doh, 1998;
Adams, this volume).

Research on evolutionary patterns in alliances suggests that as
industries evolve through the different phases of formation, matu-
rity, and reconfiguration, corresponding patterns of competitive and
cooperative strategies evolve (Demers, Hafsi, Jorgensen, & Molz,
1997). Again, this perspective would support the view of continu-
ously evolving patterns of alliance relationships between and among
NGOs, government, and businesses as NGOs become a more fixed
presence in the evolving system. As NGOs grow and expand their reach
beyond local or regional geographies, international alliance relationships, a longstanding research topic of managerial investigation (e.g.
Buckley & Casson, 1988, 1996; Contractor & Lorange, 1988; Dyer,
1997; Harrigan, 1986, 1988; Inkpen, 1995, 1996), may be useful in understanding relationships and connections between and among various NGOs and governments and business. An example of this
phenomenon is the global climate change coalition, which includes
a number of individual companies, industry associations, individual
environmental nongovernmental organizations, and consortia of such
organizations, along with local, national, and international governmental agencies, all working to promote a comprehensive global
solution to atmospheric warming. This example demonstrates the
complex, multilevel, and multidimensional relationships that are
emerging as NGOs become important and even critical players in
major social, political, and economic policy issues.

SUMMARY

NGOs are increasingly influential actors on the political–economic
landscape. Their emergence has disrupted traditional relationships
between business and government. Using a simple statistical model
as a reference point and three important theoretical perspectives from
the social and behavioral sciences, NGO activity can be thought of
as having direct influences on corporate strategy and public policy,
mediating or moderating business–government bargaining behavior, or serving as an integrated component in a trilateral relationship
among business, governments, and NGOs. The following is a summary of the multiple roles NGOs appear to play in the business–

government interface and the relevant theoretical perspectives that help to inform those roles:

Role of NGO in Business–Government Interface	Relevant Theoretical Perspective(s)
NGOs as Zs: Direct effects	Agency
NGOs as mediators and moderators	Stakeholder–agency
NGOs as nodes within business–government–NGO network	Networks and alliances
Future NGO–business–governmental–societal roles	Complexity, neural networks

As the broad NGO movement takes more permanent shape and as individual NGOs gain a more enduring status on the social and political scene, the role of nongovernmental actors will continue to transition from a simple stakeholder pressing government agents for a hearing to a more complex set of interactions and networked relations in which NGOs play a more integral role in a complex web of interactions and connections. Such evolution will naturally require more sophisticated theoretical perspectives and frameworks to properly evaluate the role of NGOs in relation to other key actors in the societal–business–government interface. Rowley's (1997) discussion of a network approach to stakeholder theory accounts for interdependent stakeholder demands and illustrates how organizations respond to the simultaneous influence of multiple stakeholders. Such a model may bridge the various theoretical perspectives introduced here. Indeed, there appears to be increasing evidence of multistakeholder alliances between firms, governments, and their respective external constituents.

CONCLUSIONS AND FUTURE RESEARCH DIRECTIONS

In this chapter I have attempted to introduce a conceptual framework for understanding and positioning nongovernmental organizations within the business–government interface. Drawing from a simple statistical model and several critical perspectives on management theory and organization, I have suggested how NGOs may influence business or governmental entities directly, how they may moderate or mediate the interaction between business and government and how they may assume a position that is integrated with business and government in a complex, adaptive system of relationships between and among governments, business, and NGOs.

As the role of NGOs within the business–government–societal system becomes more complex and dynamic, additional theoretical perspectives may be in order. In particular, those drawn from game theory (competitive dynamics), evolutionary biology (complexity theory, evolutionary theory of the firm), and computer science (dynamic systems theory, neural network analysis) may be appropriate vehicles for positioning NGOs within broader social and political systems. Complexity theory could help inform the dynamic nature of NGO interactions with government and business. As Kostova and Zaheer (1999) have posited, the interaction between organizations and the environment is a complex social and cognitive process. Complexity theory and the study of complex adaptive systems offers managers and researchers an approach for understanding nonlinear systems in which outcomes are hard to predict (Axelrod & Cohen, 2000). Neural network theory focuses on systems as parallel, interconnected networks of adaptive elements that interact in the same way nervous systems govern interactions among physiological systems (Haykin, 1994; Kohonen, 1988). Because of the complex, reflexive nature of the NGO role within a multinodal network of business-societal relationships, complexity and neural network theories may be particularly useful theoretical reference points for informing this emerging model of NGO relationships.

The role of NGOs in the business–government interface is evolving. This evolution appears to be occurring both in a broad macroinstitutional sense and in the progress of specific NGO activities in relation to particular issues, laws, regulations, or campaigns. As the role of NGOs as institutional actors continues to mature and the specific position of individual NGOs gains credence and legitimacy, NGO roles will evolve and progress. Moreover, as the number and type of NGOs continues to expand, it seems likely that governments and business will need to practice selective differentiation in evaluating the legitimacy and credibility of particular NGOs in order to determine the efficacy of working with and responding to NGO pressure. No longer will some business groups be able to dismiss NGO activism as only representative of a small minority of interests frustrated by aspects of modern capitalism. Efforts to sift through the myriad organizations and interests may pose challenges for many business firms and government agencies. As previously noted, stakeholder theory may provide some insight into how to approach such a daunting task. Mitchell, Agle, and Wood (1997) provide some guidance regarding how to evaluate stakeholder interests that should command managerial attention based on exchange transactions, power dependencies, legitimacy claims, or other claims. Another implication for practice is the potential for NGOs to replace or supplant traditional government roles. The increasing range of business–NGO collaborations referenced here, many with little explicit government involvement, has substantial implications for corporate political strategies.

The insertion of NGOs into the business–government interface requires new and innovative approaches to scholarly investigation, as well as practical insights for managers seeking to navigate a substantially transformed business environment. The proliferation of NGOs will continue and their power and influence is likely to grow, especially in developing countries where the wave of transitions from authoritarian to democratic regimes is rapidly opening up political and social space for NGOs. Scholars, corporate officers, and government officials must collectively work to reframe the business–government relationship in a manner that fully appreciates the role of these nonstate, nonfirm actors. Such an exercise is important so that research and practice in the business–government interface fully incorporate all relevant stakeholders in the emerging network of societal, organizational, and individual relationships.

REFERENCES

After Seattle: The non-governmental order. (1999, December 11). *The Economist*, 20–21.

Aubert, J. E. (2000). NGOs on GMOs: The reason for resistance. *The OECD Observer, 220*, 25–27.

Axelrod, A., & Cohen, M. D. (2000). *Harnessing complexity: Organizational implications of a scientific frontier*. New York: Free Press.

Baron, D. (1995). Integrated strategy: Market and nonmarket components. *California Management Review, 37*, 47–65.

Boddewyn, J., & Brewer, T. (1995). International-business political behavior: New theoretical directions. *Academy of Management Review, 19*, 119–143.

Brandenburger, A. M., &. Nalebuff, B. J. (1996). *Co-opetition*. New York: Doubleday.

Buckley, P. J., & Casson, M. (1988). A theory of cooperation in international business. In F. Contractor & P. Lorange (Eds.), *Cooperative strategies in international business* (pp. 31–54). Lexington, MA: Lexington Books.

Buckley, P. J., & Casson, M. (1996). An economic model of international joint venture strategy. *Journal of International Business Studies, 27*, 849–876.

Carlton, J. (2000, September 26). How Home Depot and activists joined to cut logging abuse. *Wall Street Journal*, p. A1.

Chandler, A. (1962). *Strategy and structure: Chapters in the history of industrial enterprise*. Cambridge: MIT Press.

Contractor, F. J., & Lorange, P. (Eds.). (1988). *Cooperative strategies in international business*. Lexington, MA: Lexington Books.

Cummings, J. L., & Doh, J. P. (2000). Identifying who matters: Mapping key players in multiple environments. *California Management Review, 42*, 83-104.

Das, T. K., & Teng, B. S. (1998). Between trust and control: Developing confidence in partner cooperation in alliances. *Academy of Management Review, 23*, 491–512.

Demers, C., Hafsi, T., Jorgensen, J., & Molz, R. (1997). Industry dynamics of cooperative strategy. In P. W. Beamish & J. P. Killing (Eds.), *Cooperative strategies: North American perspectives* (pp. 111–132). San Francisco: New Lexington Press.

Demsetz, H. (1983). The structure of ownership and the theory of the firm. *Journal of Law and Economics, 26*, 375–390.

Doh, J. P. (2000). Entrepreneurial privatization strategies: Order of entry and local partner collaboration as sources of competitive advantage. *Academy of Management Review, 25*, 551–572.

Doh, J. P. (1999). Regional market integration and decentralization in North America and Europe: Implications for business–government relations and corporate public affairs. *Business and Society, 38*, 474–507.

Doh, J. P. (1998, August). *Strategic choice and stakeholder assessment in state-owned industry restructuring.* Paper presented at the Academy of Management annual meeting, San Diego, CA.

Donaldson, T., & Preston, L. E. (1995). The stakeholder theory of the corporation: Concepts, evidence and implications. *Academy of Management Review, 20*, 65–91.

Dyer, J. H. (1997). Effective interfirm collaboration: How firms minimize transaction costs and maximize transaction value. *Strategic Management Journal, 18*, 535–556.

Dyer, J. H., & Singh, H. (1998). The relational view: Cooperative strategy and sources of interorganizational competitive advantage. *Academy of Management Review, 23*, 660-679.

Eisenhardt, K. M. (1989). Agency theory: An assessment and review. *Academy of Management Review, 14*, 57–74.

Freeman, R. E. (1984). *Strategic management: A stakeholder approach.* Boston: Pittman.

Galaskiewicz, J., & Wasserman, S. (1989). Mimetic processes within an interorganizational field: An empirical test. *Administrative Science Quarterly, 34*, 454–479.

Harrigan, K. R. (1986). *Managing for joint venture success.* Lexington, MA: Lexington Books.

Harrigan, K. R.(1988). Strategic alliances and partner asymmetries. In F. Contractor & P. Lorange (Eds.), Cooperative strategies in international business (pp. 205–226). Lexington, MA: Lexington Books.

Haykin, (1994). *Neural networks: A comprehensive foundation.* New York: Macmillan.

Hill, C.W.L., & Jones, T. M. (1992). Stakeholder-agency theory. *Journal of Management Studies, 29*, 131–154.

Hillman, A., & Hitt, M. A. (1999). Corporate political strategy formulation: A model of approach, participation and strategy decisions. *Academy of Management Review, 24*, 825–842.

Hillman, A., & Keim, G. (1995). International variation in the business–government interface: Institutional and organizational considerations. *Academy of Management Review, 20*, 193–214.

Independent Sector. 2001. *The new nonprofit almanac.* Washington, DC: Independent Sector.

Inkpen, A. C. (1995). *The management of international joint ventures: An organizational learning perspective.* London: Routledge.

Inkpen, A. C. (1996). Creating knowledge through collaboration. *California Management Review, 39*, 123–140.

Inkpen, A. C, & Beamish, P. W. (1997). Knowledge, bargaining power and the instability of international joint ventures. *Academy of Management Review, 22*, 177–202.

Jensen, M. C., & Meckling, W. H. (1976). Theory of the firm: Managerial behavior, agency costs and ownership structure. *Journal of Financial Economics, 3*, 305–360.

Jones, T. M. (1995). Instrumental stakeholder theory: A synthesis of ethics and economics. *Academy of Management Review, 20*, 404–437.

Kaufman, A. M., Englander, E. J., & Marcus, A. A. (1989). Structure and implementation in issues management: Transaction costs and agency theory. In L. Preston & J. Post (Eds.), *Research in Corporate Social Performance and Policy* (11: 257–271). Greenwich, CT: JAI Press.

Kellow, A. (1999). Norms, interests, and environmental NGOs: The limites of cosmopolitanism. *Environmental Politics, 9(3)*, 1–22.

Kohonen, T. (1988). An introduction to neural computing. *Neural Networks, 1*, 3-16.

Kostova, T., & Zaheer, S. (1999). Organizational legitimacy under conditions of complexity: The case of the multinational enterprise. *Academy of Management Review, 24*, 64–81

Lado, A. A., Boyd, N. G., & Hanlon, S. C. (1997). Competition, cooperation and the search for economic rents: A syncretic model. *Academy of Management Review, 22*, 110–141.

Lenway, S. A., & Murtha, T. (1994). The state as strategist in international business research. *Journal of International Business Studies, 25*, 513–535.

Manzo, K. (2000). Nongovernmental organizations and models of development in India. *Journal of Environment and Development, 9*, 284–313.

Marcus, A., Kaufman, A., & Beam, D. (Eds.). (1987). *Business strategy and public policy.* Westport, CT: Quorum.

Meznar, M., & Nigh, D. (1995). Buffer or bridge? Environmental and organizational determinants of public affairs activities in American firms. *Academy of Management Journal, 38*, 975–996.

Mitchell, R. K., Agle, B. R., & Wood, D. J. (1997). Toward a theory of stakeholder identification and salience: Defining the principle of who and what really counts. *Academy of Management Review, 22*, 853–886.

Mitnick, B. (1993). Choosing agency & competition. In B. Mitnick (Ed.), *Corporate political agency* (pp.1–12). Newbury Park, CA: Sage.

NGOs: Sins of secular missionaries. (2000, January 29). *The Economist*, 25–27.

Nohria, N., & Eccles, R. C. (1992). *Networks and organizations: Structure, form and action.* Boston: Harvard Business School Press.

North, D. (1991). *Institutions, institutional change and economic performance*. Cambridge: Cambridge University Press.

Olson, M. (1982). *The rise and decline of nations*. New Haven, CT: Yale University Press.

Ring, P. S. (2000, November 17). *Roles for states in fostering cooperative exchanges*. Presentation to the Academy of International Business annual meeting, Phoenix, AZ.

Ring, P. S., & Van de Ven, A. H. (1992). Developmental processes of cooperative interorganizational relationships. *Academy of Management Review, 19*, 90–118.

Rowley, T. J. (1997). Moving beyond dyadic ties: A network theory of stakeholders' influences. *Academy of Management Review, 22*, 887–910.

Rugman, A. M., & Verbeke, A. (1990). *Global corporate strategy and trade policy*. London: Routledge.

Shaffer, B., & Hillman, A. (2000). The development of business–government strategies by diversified firms. *Strategic Management Journal, 21*, 175–190.

Tax Report. (2001, September 26). *Wall Street Journal*, p. A1.

Thorelli, H. B. (1986). Networks between markets and hierarchies. *Strategic Management Journal, 7*, 37–51.

Tocqueville, A. de. (2000 [1835]). *Democracy in America*. Edited and translated by H. C. Mansfield and D. Winthrop. Chicago: University of Chicago Press.

Union of International Associations. (2001). http://www.uia.org/homeorg.htm

van Tujil, P. (1999). NGOs and human rights: Sources of justice and democracy. *Journal of International Affairs, 52*, 493–512.

Vogel, D. J. (1996). The study of business and politics. California Management Review, 38, 146–158.

Wasserman, S., & Faust, K. (1994). *Social network analysis: Methods and applications*. Cambridge: Cambridge University Press.

Wasserman, S., & Galaskiewicz, J. (1994). *Advances in social network analysis: Research in the social and behavioral sciences*. Thousand Oaks, CA: Sage.

Weidenbaum, M. (1980). Public policy: No longer a spectator sport for business. *Journal of Business Strategy, 1*, 46–53.

CHAPTER 2

Nongovernmental Organizations and Business–Government Relations: The Importance of Institutions

Gerald Keim

Nongovernmental organization is a twenty-first century term for what James Madison (1961) described in the *Federalist Papers* more than two centuries ago as "factions." Significant differences between the NGOs of today and the factions of Madison's time include (1) the ease of organizing brought about by the Internet and digital communication technology, (2) the expanded geographic scope of membership of some NGOs, and (3) the variety of venues in which modern NGOs operate in efforts to advance their interests. NGOs exist today to pursue a wide variety of goals, from influencing the terms of world trade to providing humanitarian relief to destitute people. In this chapter I will consider only those NGOs that seek to influence public policies and discuss how their efforts can affect business–government relations in various political arenas.

In some instances, nonbusiness NGOs can be significant competitors or collaborators for businesses or business groups. In other cases, they may be of little consequence. From a business–government relations perspective, the importance of NGOs depends very much on the institutional setting in which they are encountered. Organized groups of individuals have often played an important role in the public policy process in democracies around the world. In the first section of this chapter I discuss the general advantages organized groups enjoy relative to unorganized individuals in democracies and other political–institutional settings. Next, a simple framework for examining differences in institutional features of democracies in different countries is developed. Examples demonstrating how different institutional settings can affect NGO opportunities and operations are discussed. This is followed by a review of the nature and goals of business–government relations activities in democratic governments. Finally, the discussion turns to how modern NGOs can affect business–government relations.

ORGANIZED INTERESTS AND THE PUBLIC POLICY PROCESS

The relative effectiveness of organized interests vis-à-vis the unorganized public has been described in detail by political scientists (Bentley, 1935; Truman, 1951; Schattschneider, 1960; Key, 1964; Lowi, 1969; Salisbury, 1969; Walker, 1983; Berry, 1984; Loomis & Cigler, 1991; Jackson & Kingdon, 1992) and by political economists since Anthony Downs (1959) and James Buchanan and Gordon Tullock (1962). The work of Downs and Mancur Olson (1965, 1982), in particular, provide a logic for explaining why individuals who join organized groups are more likely than unorganized voters to be informed about and involved in governmental processes when policies concerning their interests are being considered. Groups are able to economize on the costs of information gathering and dissemination for their members. Informed and organized voters are more likely to participate in democratic politics by working for parties or candidates, expressing their opinions in public forums, and voting. Individuals who are not part of politically active groups are less likely to be informed or involved in public policy processes.

Information Acquisition: Groups and Channels

In considering an individual's rationale for gathering information to become better informed about certain public policy issues, the conditions for information acquisition have evolved substantially. Prior to the era of electronic communication, one became better informed by reading newspapers and other publications and listening to speeches and discussions about issues. In the twenty first century, information sources have expanded to include television, radio, and (most significantly) the Internet. As sources of information have expanded, so have the number of increasingly complex public policy issues. Likewise, the number of political decision makers and the levels of government that may be involved in deciding policy issues have increased. This complexity and a commensurate rise in voter apathy and alienation may result in lower participation rates. Hence, it is not surprising that many voters remain ignorant about policy details and policy positions of politicians and bureaucrats, despite the increase in sources of information in the new century.

Downs (1959) showed that the value of gathering information pertaining to the details of alternative policy options as well as information about the position and behavior of legislators or bureaucrats, even when voters feel strongly about a particular policy issue, might be very low. Spending significant time and energy becoming informed is not worth much, according to Downs, if the probability that an individual voter can influence a policy decision is very small. Certainly this is the case in most federal and state elections, when more than 10,000 individuals are expected to vote. The 2000 U.S. presidential election notwithstanding, the statistical probability that one person's vote will determine an election outcome is close to zero. Thus many voters in democracies are *rationally ignorant* about the details of policy options or even the voting records of elected officials (Downs, 1959). That is, Downs's work suggested that people will be reluctant to spend a lot of time and effort becoming better informed about public policy issues when it is unlikely that acquiring additional information will enable them to influence the outcome of most public policies. Evidence from the United States seems to support Downs's contention. A recent poll taken during the 1996 presidential election in the United States found that less than one in three Americans could name their incumbent member of the House of Representatives who was facing reelection at that time (Morin, 1996). It seems reasonable to infer that relatively few voters would be familiar with the voting records of their legislators if so few of them even know their legislator's name.

For those individuals who join organized groups, the situation is different. Olson (1965, 1982) argued that while the costs of organizing were substantial, once groups were organized and information had been assimilated the incremental costs of producing and transmitting information to their members were very small. In addition, being informed changes the incentives to participate in the public policy process. Informed voters are more likely to participate in the public policy process and members of organized groups are more likely to be informed about the issues that affect their interests (Lipset, 1981). More recently, the Internet has significantly reduced the costs of finding individuals with similar policy concerns and sharing information among such individuals. The costs of organizing individuals with similar interests into groups have declined substantially as a result.

Organizational Affiliation:
Individual Choices and Benefits

In considering group membership from the perspective of the individual, there are myriad choices and options that are now available, each of which brings with it a rich and extensive channel of information. Being part of a group like the National Rifle Association in the United States or the Bund fur Umwelt und Naturschutz Deutschland (Friends of the Earth, Germany) makes it very easy for a member to be informed on public policy issues of concern. Newsletters, Web sites, and email can provide current and specific information on such issues as well as the public policy processes by which the issues are considered, including the time and location of rallies and protest movements pertaining to the issue of interest (Price, 2000). This reduces the costs to each member of being informed. Being a member of one of these groups, however, also increases the benefits of being informed. Political decision makers in democratic governments understand that many of their constituents are rationally ignorant about the details of many policy issues and the actions taken by political decision makers. They also understand that members of an NGO are more likely to be informed about the issues of concern to the specific organization. The logic behind more-informed voters being more powerful is straightforward. Making a policy decision on an issue about which voters are largely ignorant is less likely to affect the opportunities of those in government who seek to remain in government than making a decision that is contrary to the expressed interests of voters who have joined organized groups to further their policy interests.

The number of organized groups or NGOs has grown rapidly during the Internet era ("The non-governmental order," 1999), and some have estimated that the number of lobbyists in Washington representing individual businesses or groups has increased fivefold since the 1960s (Rauch, 2000). In the simplest sense, NGOs can reduce the costs of being informed and increase the benefits to members of being active in the political process of influencing government decision makers.

The specific nature of efforts by NGOs to influence government decision makers is a function, however, of the institutional setting in which government policy making takes place. I will discuss briefly how institutional arrangements may affect the tactics and strategies used by NGOs with special attention to parliamentary systems, the U.S. presidential–congressional system, and supranational institutional settings like the European Union and the World Trade Organization. First it may be helpful to introduce a simple framework for thinking about different institutional settings in which public policy issues are decided.

INSTITUTIONAL SETTINGS, NGO ACTIVITIES, AND ADVOCACY ORGANIZATIONS

Nobel Laureate Douglas North (1991, 1994) argues that institutional settings can be divided into three related categories. *Formal institutions* are the constitutions, laws, policies, and formal agreements that citizens of different locales create. In addition to the descriptive details of formal institutions, it is also important to understand that there is variance in how laws and policies are enforced in different locales. That is, the ability of institutional actors to arbitrarily change the rules of the game and for enforcement of rules and laws in some countries to be subject to the discretion of the enforcing agent poses risks for private actors. Some researchers have quantified these differences in the form or regulatory or political constraints (Henisz, 2000). *Informal institutions*, according to North, are the behavioral norms and mental models of individuals who may have different cultural heritages and religious or political beliefs or reside in different geographic areas. Informal institutions evolve slowly over time and are more difficult to change than formal institutions. Within any institutional setting, the third important category of this framework is the *organizations* that individuals form to advance their interests. These organizations may range from political parties and government agencies to business corporations or groups advocating issues of interest to factions of workers, environmentalists, those concerned with animal rights, or a myriad of other issues. Organizations like these are often key players in the process by which policy issues and other formal institutions, including changes in decision-making processes themselves, are considered. The implications of various institutional settings for NGO operations can be understood by focusing attention on the existing formal institutions, the informal institutions, and the organizations that operate within alternative institutional settings.

Institutions and NGOs: Opportunities and Constraints

Existing institutional arrangements and organizations affect the opportunities for new NGOs to form and exercise influence. Formal institutions often promulgate rules requiring political parties to garner a minimum percentage of votes cast in an election before a party can win seats in a legislature. These procedures tend to reduce the effectiveness of small, narrowly focused parties. For example, winner-take-all rules for electing legislatures in Great Britain, Canada, and the United States make it very difficult for new parties to be formed or have any chance of getting candidates elected. Laws pertaining to reporting requirements for various tax classifications make it easy to determine sources of funding for NGO operations. Such laws also make it easy for NGOs to acquire information about other groups, businesses, or government agencies that may affect the policies of interest to a specific NGO. These are a few examples of how formal institutions in different settings may affect NGO opportunities and activities. Of course, there will be variation and the relevant formal institutions in specific locales of operations will affect each NGO differently.

Organizations in different institutional settings are similarly important to NGO operations. For example, many parliamentary systems have strong political parties that appeal to large segments of the population and strong umbrella associations that typically represent the established interests of business and labor, such as the large trade and industry associations in France and Germany. These existing organizations create entry barriers that affect opportunities for new NGOs to participate in public policy processes (Hillman & Keim, 1995). Let us consider each of these separately.

Strong political parties in parliamentary systems like Germany exercise discipline over their elected and appointed members, requiring members to follow the party agenda. If members stray from the party line on policies, they will find it difficult to gain the party support that is necessary for reelection or reappointment. This minimizes the discretion of elected or appointed members to respond individually to pressures or incentives provided by NGOs in an effort to influence policy decisions. Instead, NGOs often must direct their efforts to influencing the agendas on which parties campaign for election. This requires more advanced planning and organization and moves advocacy efforts farther away from specific public policy decisions. In the United States, on the other hand, party discipline is much weaker and members of a party often vote against party leaders. President Clinton, for example, found many Democrats would not support his request for "fast track" authority to negotiate trade policy. Many Republicans also voted against their Speaker's position on protection for the steel industry in 1999. As a result, groups like the National Rifle Association or the Sierra Club can target individual members of Congress from both parties in their efforts to influence a pending public policy decision pertaining to gun control or the environment. Hence, the opportunities for influencing public policies may be more diffuse in some systems and there may be natural constraints in some instances because of the necessity to influence policy makers both directly and indirectly and in different levels of government and various political sectors.

The Status of NGOs in Different Institutional Settings

In the United States interest groups have no formal or traditional standing in the public policy process, although interest groups or factions have been participants in American politics since the administration of George Washington. In some countries (like Austria, for example) umbrella organizations like the chambers of labor and commerce enjoy mandatory membership laws that require every worker or every business owner to join. The umbrella associations are seen under existing laws as the legitimate representatives of workers and businesses and have an accepted role in the public policy process. This can make it difficult for new NGOs without mandatory memberships to be effective and make it difficult for them to participate in the established public policy process. The established umbrella associations have the effect of crowding them out.

As the European Union expands its scope of decision making, on the other hand, the absence of strong Europeanwide political parties or umbrella organizations enables new NGOs to be more effective in recruiting members and in participating in the policy formation process. Similarly, other supranational policy-making organizations like the United Nations or the World Trade Organization may offer more opportunities for new NGOs to participate with less competition from older or more established organizations, since most of the entrenched organizations operate at the national, state, or provincial level.

BUSINESS–GOVERNMENT RELATIONS

Public policy decisions affect current operations and future opportunities wherever businesses operate. Businesses can choose from three different postures for dealing with public policy decision making. A purely reactive posture is pursued simply to respond to new policies or changes in existing policies as they occur. This posture requires no resource expenditures for involvement in the public policy process, but the adjustment costs may be quite high in terms of required and sometimes unanticipated changes in operations or investment plans. A second and more active form of participation in the public policy process is to actively monitor the progress of initiatives to change existing policy or institute new policy. Although this monitoring posture requires some resource expenditures, it may provide more time to anticipate and adjust to new policies. The benefits of gaining lead time may more than offset the costs of monitoring and result in net cost savings over the purely reactive posture. Joining a trade or industry association that monitors policy developments affecting members is often a lowcost way to engage in issue monitoring at the state, provincial, national, or supranational level.

Business–Government Relations and Issues Advocacy

The third and most aggressive business–government relations posture for a firm is to engage in issue advocacy in order to bring about new policies that are more favorable or to resist proposed changes in existing policy that would be less favorable to the business's interests. This posture includes monitoring efforts to assess what is occurring in the public policy process and to identify new opportunities and threats. Some of the opportunities and threats will be chosen for advocacy efforts by a firm or coalition of firms and other NGOs. The choice of which issues to select for advocacy efforts depends in part on the likely impact an issue may have on a business or set of coalition partners and on the probability that a business or coalition can influence the outcome of an issue by influencing relevant policy decision makers as they decide on specific issues (Keim, 2001). In addition, the ability of an NGO or NGO coalition to influence government and public policy may be a function of the number and power of the coalition partners, as pointed out elsewhere in this volume.

Issues Life Cycles

Many problems, disputes, or disagreements that become public policy issues seem to follow a similar life cycle (Baron, 2000). The issue begins as in the lower left corner of Figure 2.1 with some initial event. For example, such an event may be journalistic coverage of genetic science as it is applied to agricultural products, as discussed by Soule (this volume), or a protest about labor issues in some developing nation. Many events go no further but some will continue to attract attention. Continuing media interest is most likely if an event arouses interest in some group of citizens. This may occur when there is a group of citizens who are intensely interested in implications of the event. In other cases discussion of the event may be added to the advocacy agenda of existing interest groups or NGOs. Interest in the issue by such groups tends to move the issue along the life cycle from left to right. If the event or the implications of the event for existing policy or future policy continues to attract inter-

Figure 2.1
Issue Life Cycle

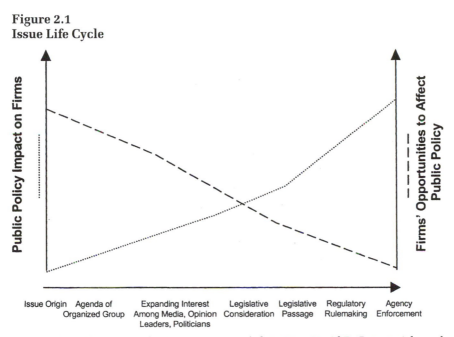

Source: From *Business and Its Environment*, 3/E by Baron, David P., © 2000. Adapted by permission of Pearson Education, Inc., Upper Saddle River, NJ.

est from NGO members, some media coverage is likely to continue. If the group or groups concerned with the issue are able to expand interest in the issue to politicians, then policy proposals will be debated. This is a substantial step forward and moves the issue into the actual policy-making arena. Sufficient organized interest in a particular policy proposal may lead to the adoption of such a policy by the government and new rules and regulations may be promulgated as a result.

In the case of NGOs, the model of business–government relations and issues advocacy provides the framework within which NGOs advocate their issues with governments and the issues life cycle offers a system for understanding the progress and sequence of issue development. In the next section I describe how NGOs use various tools and techniques to advance their interests within this framework.

NGOs AND BUSINESS–GOVERNMENT RELATIONS

As widespread access to the Internet has increased, information about events that may become public issues is easier to access and disseminate and the costs of organizing group action have been reduced substantially. Thus, for any given issue arising in the twenty-first century it is easier to generate interest by an NGO or to form an NGO specifically to deal with the issue, than was the case in the pre-Internet era. It is also true that due to the increased number of NGOs in operation, there are more groups monitoring more aspects of business operations. This in turn leads to more NGOs discovering new issues that may lead to new controversies for businesses than was the case before the Internet was so widely used.

NGOs and the Issues Life Cycle

NGOs are important players early in the issue life cycle by identifying new issues through their extensive monitoring of business activities. One example is a Web site that provides information about the quantity of environmental emissions a firm may produce in various geographic locales. The Environmental Defense Fund maintains a Web site, Scorecard.org, which is both a provider of existing information and a collector of new information (Price, 2000). This site enables U.S. residents to monitor which firms are emitting pollutants in their local environment. The site also provides a means for individuals accessing the site to provide new information pertaining to emerging issues in their local area about which the Environmental Defense Fund may not be informed. Scorecard.org also provides information on how to join the environmental movement. Since new information often builds interest and leads to a desire to take some action, this can be an effective recruiting device for new members. In addition, since larger coalitions inherently signal greater credibility and legitimacy, such organizational growth and expansion can be important to NGO effectiveness.

NGOs and Collective Actions

Collective actions can be organized more easily as a result of the Internet as well. As discussed in the chapter by Domask (this volume), simultaneous protests in front of Home Depot stores across the United Sates coordinated with critical advertisements publicizing the company's purchases of timber from old-growth forests led to a change in purchasing policy by the firm (Alden, 2001). This in turn led a major Canadian forest-products supplier to announce an end to cutting old-growth forests.

The ease with which information can be gathered and disseminated means that all information, regardless of its veracity, can be spread quickly to interested parties. Information that is unverified, distorted, exaggerated, or simply false can be disseminated and may lead some groups to take action as if the information was accurate and verified by other sources. The attack on Royal Dutch Shell for proposing to sink the Brent Spar oil drilling platform in deep ocean water was led by Greenpeace and based on allegations of environmental damages that later proved to be questionable (De Jonquieres, 2001). As a result, businesses and other organizations concerned with public policy must develop capabilities to quickly respond to the dissemination of new information. In a world where rational ignorance among unorganized voters is widespread, perceptions based on misinformation may be as important for some public policy issues as carefully researched facts.

NGOs and Political and Legislative Action

NGOs are also important players in the evolving process that brings some issues to the attention of politicians and provides political support for passage or defeat of new policies. In the United States, NGOs can provide a candidate or elected official with support from segments of interested voters in return for the politician supporting the issues or policies of interest to the NGO members. NGOs organized to deal with environmental or labor issues, for example, can provide political support that may substitute for the support that would be provided by political parties in some democracies. Support from organized groups other than political parties enables elected officials to be more independent of their parties, which in turn provides more opportunity for organized groups to directly influence elected decision makers when policies of interest are being considered. Although such status is not common in the United States, the maverick independent Representative Bernard Sanders (I–Vt.) is an archetype of a politician whose political support and constituencies depend much more heavily on informal citizen groups and NGOs than on formal political parties.

In democracies where parties maintain strong discipline over their elected members, NGOs must direct their influence efforts at the formation of party agendas. Parties in such countries develop agendas before elections with a view toward focusing on issues that will attract the interests of likely voters. Trying to influence party agendas is a more indirect means of influencing public policies, but it is often the best opportunity provided to NGOs in countries, like Great Britain, with strong parliamentary systems. If a party adopts agenda items supported by an NGO or coalition of NGOs and then wins election, the supporting NGOs stand to benefit directly. Not only will the new party in power advocate their preferred policy positions, but they also may receive assistance directly from the government to implement policy actions. Some British NGOs concerned with debt relief for developing nations enjoyed a symbiotic relationship with the British treasury in the late 1990s. The treasury used the NGOs to generate popular support for the government's position on debt relief, and in turn the British government was a champion for debt relief with the International Monetary Fund (Beattie, 2001).

NGOs and National and Supranational Institutional Settings

As mentioned earlier, some parliamentary systems also have very well established umbrella interest groups that have a long tradition of participating in the public policy process to represent the interests of established groups like business, labor, and agriculture. The existence of these groups and the widespread acceptance of their traditional role in the public policy process are entry barriers to the policy influence of newly formed groups in these institutional settings.

The emergence of new policy venues, often at the supranational level, like the EU and the WTO, create opportunities for NGOs precisely because strong parties and established umbrella groups do not exist for such venues. Thus, entry into the policy-making arena for NGOs is far easier and there may be fewer competitors in these newer venues.

Because political parties and established umbrella groups are anchored in the institutional arrangements of a particular country, these organizations are often not as successful when trying to operate in supranational policy venues. NGOs with experience operating in numerous national settings and that draw members from various countries may be more effective in supranational venues because of their cross-national experience.

NGO Collaborations and Coalitions

Individual NGOs are likely to be more successful in political arenas when they can form coalitions or otherwise work in concert with other groups and, in so doing, broaden their representative base. An obstacle to closer coordination in the past has been competition among NGOs. Many politically active NGOs depend on members to provide or attract financial resources. Because NGOs compete for members with other groups, many were afraid to share membership lists. New software that enables groups with similar agendas to activate members in unison without sharing membership lists has greatly facilitated coordination among NGOs with similar policy interests (Price, 2000).

This example of guarding membership lists illustrates another often-overlooked aspect of NGO operations. Consider whose interests are served by not sharing membership lists. It is hard to argue that NGO members are better served. Suppose some members of one NGO found another group to be more attractive after working together on some coordinated campaign effort and joined the other NGO. Clearly the members who switched groups would have improved their position by their action. The old group, however, would now have fewer members.

The total number of individuals working for the same cause or issue, however, would not be smaller. In fact the number may be larger if the coordinated advocacy effort led to more publicity than the NGOs could attract individually and the increased publicity attracted new members to work for the cause. In fact, it is hard to imagine circumstances under which members of one group would not want to share rosters with other like-minded groups to unite in action for their common cause. But as Benjamin Smith, Environmental Defense outreach coordinator, said in an interview with Tom Price, "The reality of the nonprofit membership world is that groups like ours are very cautious about how they share membership databases . . . they fear other groups might lure their members away" (2000, p. 28). This is competition, plain and simple, and leaders of NGOs do not like competition any more than leaders of businesses or labor unions or other groups.

As principal–agent theory suggests, just as in private corporations shareholders' and managers' interests may differ, the interests of NGO leaders and managers also may diverge from those of their membership base. Some leaders may even be professional organizers whose primary goal is maintaining, if not growing, the group they lead. Leaders may not be true believers in the cause for which the NGO was originally founded. On the other hand, there may be instances in which the staffs of NGOs are more "hard core" than their membership constituents, suggesting that members and donors have the opportunities to "shop around" for NGOs that most closely represent their interests (Teegen, this volume).

This potential difference in interests between members and leaders of some NGOs is important because it can provide opportunities for businesses to gain access to or otherwise participate in some NGO activities. Leaders seeking to grow their NGOs are interested in gaining more members and more resources to support expanded activities and future growth. By joining an NGO as a member or by providing support, either through a contribution directly or from a corporate-sponsored foundation, a business can establish a relationship with an NGO. This, in turn, opens lines of communication through which opportunities for sharing information or determining common ground may be explored. Agreeing to disagree on some issues may enable business firms and NGOs to work together on an occasional basis where similar issue positions can be negotiated. Working together occasionally and communicating more regularly can provide information useful in monitoring the progress of issues. Such interaction provides opportunities to shape advocacy efforts when policy changes by business are sought or are to be resisted. It also provides opportunities to affect market opportunities directly. In 1992, Greenpeace endorsed a new environmentally friendly refrigerant to replace coolants that damaged the ozone layer (Houlder, 2001). In this case, early participation in environmental groups by some producers of coolants alerted them to the market potential of developing products that were more environmentally friendly. When these products were introduced, some environmental NGOs' public statements helped with the marketing of these products. Both parties seem to have benefited from these interactions. Companies that view such NGOs as "the enemy" and have no dialogue or interaction miss such opportunities. Indeed, NGOs can and do draw attention to the fact the while company A and company B are doing the right thing, company C still has failed to change its ways.

SUMMARY AND CONCLUSION

In the early years of the twenty-first century, politically active NGOs are more numerous than they have ever been before. The Internet has reduced the costs of organizing and made it easier to monitor issues, disseminate information about issues, attract new members, and organize members in efforts to influence public policy at all levels of government. Organized groups have always been participants in the public policy processes of democracies. Opportunities for participation do vary from one institutional setting to another. Parliamentary systems with strong political parties and well-established umbrella organizations generally present reduced opportunities for NGOs to directly affect public policy decision making compared to democracy in the United States. NGOs in parliamentary systems are, however, more likely to be valuable sources of information and support as parties assemble agendas prior to elections. The issues of well-organized effective NGOs will increasingly affect election outcomes in these systems. Supranational venues like the European Union and the WTO, on the other hand, are venues where NGOs may be particularly successful as policy advocates in a very direct way. The absence of strong parties and umbrella groups in these settings enables NGOs to exert their influence directly with policy makers.

Thus, in many institutional settings organized groups are often key players in the public policy process, either as drivers of change or as sources of resistance to change, depending on the groups and the policies. As a result, businesses participating in government relations activities must be aware of existing and newly formed NGOs that may be active on issues of interest. NGOs can, through their efforts, move issues along the issue life cycle or retard their movement, effectively stopping the progress of an issue in its tracks. They may be able to prolong interest in an event that may have faded from public attention in past years. NGOs may work actively to oppose business interests in their efforts to influence political decision makers. Some firms, however, may be able to find common ground with some NGOs and form useful political coalitions with them. Understanding the differences in interests between members and leaders of NGOs can lead to the discovery of opportunities to help selected leaders with funding or other important resources. In return, firms can gain access, information, and opportunities to shape advocacy efforts.

From the NGO perspective, businesses can likewise be seen as adversaries in some cases and allies in others. Businesses can be important sources of information, resources, and influence. Seeking to find common ground can lead to broader coalitions and increase the likelihood of common interests being translated into public policy.

REFERENCES

Alden, E. (2001, July 18). Brands feel the impact as activists target customers. *Financial Times*, p. 7.

Baron, D. (2000). *Business and its environment*. Upper Saddle River, NJ: Prentice Hall.

Beattie, A. (2001, July 17). Campaigners offer moral integrity for influence. *Financial Times*, p 11.

Bentley, A. (1935). *The process of government*. Bloomington, IN: Principia Press.

Berry, J. M. (1984). *The interest group society*. Boston: Little, Brown.

Buchanan, J. M., & Tullock, G. (1962). *The calculus of consent: Logical foundations of constitutional democracy*. Ann Arbor, MI: University of Michigan Press.

De Jonquieres, G. (2001, July 19). Appealing to emotions to get the message across. *Financial Times*, retrieved October 20, 2001, from FT.com.

Downs, A. (1959). *An economic theory of democracy*. New York: Harper & Row.

Henisz, W. J. (2000). The institutional environment for economic growth. *Economics and Politics, 12*, 1–31.

Hernson, P. S., Shaiko, R. G., & Wilcox, C. (1998). *The interest group connection.* Chatham, NJ: Chatham House.

Hillman, A. J., & Keim, G. D. (1995). International variation in the business–government interface: Institutional and organizational considerations. *Academy of Management Review, 20*, 193–214.

Houlder, V. (2001, July 23). Campaigners learn lesson of business advantage. *Financial Times*, p. 9.

Jackson, J. E., & Kingdon, J. W. (1992). Ideology, interest group scores, and legislative votes. *American Journal of Political Science, 36*, 805–823.

Keim, G. D. (2001). Managing business political activities in the United States: Bridging between theory and practice. *Journal of Public Affairs, 2* (1), 362–375.

Key, V. O., Jr. (1964). *Politics, parties and pressure groups* (5th ed.). New York: Crowell.

Lipset, S. M. (1981). *Political man: The social bases of politics.* Baltimore, MD: Johns Hopkins University Press.

Loomis, B. A., & Cigler, A. J. (1991). Introduction: The changing nature of interest group politics. In A. J. Cigar & B. A. Loomis (Eds.), *Interest group politics* (3rd ed.). Washington, DC: CQ Press.

Lowi, T. J. (1969). *The end of liberalism* (2nd ed.). New York: Norton.

Madison, J., et al. (1961). *The Federalist papers*, edited by C. L. Rossiter. New York: New American Library.

Morin, R. (1996, January 29). Who's in control? Many don't know or care: Knowledge gap affects attitudes and participation. *Washington Post*, p. A1.

The non-governmental order. (1999, December 9). *The Economist.*

North, D. (1991). *Institutions, institutional change and economic performance.* Cambridge: Cambridge University Press.

North, D. (1994). Economic performance through time. *American Economic Review, 84*, 359–368.

Olson, M. (1965). *The logic of collective action: Public goods and the theory of groups.* Cambridge: Harvard University Press.

Olson, M. (1982). *The rise and decline of nations.* New Haven, CT: Yale University Press.

Price, T. (2000). *Cyber activism: Advocacy groups and the Internet.* Washington, DC: Foundation for Public Affairs.

Rauch, J. (2000). *Government's end: Why Washington stopped working.* New York: Public Affairs Press.

Salisbury, R. (1969). An exchange theory of interest groups. *Midwest Journal of Political Science, 13*, 1–32.

Schattschneider, E. E. (1960). *The semi-sovereign people: A realist's view of democracy in America.* New York: Holt, Rinehart and Winston.

Truman, D. B. (1951). *The governmental process.* New York: Knopf.

Walker, J. (1983). The origins and maintenance of interest groups in America. *American Political Science Review, 77*, 390–406.

CHAPTER 3

After Seattle: How NGOs Are Transforming the Global Trade and Finance Agenda

Jacqueline Deslauriers and Barbara Kotschwar

This volume examines, in part, the way in which nongovernmental organizations are affecting traditional business–government bargaining by "transforming it from a two-way exchange into a trilateral system of relationships and entanglements" (Doh, this volume). In this chapter the role of NGOs in country-to-country bargaining in the international economic arena is addressed, taking into account the steps that the international organizations responsible for guiding these international economic relations have taken in response to the rising demands for involvement of NGOs in the areas of trade and finance.

Throughout this chapter the term NGO refers to organized groups not affiliated with a government or international organization and not part of a corporation with particular interests or objectives. NGOs include environmental organizations, human rights groups, business associations, labor unions, academic organizations, and other interest groups. Within the existing literature and in policy discussions, the term "civil society" is often used interchangeably with NGO, particularly in the discussions of the Free Trade Area of the Americas (FTAA). Here, civil society should be understood as a broader category that includes NGOs as well as businesses and individuals.

Much of the information available on this topic is anecdotal and in several cases the mechanisms for incorporating NGO input into trade and finance policy fora are relatively new. The case studies presented in this chapter are descriptive. We do not pretend to assess whether the mechanisms are functioning well, but rather aim to provide a snapshot of the mechanisms that institutions and governments have put into place to accommodate the views and objectives of this new set of actors within the existing international framework. An assessment of these mechanisms is made more difficult, not only by the short reference period and scarcity of objective information on the subject, but also by the diverse range of organizations included under the aegis of the term NGO; it would be nearly impossible to come up with a majority opinion even if a thorough survey of all actors involved on all sides were possible.

While the chapter addresses the role of NGOs in the international economic arena, the analysis is done through the lens of changes in international organizations related to international trade and national trade policy consultative mechanisms. We also look at a number of international organizations active in international macroeconomics and finance: the World Bank and the International Monetary Fund (IMF), as well as the Organization of American States (OAS), whose mandate includes trade as part of a broader agenda.

When discussing the role of NGOs in trade and financial policy, the picture that often comes to mind is that of protesters rallying at the site of international meetings of economic policy makers. Effigies of World Bank and World Trade Organization (WTO) heads, mailboxes thrown through the windows of Starbucks, and students in turtle costumes throwing rocks are certainly one part of the picture. Also significant, however, although less visible, are those NGOs that have long worked to create a space for their views within the international economic decision-making process (Foster 2001). In identifying the actors under discussion, it would be misleading to talk about a single category of NGO with a stake in trade issues. These groups span a wide range of interests, from environmental groups to industry associations to human rights activists to groups of student dissatisfied with the current state of the world. As their objectives and interests differ, so do their tactics. Some groups have specifically articulated positions that they would like to see incorporated in governments' or international economic organizations' policies. Others would simply like these governments and organizations to stop what they are doing and, in the case of the trade and finance institutions, to cease existing. Korzeniewicz and Smith (2001) divide these into "insiders"—those groups favoring cooperation— and "outsiders"—groups that employ more confrontational strategies. This diversity makes it more difficult for policy makers who would like to address their concerns in a reasonable manner to constructively utilize their input. As Hoekman and Kostecki (2001, p.

2) note in their volume on the WTO, "Contradictory demands by these groups pose a great challenge for WTO members." A closer look at some of the means used to incorporate these groups will show the various ways in which NGOs are currently participating in the realm of trade policy.

THE CHANGING FACE OF TRADE POLICY

Trade policy has of late become an increasingly prominent subject of public discourse. Students who have followed the popular press over the past few years and were thus exposed to extensive media coverage of street protests and sit-ins aimed at stopping trade and financial talks may be surprised to hear that this has not always been the case. Traditionally, trade policy was the province of specialized bureaucrats. In fact, as late as the last completed round of multilateral trade negotiations, references to trade policy decisions were not normally seen as galvanizing news items and were relegated to the inside pages of most major newspapers. Silvia Ostry (2001) quotes the WTO director general's characterization of the launching of the Uruguay Round as being done in "the silence of public apathy." This is no longer the case: The silence on trade has quite decisively been broken. Judging from the front-page coverage received by the 1999 Seattle WTO Ministerial (often referred to as the "battle in Seattle") and the July 2001 G-8 summit in Genoa, trade is now a hot item.

While trade policy has always been of interest to particular domestic interest groups and coalitions—farmers, textile producers and steelworkers immediately come to mind—NGOs and civil society groups of various stripes and colors now claim an expertise on and an interest in trade and the shaping of the international trading system. University students engage in heated debate about the environmental impacts of WTO panel results, local newspapers run human interest stories on the impacts of liberalizing trucking services, and, according to one anecdote from Swiss television, journalists report that parents feel compelled to reassure their children that there is no WTO monster hiding underneath the bed (Hoekman & Kostecki, 2001). Numerous Web sites have sprung up touting the evils of free trade and collecting anti-MAI (Multilateral Agreement on Investment), NAFTA, FTAA, or WTO anecdotes. As regularly as meetings gathering trade technocrats are held, protesters mobilize in parallel to rise up against trade and globalization. Many may wonder how this sudden widespread interest in economic policy making has come about and why there was such a significant mobilization of NGOs interested in trade in the 1990s. The first part of this chapter addresses some of the factors that have come together to make trade a more prominent issue and to enable NGOs to be propelled into the international policy-making arena.

Growth of Trade

Statistically, trade's increased importance is reflected in the fact that trade has grown both in magnitude and as a percentage of world output. Over the past quarter century global trade flows have doubled and the ratio of world trade in goods and services has increased, rising by 10 percentage points since 1990 to reach nearly 30 percent in 2000 (WTO, 2001b). At the same time, cross-border foreign direct investment has increased, growing even faster than world production, capital formation, and trade, reaching a record $1.3 trillion in 2000 (UNCTAD, 2001). Multinational and transnational corporations have grown in number and the number of people employed by such corporations has grown. In the year 2000 there were more than 60,000 transnational corporations with more than 800,000 affiliates abroad (UNCTAD, 2001).

Trade and Technology

This rise in the trade of goods and services across countries has been spurred by several phenomena of the modern economy. Advances in communications, information processing, and transport have been essential to the explosion of trade and for increasing the ease in establishing foreign direct investments. The cost of long-distance telecommunications has fallen substantially over the past few decades. The introduction of the facsimile machine and even more so of electronic communications such as email has enabled inexpensive and nearly instantaneous transmission of large amounts of information. By the year 2000 it was possible, even commonplace in most advanced industrial countries, for people to communicate at minimal cost, or even for free, through the Internet. Falling personal-computer costs—a personal computer in 1990 was about a third of the cost in 1980—have dramatically cut the costs of doing business; and easy access to electronic monitoring (i.e., barcodes, electronic inventories, etc.) has enabled companies to move stock in previously unforeseen ways and to new trading partners. In addition, the cost of transportation, particularly air transport, has made previously difficult-to-reach markets readily accessible. Capital now flows nearly effortlessly across borders and goods distribution is less subject than ever to geographic constraints.

Trade and Public Policy

Government and intergovernmental policy actions have supplemented the impact of technology on the growth of trade. Governments have liberalized their economies through unilateral policy actions and by increasing their participation in multilateral negotiations. The General Agreement on Tariffs and Trade (GATT) was initiated in 1947 with 23 founding countries; at the end of the Uruguay Round establishing the WTO in 1994 there were 128; as of January 2002 the number of members had grown to 144. More trade and more trade agreements have meant more attention paid to trade. In addition, the issues on the trade negotiating agenda have grown progressively more complex and have moved away from the traditional border measures. During the first few GATT rounds, negotiators focused on bringing down tariff barriers to goods trade. Subsequent rounds introduced new agenda items, such as investment measures relating to trade policy, trade in services, and trade in ideas or intellectual property rights. More recently, other new issues, such as competition policy and electronic commerce, have been identified as candidates for discussions within the WTO. Most recently, trade policy and domestic regulations have become inextricably intertwined, and as the international trade regime comes into contact with domestic laws, people take greater notice. Changes in one government's policies more readily affect citizens in another country, and international economic negotiations now touch on more domestic aspects of society than ever before.

Trade and Multilateral Institutions

In addition to the dynamics underlying trade among companies in the international market, some important changes were made to the operations of the multilateral trading system. In the wake of the Uruguay Round, the institutionalization of the multilateral trading system has brought disputes into the international arena that had previously been addressed privately or bilaterally among companies or countries. Since the establishment of a system to regularize the undertaking of trade disputes, trade appears to have become more contentious, with disputes among nations growing (this increase in disputes could also be the result, however, of the increased access to trade-resolution mechanisms that had previously not existed). During the first year of its operation, the WTO Dispute Settlement Mechanism handled 22 disputes. By the end of 2000, more than 240 cases in total had been handled (WTO, 2001a). While the United States and the European Union continue to be the largest players in this process, developing countries have increasingly taken part, including instances of cases lodged by one developing country against another.

The Empowerment of the International NGO Community

The same factors increasing the reach of trade have contributed to the rise and empowerment of the international NGO movement. Trade-oriented NGOs have been able to mobilize and transnationalize themselves very effectively through the use of the Internet, fax, and cheap air tickets. Technological innovations have brought together like-minded groups from different regions. Mobilization has been greatly facilitated through rapid electronic and wireless communications and decreased costs of transport. The ease of international communications through the Internet is often mentioned as one of the factors that helped to bring about the demise of talks toward a multilateral framework on investment, as domestic interest groups joined across borders to jointly rally against the MAI. Farmers in mid-Saskatchewan have been able to share views and ideas with like-minded groups in France; environmental groups have teamed with trade lawyers in otherwise unimaginable alliances to fight against common economic foes; and, in advance of the Seattle Ministerial and Quebec City Summit meeting, U.S. NGOs offered training courses on trade issues, on mobilization, and on protest methods to potential demonstrators in meeting sites (Harding, 2001; Longworth, 1999). Tutorials advertised on various antitrade Web sites included how to hang a banner from a tall building, how to mitigate the effects of tear gas, and how to resist being lifted by the police.

As policies led to the economic opening that stimulated trade, openings in the political realm created a space for nontraditional political actors to be heard. Particularly in Latin America, democratization and liberalization in the 1980s gave rise to new grassroots movements and new networks of interest expression. This space created for civil society has allowed domestic as well as transnational NGOs to form and to mobilize.

In recent decades these NGOs have been successful in changing business and government policies by applying pressure, mobilizing resources, and increasing public attention. NGOs with an interest in trade issues have taken a cue from earlier NGOs, generally environmental and human rights groups that were successful in changing government and business behavior. The antiapartheid movement that convinced companies, national governments, and consumers to boycott South African goods until the apartheid system was abandoned was a principal example, as were the NGOs that mounted campaigns to convince Nike to change labor conditions in overseas plants and to make Nestlé revise its marketing of baby formula. Other examples include the boycott and actions against the Texaco corporation by the 1993 indigenous peoples' movements in Ecuador (see Ward, 2001), NGO activism against environmental degradation of the Amazon region in Brazil (see Barbosa, 1996; Hunter, 1996) and movements to gain recognition for unions in *maquiladoras* in Guatemala (Carr, 1999, p. 54). NGOs found that in international discussions they could perform the following functions:

- Raise awareness of issues, particularly to bring to a popular level information about technical issues.
- Mobilize support for or opposition to issues on the international agenda.
- Provide technical expertise and specific technical information.
- Monitor and oversee implementation.

Employing these techniques, NGOs have demonstrated their effectiveness and become players on the international stage. As such, economic integration, political liberalization and globalization have paved the way for NGOs to play an unforeseen role in the negotiations among states. As political scientist John Odell observes, "With this liberalizing policy trend, governments have constrained their abilities to decree economic and political outcomes and empowered other actors: commercial firms, banks, international agencies and nongovernmental organizations concerned with the environment, human rights and peace. All these actors are destined to be thrown together repeatedly in multiple, overlapping processes of conflict and bargaining" (2000, p. 2). The challenge to international organizations and national governments is how to use these interactions in a positive manner to enable them to achieve outcomes that will further their society's welfare.

The Emergence of NGOs: Implications for Trade Negotiations

The changes in the international economic arena are reflected by the acknowledgment in an IMF forum on civil society that "civic associations have undertaken initiatives to change and shape global laws and institutions. This development is certainly a change, if not a shift, in how and who governs in international relations and it has also been described as enlarged or complex multilateralism" (Schnabel, 2001, p. 2).

Historically, national negotiators—in this case we look at those engaged in setting the international trade and financial frameworks— have played a two-level game, negotiating with each other at the international level while at the same time receiving input from domestic coalitions. Now there is a third level, or at least a third actor, engaged in this two-level game: the international NGO community, which often has vast networks at play, applying pressure to advance their interests in the domestic arena as well as at the international level.

NGOs, TRADE, AND THE ROAD TO SEATTLE

Long active in the areas of environment and human rights, NGO mobilization in the area of trade began in earnest during the early 1990s. One early sign of interest by the NGO community in the operation of the multilateral trading system came from the environmental community as a result of the so-called tuna–dolphin case. This case, brought before the GATT dispute-settlement mechanism, was stimulated by a U.S. ban on tuna from Mexico under the provisions of a 1972 domestic U.S. law. This law, the Marine Mammal Protection Act, banned the importation of tuna from countries that did not use certain procedures to prevent the killing of dolphins. In 1991 Mexico complained under the GATT dispute-settlement procedure that it was being treated unfairly. The GATT panel held that the United States was behaving in a discriminatory manner toward trade from Mexico, thus violating a fundamental principle of the multilateral trading system, national treatment (nondiscrimination). According to the panel, the United States could not embargo imports of tuna products simply because Mexican regulations on the way tuna was produced did not conform to U.S. regulations. The panel report was not ultimately adopted. However, environmental NGOs saw this decision as favoring free trade over environmental protection and led them to become increasingly conscious of and involved in the NAFTA negotiations going on at the time, as well as to mobilize efforts toward increasing the profile of environmental issues at the WTO. Lawyers, specialists, and activists bombarded negotiators with information, launched public education campaigns, and lobbied legislators. At the conclusion of the NAFTA negotiations, environmental issues were eventually addressed explicitly in a side agreement on environmental cooperation and a nonnegotiating Committee on Trade and the Environment (CTE) was subsequently established in the WTO.

NGOs and the MAI Negotiations

The most prominent case of organized NGO mobilization against a trade-related initiative was that of the negotiations on the Multilateral Agreement on Investment within the Organization for Economic Cooperation and Development (OECD). This movement generated countless Web sites, slogans, and press reports, as well as an anti-MAI rock concert. By 1997 it had turned the streets of Paris into a site for demonstrations and rallies against the OECD. A leaked version of the draft MAI text was placed on various NGO Web sites, where it became fodder for the critics of the agreement. Much of the MAI opposition originated in Canada, when a number of environmental groups reacted to a dispute brought in the context of NAFTA between the government of Canada and a U.S. firm, the Ethyl Corporation (see Graham, 2000, pp. 37–39; Soloway, 1999). Characterizing the MAI as "NAFTA on steroids," NGOs launched an unprecedented effort of lobbying and protests against the agreement. As Graham states in a book that explores the breakdown of these negotiations, "The phenomenon of large-scale, street-fighting opposition to a multilateral commercial agreement was something that the world had never seen before the anti-MAI demonstrations and it poses an enigma" (2000, p. 9). Ultimately, the attempt to negotiate the MAI failed. Most analysts attribute the inability to reach consensus on the MAI as the result of a combination of factors, including vast differences in negotiating positions, an inappropriate choice of forum that did not incorporate the majority of developing countries, and poor timing. However, anti-MAI NGOs were quick to take full credit and advertise their success, and this episode became a claim of victory for the antiglobalization NGOs.

NGOs and Trade Advocacy: Insiders and Outsiders

In his discussion of the MAI episode, in which NGOs were ultimately invited to come into the room and share their concerns with the negotiators, Graham (2000) classifies the opposition NGOs into three main categories: those that refused to participate, claiming that the only acceptable agreement is no agreement; those that accepted the invitation to meet with OECD representatives, but used this space to shout denunciations; and those that sought to work with the OECD secretariat to see where their concerns could be addressed. This classification agrees with Korzeniewicz and Smith's (2001) classification. The first of these groups encompasses the "outsiders" who want to stop the process and to halt negotiations among countries toward what they see as an unfair or undesirable world order. The other group is composed of NGOs who work within the parameters of the system to create a space for participation, often remaining critical of the system in which they are participating and at times using the same techniques as the outsiders. The NGOs in this group try to advance their objectives from the inside through the creation of formal mechanisms for their participation in international fora and by making use of the space ceded by national and international institutions.

While the failure of the MAI negotiations cannot be attributed solely to NGOs, there is little doubt that they played a major role, that their voices were heard, and that the NGO antitrade movement was strengthened as a result. The perceived success of the MAI protests served as a launching pad for the subsequent demonstrations in Geneva, Seattle, Washington D.C., Prague, and Genoa, as well as a calling to consciousness of the world to the burgeoning antiglobalization movement. In Seattle, NGOs hoped to take advantage of similar internal weaknesses as seen in the MAI.

INSTITUTIONAL STEPS TO ACCOMMODATE NGO VIEWS

NGOs that have chosen to use "insider" techniques use a number of methods to influence policy. Among others, these include

- Reports and studies containing technical information, including legal briefs and opinions to be used in legal fora.
- Web sites for the dissemination of information and informational campaigns.
- Training in technical areas.

As NGOs have increased the scope and strategy of their trade-related activities, countries and international organizations have begun to take their views into account. They have also been able to work in cooperation with and to benefit from these organizations. Increasingly, organizations and governments have sought to use input from NGOs to gather technical information to which they themselves may not have easy access and to gauge the tenor of potential popular reaction to proposed policies. The number of NGOs participating in international debates has risen over the years. The Union of International Associations puts the number of international NGOs at 26,000 in 1999, up from 6,000 in 1990. Their activity in the international economic arena has also grown dramatically: In 1948 the United Nations, the first international organization to have incorporated NGO participation, listed 41 consultative groups formally accredited to the U.N. Economic and Social Council; by 1998 this number had exceeded 1,500 (Simmons, 1998). Over the past few decades numerous groups with specific interest in trade and finance have surfaced.

The WTO: From Marrakech to the
Battle in Seattle and Beyond

The World Trade Organization is a member-driven international organization set up to oversee trade policy and set the international framework of rules within which members conduct trade. The WTO's rule of consensus in decision making has prompted some to argue that NGO activity and influence should be concentrated on—or even limited to—input at the national level. Given the huge disparity of resources between NGOs in rich countries and those in poor countries—and even the potential disparity in resources between rich-country NGOs and poor countries themselves—there is a sense among some that despite the advances discussed in the preceding section, participation by rich-country NGOs in the WTO could overwhelm poorer countries and undermine the consensus nature of the multilateral trade realm. Others see NGOs as able to provide additional technical information not accessible to any but the most developed countries in a more equitable manner, and as providing a range of views that would offer countries a balance to official positions (Charnovitz, 2000).

While NGO participation in and interest about WTO activities has increased of late, such actors have been recognized since before the inception of the organization. The 1948 Havana Charter of the proposed International Trade Organization (ITO) (which was ultimately rejected in favor of a looser institutional structure in the form of the General Agreement on Tariffs and Trade) contained provisions on consultations and cooperation with nongovernmental organizations. GATT/WTO cooperation with other bodies concerned with similar issues has grown over the years. In the original GATT only one other body was explicitly mentioned, the IMF, which governments were to contact for matters regarding foreign exchange transactions and in connection with the invocation of the balance of payments provisions.

The Uruguay Round agreements, however, make reference to various intergovernmental institutions. These include the World Bank, the World Intellectual Property Organization, and the World Customs Organization, as well as various nongovernmental or quasi-nongovernmental organizations such as the International Organization for Standardization, the Codex Alimentarius Commission, the International Office of Epizootics, and the International Plant Protection Convention. Although the International Chamber of Commerce (ICC) has traditionally actively followed the work of the GATT and the WTO, the first formal agreement between the WTO and an NGO was concluded by the International Federation of Inspection Agencies

(IFIA). This agreement concerned preshipment inspection. In 1995 the WTO established an independent entity to oversee arbitration in preshipment inspection through an agreement with the IFIA and the ICC.

In addition, the agreement explicitly makes provisions for general cooperation with NGOs. In the Uruguay Round Agreement establishing the World Trade Organization, Article V(2), "On Relations with Other Organizations," states, "The General Council may make appropriate arrangements for consultation and cooperation with non-governmental organizations concerned with matters related to those of the WTO" (WTO, 1995). This language is almost identical to that proposed for the ITO in 1948. The following year the *Guidelines for Arrangements on Relations with Non-Governmental Organizations* directed the WTO secretariat to seek more active interaction, through symposia and briefings, with NGOs (WTO, 1996). While these guidelines mandated an expanded communication with NGOs, they also emphasized the intergovernmental nature of the organization, underlining the importance of national consultation mechanisms with NGOs, and rejected direct involvement of NGOs in WTO work.

Over the past decade, particularly since the Uruguay Round, many more NGOs that consider they have relevant interests in WTO work have become active in the discussion on the operations of the WTO. The most vocal have been those representing labor and environmental groups and others that would like to use the WTO as "an instrument to enforce norms and rules" in nontrade areas (Hoekman & Kostecki, 2001, p. 71).

The first incidence of a mobilized opposition presence of NGOs at a GATT meeting took place in Brussels at the 1990 ministerial meeting, where large numbers of groups opposed policies they considered unfavorable to developing countries, terming the launching of a new round of trade liberalization a "GATT-astrophe" (Croome, 1995, p. 276). Since this event, subsequent WTO ministerial meetings have nearly all been accompanied by protestors espousing a variety of causes.

Shortly after its inception, the WTO began to take steps to include the views of NGOs with an interest in trade issues. In November 1996 the International Center for Trade and Sustainable Development (ICTSD) was formed. The ICTSD's mandate is to improve relations between the WTO and NGOs involved in trade and sustainable development issues. In 1996 NGOs were first able to attend the WTO ministerial meeting, held that year in Singapore. The following year the WTO began sponsoring symposia for NGOs on issues of interest to them.

One area in which NGOs expressed a great deal of interest was in the dispute-settlement mechanism. Starting with the so-called shrimp–turtle case, NGOs began submitting amicus briefs, or unsolicited position papers. The dispute settlement panel for the shrimp-turtle case did not take these briefs into account, as it felt that it did not have authority to consider them under the WTO Dispute Settlement Undertaking (DSU). In 1998 NGOs took another approach to sharing their views on this case by forwarding their briefs to the U.S. government, which was appealing the shrimp–turtle decision. The U.S. government submitted these NGO briefs as an attachment when it submitted its appeal, thus making them part of the U.S. government submission. The Appellate Body accepted these attachments, as well as an additional brief submitted directly by an NGO. Later in the year, the Appellate Body issued a decision that basically stated that NGOs could submit briefs but the panel was not under obligation to consider them. After a subsequent panel (the asbestos case) in which amicus briefs were submitted, the Appellate Body established a mechanism for submission of NGO briefs, in which submitting parties must make clear their objectives, affiliation, and financing, as well as provide a summary of their contribution to the issue at hand and an explanation of why their material does not repeat material already received by the body from countries (see Charnovitz, 2000; WTO, 2000a, 2000b).

The WTO has attempted to respond to criticisms and concerns from NGOs and has made strides to cooperate with NGOs. As Richard Blackhurst asserts, such cooperation can help bring "new views and arguments to bear on the wide range of issues covered by the WTO's rules and procedures" (1998, p. 37). The WTO has made these rules and procedures more transparent to the public by making many documents, including previously restricted documents, available to the public. While the GATT was criticized for being secretive, opaque, and stingy with information, the WTO has made efforts to disseminate information, although some important data remain restricted to countries. In 1995, the WTO launched its public Web site, on which it has placed a great deal of information, including the full text of all public and derestricted documents, an explanation of the WTO agreements and issues, a list of member countries and countries in accession, schedules of meetings and various studies and statistics. This Web site has been overhauled to make it more user friendly and the process of document derestriction has been made much quicker. On the new site, information is provided regarding the date of derestriction, so the speed of this process can be monitored. In addition, there is a monthly listing of documents received by NGOs and a specific section devoted to information regarding NGOs and trade.

In an additional attempt to engage a range of views, the WTO has sponsored various symposia for participation of NGOs and other civil society groups. Beginning in 1998, these symposia, which were also Web-cast, involved a broad spectrum of NGOs from business, environmental groups, academics, and so on. Governments also attended. In subsequent years, open symposia have been held addressing the relationship between trade and sustainable development, the role of developing countries in the next round of trade negotiations, regionalism, and other issues such as financial services and intellectual property rights. Discussions are public and supporting documents are made available at http://www.wto.org.

Multilateral Financial Institutions and NGOs

Over the past decade, the World Bank and the International Monetary Fund have seen increased NGO interest in their projects and policies, in terms of NGO participation in projects as well as those who would most like to see the organizations shut down. Since the early 1990s, Bank–Fund annual meetings—whether in Madrid, Prague, or Washington—have been accompanied by street protestors and mass demonstrations. Over this same period of time, both institutions have worked together in closer cooperation with nongovernmental groups and have greatly increased the amount of information they make publicly available. The international financial institutions have, over the past decade, used three basic mechanisms to work with NGOs. First, they have taken steps to increase transparency and make more of their materials available to civil society groups. Second, they have oriented some resources toward activities involving NGOs and civil society actors. Third, they have established consultative mechanisms on specific projects and activities.

The World Bank: Gateways and Participation

In the early 1980s, nongovernmental organizations were active in commenting on World Bank activities in areas relating to debt and debt rescheduling; and in the 1990s, social and environmental issues assumed center stage (Brown & Fox, 2000). In 1994 a coalition comprising more than 200 NGOs with the catchy title of "Fifty Years Is Enough" mobilized at the annual meetings in Madrid with a well-organized campaign protesting World Bank and IMF policies. Increasingly vocal NGOs prepared reports and disseminated information about Bank projects that they saw as contradictory to the Bank's own policies, especially some high-profile projects.

The World Bank began to form a mechanism for relationships with nongovernmental actors in the 1980s. In 1981 the first operational policy note on relations with NGOs was approved by the board of directors. In 1982 an NGO–World Bank committee was formed to engage NGOs in dialogue on issues considered of importance to civil society. In the early 1990s, in response to mounting criticism by NGOs mainly with respect to environmental aspects of various World Bank projects as exemplified by the implementation of the Sardar Sarovar (Narmada) projects in India, the World Bank commissioned studies on internal lending policies and on the environmental and resettlement effects of its projects. The results of these studies (see World Bank, 2001a; Hunter & Udall, 2001) included the creation of a three-member inspection panel that would serve as an independent forum for private citizens whose interests have been directly harmed by a World Bank–financed project (IBRD, 1993). Since then, NGOs have been actively consulted in many World Bank projects, especially in environmental issues. The World Bank has gone so far as to join a formal global partnership (1998) with the world's largest environmental organization—WWF—to help protect the world's forests. The World Bank–WWF Forest Alliance includes a management team and steering committee jointly staffed by both organizations and under one operational budget.

Institutionally, the World Bank has dedicated human and financial resources to focus on civil society issues. The World Bank, according to its Web site, defines civil society as "development and advocacy NGOs," as well as "trade unions, faith-based organizations, community-based organizations, foundations and other groups that shape local and global society" (see http://www.worldbank.org/html/extdr/pb/pbcivilsociety.htm). The Environmentally and Socially Sustainable Development Network and the Office of the Vice President of External Affairs, based in Washington, D.C., spearhead the World Bank's NGO initiatives, placing more than seventy civil society specialists in Bank offices in developing countries. This effort was undertaken to "facilitate a global, regional, national and local policy dialogue and outreach with civil society and to generally ensure a two-way flow of information between the World Bank and civil society on a range of issues" (World Bank, 2001b). Even in developing its own broader operational policies and directives, the World Bank has gone to great lengths to incorporate nongovernmental voices through briefings, consultative rounds of discussion with NGOs, draft policy releases for feedback, and even paying to fly developing-country NGO representatives to these meetings. The Indigenous Peoples Policy, the Resettlement Policy, and the Forest Policy are a few of the major World Bank guiding policies that included such extensive outreach and consultation.

In addition to consulting NGOs on project matters, the Bank has moved to increase transparency regarding its operations. In 1993 the World Bank increased the types of documents available to the public and established Public Information Centers (PICs), enquiry points for the public, located in various member countries to make these documents more widely available. Following steps in 1998 and 2000, The Bank released Heavily Indebted Poor Country (HIPC) documents, Country Assistance Strategies (1998), Poverty Reduction Strategy Papers, Bank–IMF Joint Staff Assessments (2001), as well as papers prepared for International Development Agency (IDA) meetings (2001) (see World Bank, 2002).

The World Bank also funds small-scale activities in developing countries for which NGOs serve as executing agencies. According to the World Bank Web site, between 1985 and 1997 nearly $900 million was approved to support activities involving nongovernmental organizations. In 1999 the NGO and Civil Society Unit of the social development arm of the World Bank prepared general guidelines for World Bank staff to conduct consultations with civil society organizations. An additional tool, the World Bank's *Consultations with Civil Society—A Sourcebook* was published in 2001 (World Bank, 2001b). For fiscal year 2000, a portfolio review conducted by social development staff of the Bank showed that 71 percent of the projects considered by the Bank's board reported intended civil society involvement (World Bank, 2001b).

The International Monetary Fund

The main mechanism used by the IMF with respect to NGOs is the increased provision of information. The number of IMF documents, which also includes country staff papers and details about country financing arrangements that are publicly available, has increased markedly. The director of the IMF's office in Europe addressed these issues in an editorial written to inform NGOs of the will of the IMF to work with them. In this editorial, Fleming Larsen (2000, p. 281) writes, "Our dialogue with the NGOs is helping us to better understand their points of view and it is clearly having an impact on our policy formulation and presentation. This impact has been particularly visible in the huge quantity of information the IMF now releases."

The Organization of American States:
Civil Society Accreditation

The Organization of American States is an intergovernmental organization that brings together the countries of the Americas. Since 1994 the OAS has received mandates from the Summit of the Americas process that address issues relating to the strengthening of democracy; the promotion of growth and prosperity, including the growth of trade; better labor conditions; and protection of the environment and social matters, including poverty, health, education, and gender equality.

Various attempts had been made over the years to devise a single mechanism through which nongovernmental groups with relevant interests could participate in the activities of the OAS. The challenge lay in devising a flexible framework for the participation of a varied and highly diversified NGO community with interests in the work of the OAS.

In 1994 a working group was created under the aegis of the Permanent Council, the body responsible for carrying out the work of the OAS, to study the possibility of granting formal status to NGOs in the OAS. The working group labored for several years to reach consensus on the issue but was unable to come to an agreement. As with most political initiatives, timing played an important role in bringing about success: The 1998 Santiago Summit of the Americas called for governments to promote the formation of civil society organizations and to foster public sector–civil society dialogue and partnerships (Summit of the Americas, 1998). This signal helped to provide the impetus to move beyond the status quo and devise a mechanism within the OAS to grant civil society participation in its activities.

The June 1999 OAS General Assembly approved Resolution 1661, which established within the Permanent Council a Committee on Civil Society Participation in OAS Activities. The special committee was tasked with preparing guidelines for the participation of civil society in OAS activities, and the deadline for completion and adoption of these guidelines was set for December 31, 1999.

Prior to the establishment of these guidelines, civil society participated in the activities of the OAS as invited guests or observers (see OAS, 1971). The procedure required interested groups to petition to attend a specific meeting or conference. Civil society organizations over the years had developed relationships with individual agencies and departments within the OAS, but a regulatory framework for the organization as a whole was lacking. The *Guidelines for the Participation of Civil Society Organizations in OAS Activities* (OAS, 1999) covers the procedural requirements for organizations to become accredited as well as the broader issues of the scope and principles for participation. The purpose in establishing the guidelines was to bring to the deliberations of the OAS the benefit of a pool of advice from organizations with expertise in their respective areas of competence.

The OAS maintains a register of civil society groups that have presented applications and been accepted through the accreditation process. It remains the case that any group that has not chosen to become accredited may still apply to attend specific meetings of the organs, agencies, and entities of the OAS. Those organizations that are accredited and are included on the register must still apply, by way of a letter to the secretary general, to attend the annual OAS General Assembly.

An application from a group to become accredited must meet the criteria set out in the guidelines and is reviewed by the Permanent Council's Committee on Civil Society Participation in OAS Activities. If an application does not meet the criteria set out in the guidelines or is incomplete, the committee will notify the civil society organization, which then has the opportunity to gather the necessary information, answer any question the committee may have with respect to the petition, and then resubmit its application for further consideration.

To date, there are thirty-five civil society organizations that are accredited and listed on the OAS register.[1] These groups represent a diversity of issues relevant to the work of the OAS, including human rights, indigenous peoples, women and gender, the environment and sustainable development, democracy and electoral processes, the Summit of the Americas process, and more. They include community-based groups, universities, and policy and advocacy groups.

A recent example of civil society contributions to the Summit of the Americas process were the consultations held in the OAS Permanent Council's Special Committee on Inter-American Summit Management (known by its Spanish acronym CEGCI). The Canadian government prepared position papers on the substantive themes of the Summit Plan of Action and made these available on their Web site. Under the auspices of the CEGCI, all OAS-accredited civil society organizations as well as other civil society groups interested in the Summit process were invited to attend open meetings of the CEGCI, which were also broadcast on the Internet. The meetings were normally held in the month prior to the meeting of the government-to-government Summit Implementation Review Group (SIRG) that would be negotiating the text of each issue area. Civil society's recommendations were then presented to the next meeting of the SIRG by the chairman of the CEGCI.

The Free Trade Area of the Americas Process, Civil Society, and Transparency: A New Approach?

The Free Trade Area of the Americas process is an ongoing negotiation toward eliminating barriers to trade and investment among thirty-four countries in the Americas and is an example of an arena in which space is being created for the presentation of NGO views. Initiated at the first Summit of the Americas in Miami in 1994 and formally launched at the second Summit in Santiago de Chile in 1998, the FTAA negotiations are scheduled to conclude by 2005. The FTAA process was inaugurated subsequent to the conclusion of NAFTA and the multilateral Uruguay Round negotiations. Although the negotiations are still underway, certain operating principles have been agreed upon. The FTAA process operates on the principle of consensus in decision making, has pledged to be consistent with the obligations of the WTO, and will be implemented as a single undertaking. In preparation for launching the negotiations, FTAA ministers acknowledged that a range of views existed regarding this initiative within their own countries. In the San Jose Ministerial, they issued the following statement: "We recognize and welcome the interests and concerns that different sectors of society have expressed in relation to the FTAA. Business and other sectors of production, labor, environmental and academic groups have been particularly active in this matter. We encourage these and other sectors of civil societies to present their views on trade matters in a constructive manner" (FTAA, 1998, p. 17). Although there is no explicit mention of NGOs, the FTAA process includes specific mechanisms for the participation of civil society.

Within the institutional structure of the FTAA process, a Committee of Government Representatives on the Participation of Civil Society was created to collect these views from civil society groups, to increase transparency in the negotiating process, and to broaden public understanding and support for the FTAA. To fulfill their mandate, the committee, meeting for the first time in October 1998, extended an "Open Invitation to Civil Society," inviting members of the public to submit their views on the FTAA negotiations. The open invitation was posted on the FTAA official Web site from November 1, 1998, to March 31, 1999. The submissions received were considered by the committee, which submitted a report to ministers at their following meeting, in November 1999, summarizing the range of views expressed.

At the Toronto Ministerial meeting, the committee was directed to obtain ongoing input from Civil Society on trade matters relevant to the FTAA through written submissions (FTAA,1999a). A second open invitation was issued on April 10, 2000, with a deadline for receiving submissions in this phase of September 30, 2000. The report of the committee, summarizing the range of views contained in the submissions, was submitted to ministers at their 2001 meeting in Buenos Aires. The decision was made to maintain the open invitation on a continuing basis, with regular reporting by the committee. Ministers also instructed that the negotiating groups receive the submissions from civil society groups which refer to their respective issue areas and those related to the FTAA process in general (FTAA, 2001b). Executive summaries of the submissions from Civil Society groups from the first and second open invitations are available online (see http://www.sice.oas.org/ftaa_e.asp and http://www.ftaa-alca.org).

The first Open Invitation to Civil Society received sixty-six responses from civil society actors in sixteen FTAA countries. The submissions addressed a range of issues and came from a variety of groups. The largest category was that of "business associations and other sectors of production," which also includes professional associations, with 32 percent of the submissions; labor and environmental organizations each submitted 15 percent of the total; academics (including students) were responsible for 13 percent of submissions; and "other organizations and individuals" comprised 25 percent of submissions. Submissions ranged from those addressing specific areas of negotiation (agriculture, antidumping and countervailing duties, competition policy, dispute settlement, government procurement, intellectual property, investment, market access, services) to those addressing issues related to business facilitation, transportation, labor standards or environmental protection (FTAA, 1999a). The second Open Invitation to Civil Society received eighty-two responses, of which seventy-seven complied with the requirements.[2] For this round, submissions came from the following distribution of actors: 35 percent from business and professional associations, 13 percent from academic sources, 10 percent from environmental organizations, and 8 percent from labor organizations. The remaining 34 percent came from organizations designating themselves as "other organizations" or individuals.

In terms of geographic distribution, the majority of submissions have come from North America. For the first invitation, half of the responses came from the United States or Canada, 13 percent originated in South America, 10 percent were from the Caribbean, and 7 percent were from Central America. The remaining submissions were divided among organizations identifying themselves as international, inter-American, or Latin American (16 percent) and subregional organizations (4 percent). In the second round, 48 percent of responses came from South American countries; 47 percent from North American countries and 5 percent from Central America and the Caribbean. While Latin America seems to have vastly improved its weighting in the second round, it may be noted that over half of these submissions came from a single country: Brazil.

The Committee on Civil Society will continue to receive input from civil society groups on the FTAA process and to disseminate these views both to the FTAA negotiating groups and to the public. The committee's mandate has also been strengthened and it has been instructed to consider mechanisms to "foster a process of increasing and sustained communication with civil society" (FTAA, 2001b).

In addition to the work done in the committee, the FTAA process has taken steps to enhance transparency and the flow of information on the process to the public through a public Web site and by making available documents of the process. During the preparatory phase of the FTAA process, a Web page was created to transmit information on the process to the public. This Web page (located at http://www.ftaa-alca.org and at http://www.alca-ftaa.org) contains all the public and derestricted documents of the process, including inventories and compendia of national legislation and regional provisions in the various negotiating areas, as well as databases of statistics and technical assistance opportunities created by the Inter-American Development Bank (IDB) and the OAS, links to trade-related sources of information within the participating countries, and a list of governmental contact points.

The most innovative step taken to increase transparency was the publication of the draft FTAA agreement. Early in 2001, in anticipation of the third Summit of the Americas, which was to be held in Quebec City in April, many NGOs called for the "liberation" of the FTAA text, much as they had called for the liberation of the MAI. Domestic and transnational groups criticized the FTAA negotiators for meeting behind closed doors and not sharing their results (Shamsie, 2000). Ministers at the Buenos Aires ministerial meeting duly recommended to their leaders that this text be "liberated"; and the nearly 500-page draft text, reflecting the progress made to that date in each of the negotiating groups, was made publicly available in the four official languages of the FTAA process on July 3, 2001 (see http://www.ftaa-alca.org).

NATIONAL PRACTICES:
CONSULTATION PROCESSES WITH NGOs

International economic negotiations are conducted by and among countries. As witnessed in the previous sections, even when international organizations that deal with economic issues are trying to become more transparent and implement mechanisms that allow them to be more receptive to civil society participation and opinions, they continue to stress that transparency and interaction needs also to be addressed at the national level. In examining these mechanisms two elements become clear. One is the strides that have been taken by countries, both developed and developing, in paying attention to the public's access to information. In the FTAA process, for example, several countries, including the United States, Canada, Costa Rica, and Chile, have either placed the text of their negotiating positions or described these positions on their own national Web sites. Many other FTAA countries have provided information about their trade negotiations, including descriptions of the process, frequently asked questions, information about seminars, and space for civil society to send comments or questions to the government officials responsible for these negotiations. However, the second notable element is the remaining asymmetry between developed and developing countries in their ability to interact with NGOs and other civil society groups. Several countries are starting to develop interactive consultation mechanisms and have begun to provide their private and civil sectors with information about the agreements they are negotiating and how they are approaching these negotiations. However, a cursory examination leads to the conclusion that developing countries are less likely to have the same types of mechanisms in place as seen in the industrialized countries. This section of the chapter explores a small sample of consultative trade policy mechanisms in place in a number of FTAA participating countries. This is by no means an exhaustive list of countries; omissions are due to lack of available information and should not be seen as a comment on the validity of any particular country's mechanism.

Much has already been written about the U.S. consultation mechanisms, particularly the official advisory committee system established by the 1974 U.S. Trade Act and we will not pretend in this chapter to summarize this literature (Destler, 1995). In addition to the government's consultations with business and civil society groups, the Office of the United States Trade Representative (USTR) has made information available on its Web page regarding all trade negotiations under way. This information includes the text of U.S. positions being taken in the various negotiating groups in the FTAA, requests for comments on the FTAA draft text, and the open invitation to civil society as well as the executive summaries of civil society submissions (See http://www.ustr.gov).

Other governments in the Americas employ a mix of strategies to communicate with NGOs on trade-related matters. These mechanisms all include some form of consultation with government trade delegations, information and opinion-sharing opportunities, and information dissemination, now often through national official Web pages.

Canada

Canada's methods for consultation with nongovernmental actors evolved alongside the changing landscape of trade negotiations in the 1980s and 1990s. As tariff barriers were reduced through the successive GATT rounds, trade negotiations increasingly focused on nontariff barriers. Issues such as the environment, natural resources, and health became part of the lexicon of trade negotiations; and public concerns regarding the impact of trade agreements on the lives of their citizens took on new dimensions for the government. Concurrently, the Canadian provinces began to play an increasingly important role in the formulation and implementation of trade policy. Trade policy issues began to reach into public policy areas under shared federal–provincial jurisdiction and even areas exclusively under provincial jurisdiction. The high public visibility of agreements such as the Canada–United States Free Trade Agreement (CUFTA) and the subsequent North American Free Trade Agreement (NAFTA) marked the coming out for civil society groups, including labor and business, in the formulation of Canadian trade policy (Dymond & Dawson, 2001).

This section will focus on two of the consultation modalities employed by the Canadian government: (1) direct consultations with multistakeholders and the dissemination of Canadian government position papers on specific trade issues, and (2) the solicitation of written submissions by civil society on these issues and an Internet-based program run through the Department of Foreign Affairs and International Trade's (DFAIT) Web site.

Multistakeholder consultations have been organized to bring the ministers of trade and foreign affairs and senior government officials together with a variety of civil society groups to discuss particular issues, such as Canada's trade agenda, the 2001 Summit of the Americas, and the WTO. The purpose of these meetings is to allow for information sharing by both government officials and civil

society and for Canadian officials to answer questions from participants. Stakeholders invited to these sessions have included a variety of groups representing business, environmental interests, women,
human rights issues, and labor, to name a few.

Canada's initial foray into the virtual consultation process began
in February 1999 in preparation for the WTO's Seattle ministerial
meeting in early December 1999 and the FTAA ministerial meeting
in early November 1999 in Toronto. A notice was published in the
Canada Gazette and on the DFAIT Web site seeking Canadians' opinions on the "scope, coverage and approaches" (Dymond & Dawson,
2001) to a range of trade issues relevant to both the WTO and FTAA
negotiations. Many topics have been part of this consultation process, including the regulation of genetically modified food, the framework for the environmental assessment of trade negotiations, trade
in services negotiations, WTO transparency, and, most recently, the
WTO ministerial meeting in Doha (See http://www.dfait.maeci.gc.ca).
Other mechanisms within the consultation process include federal–
provincial–territorial trade meetings, the *Canada Gazette*, sectoral
advisory groups on international trade and public opinion research,
and the Canadian parliament's Standing Committee on Foreign Affairs and International Trade (SCFAIT).

The post-Summit report issued by the SCFAIT in June 2001 asserts that "the Summit clearly highlighted a number of key issues
including . . . to increase transparency and the engagement of civil
society which must be addressed by the Government of Canada, both
in ongoing processes of integration in the Americas and in Canadian
foreign policy more generally" (Standing Committee, 2001, p. 1). The
committee's recommendation with respect to transparency and the
engagement of civil society includes releasing Canadian position
papers submitted in trade negotiations, releasing the text of trade
agreements during the negotiation process, supporting the "People's
Summit," and encouraging future Summit hosts to follow the Canadian example of transparency and engagement of civil society in the
preparations for the Summit of the Americas.

Chile

In Chile, trade policy making is done through the office of the
executive, which holds, according to the 1980 Constitution, the right
to negotiate treaties with foreign countries. The congress may reject
or accept these treaties prior to ratification, but, unlike in the United
States, cannot make modifications to treaties submitted by the executive. This centralized system does not require the same extent of

consultations as in some other institutional settings, and hence a formal consultation mechanism with business and labor was not put into place in Chile until the return to democracy in the early 1990s. At this time Chile was starting to relax its previously unilateralist approach to trade policy and began to negotiate regional arrangements. In 1994 Chile requested to join NAFTA; in 1997 became an associate member of Mercosur (the regional customs union among Brazil, Argentina, Paraguay, and Uruguay); and in 1997 negotiated a free trade agreement with Canada. As a result of the increasing number of negotiations, mechanisms for intergovernmental coordination and consultation with the private sector and other interested parties were developed. A Committee of Public–Private Participation for International Economic Relations was set up to inform the private sector on issues in trade negotiations. The Chile–Canada and Chile–United States negotiations have featured parallel discussions with labor and other civil society actors. Civil society participation is generally focused on actors in economic sectors directly involved in the negotiations. Since the FTAA process has been in place, consultations with civil society groups have increased, inspired by the mechanism created in the FTAA negotiations. This has entailed a well-publicized call for civil society input, followed up by government officials meeting with civil society groups and hearing their concerns and giving these groups informational briefings on FTAA issues.

The Office of International Economic Relations (DIRECON) has created a Web site to disseminate information to the public on Chile's trade negotiations and explain the government's procedures for consultations with civil society (http://www.direcon.cl). Within the scope of this mechanism, trade negotiators have been mandated to maintain a dialogue with civil society and they often travel throughout the country, holding seminars to explain Chilean trade policy activities to interested civil society groups and to listen to their comments. In 2000, after the second Open Invitation to Civil Society in the FTAA process, the government of Chile held a seminar, along with the Alliance for Just and Responsible Trade, in which negotiators explained their negotiating objectives and accomplishments so far in the FTAA negotiations and asked for civil society opinions. Over a third of all civil society submissions to the second FTAA invitation came from Chile.

In its bilateral negotiations, such as those toward a free trade agreement with the United States, the government of Chile has solicited comments bilaterally from business, labor, professional associations, environmental groups, indigenous groups, academics, and others.

In addition, a number of seminars on different negotiating areas have been held, with information on these activities available through the Web site (http://www.direcon.cl).

Mexico

As economic policy moved from the traditional state-driven import-substitution model to a more open economic model in the late 1980s, and as the political system experienced an opening in the 1990s, consultation with groups in civil society became more important to the Mexican government. A defining moment in Mexico's trade policy decision making was the 1990 announcement that Mexico would seek to negotiate a free trade agreement with the United States and Canada. In September 1990 the government, at the request of the Mexican senate, formed an Advisory Council on the Free Trade Agreement, composed of representatives from government, the private sector, academia, labor, and the agricultural sector. As Carlos Alba and Gustavo Vega (2001, p. 1) assert, "The Mexican government understood that in order for the NAFTA negotiations to be successful it would be necessary to rally the support or at least to gain the consensus of strategic social groups and especially the willing participation and support of the Mexican private sector and foreign investors located in Mexico." A two-track consultative mechanism was created.

The first track consisted of consultations with business and business associations, including chambers of commerce and industry. This built upon an infrastructure already nominally in place. The Business Coordinating Council (CCE), which had existed since 1975 as an umbrella organization for the private sector, was convened and through this entity the Coordinating Body of Foreign Trade Business Organizations (COECE) was set up through which the private sector's input was channeled. This institution served as a forum for private-sector dialogue. COECE also undertook sectoral impact studies of the Mexican economy, which led to 140 sectoral working groups. The second track was comprised of broad-based consultations with labor, peasant organizations, academics, and business representatives. These groups were consulted prior to initiation of the negotiations, during the negotiations, and during the implementation period. This consultative mechanism was employed during NAFTA and in all subsequent trade negotiations entered into by Mexico. In terms of information diffusion, the economic secretariat, formerly SECOFI, maintains an informative Web page, with documents relating to the treaties being negotiated by Mexico, studies, and statistics (http://www.economia-snci.gob.mx/).

CONCLUSION: HAVE THE NGOs CHANGED THE FACE OF TRADE NEGOTIATIONS?

In the previous discussion we have reviewed how NGOs and broader civil society are becoming increasingly involved in global trade and financial policy. As P. J. Simmons (1998, p. 83) writes, the question facing governments and international institutions today is not whether to include NGOs in their decision-making process, but rather "figuring out how to incorporate NGOs into the international system in a way that takes account of their diversity and scope, their various strengths and weaknesses and their capacity to disrupt as well as to create."

NGOs have certainly been successful in increasing the visibility of trade and focusing attention on the actions of trade negotiators, whether they like it or not. In the area of project finance, NGOs have managed to shine a spotlight on the potential impacts, especially in the area of the environment, of large projects, an issue discussed by Adams elsewhere in this volume. NGO insistence has brought some previously undiscussed issues onto the international economic agenda.

NGOs bring with them resources that can be helpful to trade and financial policy makers. They also bring a new challenge to institutions and organizations working to represent the interests of their constituencies. While in many ways NGOs open up the debate on economic policy making and create pressure for transparency and accountability for decision makers, there is also the issue of representation in the NGO community. While the most active NGOs may reflect the views of the civil-society groups they claim to represent, this claim is difficult to test. An increased number of voices adds to the debate: The challenge to both policy makers and NGOs is to prevent chaos and to forge a space in which the appropriate groups can access the expertise, resources, and perspectives brought by NGOs. Governments and international organizations continue their own efforts to forge relations with NGOs. These mechanisms will help to determine the manner in which these actors will coexist on the new three-level playing field of international economic relations.

NOTES

The ideas, views, and opinions expressed in this chapter are the exclusive responsibility of the authors and do not necessarily reflect the views of the OAS General Secretariat or of its member states. The authors would like to thank Zuleika Arashiro for invaluable research assistance and Jos Manuel Salazar and Jorge Mario Martinez for their helpful comments.

1. The list of organizations can be found at http://www.civil-society.oas. org/accredited%20organizations/accred-org.htm

2. These requirements and a further explanation of the process can be found in FTAA (2001a).

REFERENCES

Alba, C. S., & Vega, C. (2001, September). *Trade advisory mechanisms in México.* Unpublished memo prepared for the Inter-American Development Bank/Inter-American Dialogue/Munk Centre for International Studies.

Barbosa, L. C. (1996). The people of the forest against international capitalism: Systemic and anti-systemic forces in the battle for the preservation of the Amazon rainforest. *Sociological Perspectives, 39,* 317–331.

Blackhurst, R. (1998). The capacity of the WTO to fulfill its mandate. In A. O. Krueger (Ed.), *The WTO as an international organization.* Chicago: University of Chicago Press.

Brown, L. D., & Fox, J. (2000, October). *Transnational civil society coalitions and the World Bank: Lessons from project and policy influence campaigns.* Harvard University Working Paper No. 3. Hauser Center for Nonprofit Organizations and Kennedy School of Government.

Carr, B. (1999). Globalization from below: Labour internationalism under NAFTA. *International Social Science Journal, 51,* 49–59.

Charnovitz, S. (2000). Opening the WTO to nongovernmental interests, *Fordham International Law Journal, 24,* 173–216.

Croome, J. (1995). *Reshaping the world trading system: A history of the Uruguay Round.* Geneva: World Trade Organization.

Destler, I. M. (1995). *American trade politics* (3d ed.). Washington, DC: Institute for International Economics.

Dymond, W. A., & Dawson, L. R. (2001). *The consultative process in the formulation of Canadian trade policy.* Unpublished memo prepared for the Inter-American Development Bank/Inter-American Dialogue/ Munk Centre for International Studies.

Foster, J. (2001, August). *Knowing ourselves: A brief history of emerging global civil society.* Prepared for the fourth CIVICUS World Assembly, Vancouver, B.C., Canada.

Free Trade Area of the Americas (FTAA). (1998). Fourth trade ministerial: Joint declaration of ministers. San José, Costa Rica. Retrieved March 19, 2002, from http://www.ftaa-alca.org/ministerials/costa_e.asp

Free Trade Area of the Americas. (1999a). Report of the FTAA Committee of Government Representatives on the participation of civil society. Retrieved November 4, 2002, from http://www.ftaa-alca.org/spcomm/ derdoc/cs3e.doc

Free Trade Area of the Americas. (1999b). Fifth Trade Ministerial: Joint declaration of ministers. Toronto, Canada. Retrieved November 4, 2002, from http://www.ftaa-alca.org/ministerials/minis_e.asp

Free Trade Area of the Americas. (2001a). *Report of the Committee of Government Representatives on the participation of civil society in the*

FTAA process. Retrieved April 30, 2002, from http://www.ftaa-alca.org/spcomm/derdoc/dcs8r1e.doc

Free Trade Area of the Americas. (2001b). *Sixth trade ministerial: Joint declaration of ministers.* Buenos Aires, Argentina. Retrieved April 7, 2002, from http://www.ftaa-alca.org/ministerials/BAmin_e.asp

Graham, E. M. (2000). *Fighting the wrong enemy: Antiglobal activists and multinational enterprises.* Washington, DC: Institute for International Economics.

Harding, J. (2001, September 10). Globalization's children strike back. *Financial Times*, p. 14.

Hoekman, B. M., & Kostecki, M. M. (2001). *The political economy of the world trading system* (2d ed.). Oxford: Oxford University Press.

Hunter, D. (1996). *The PLANAFLORO claim.* Retrieved April 20, 2001, from http://www.ciel.org/Ifi/planafl.html.

Hunter, D., & Udall, L. (2001). *The World Bank's new inspection panel: Will it increase the bank's accountability?* Washington, DC: Center for International Environmental Law. Retrieved April 30, 2001, from http://www.ciel.org/Publications/issue1.html

International Bank for Reconstruction and Development (IBRD) (1993, September 2). *IBRD resolution no. 93-10, IDA resolution no. 93-6.* Washington, DC: The World Bank.

Jay, B. A. (2001). FTAA and civil society: Did Toronto trade talks advance participation? Retrieved April 23, 2001, from http://www.americas net.net/Commentators/Bruce_Jay/toronto_legacy.html

Keohane, R. O., & Nye, J. S. (2000, May). The club model of multilateral cooperation and the World Trade Organization: Problems of democratic legitimacy. Paper presented at the Conference on Efficiency, Equity and Legitimacy: The Multilateral Trading System at the Millennium, Harvard University.

Korzeniewicz, P. R., & Smith, W. C. (2001, September). Transnational civil society networks and the politics of summitry and free trade in the Americas. Paper delivered to the Inter-American Dialogue, Washington, DC.

Larsen, F. (2000). The IMF's Dialogue with the NGOs. *Transnational Associations, 6*, 278–281.

Longworth, R. C. (1999, July 5). Activists on Internet reshaping rules for global economy. *Chicago Tribune*, p. 1.

Odell, J .(2000). *Negotiating the world economy.* Ithaca: Cornell University Press.

Organization of American States (OAS). (1971). AG/RES.57 (I-O/71).

Organization of American States. (1999). CP/RES. 759 (1217/99).

Ostry, S. (2001). World Trade Organization: Institutional design for better governance. In R. Porter, P. Sauvé, A. Subramanian, & A. B. Zampetti (Eds.), *Efficiency/equity/legitimacy: The multilateral trading system at the millennium).* Washington, DC: Brookings Institution Press.

Schnabel, A. (2001). *Governing global finance: The role of civil society* (Transcript of economic forum). Retrieved April 5, 2001, from http:/// www.imf.org/external/np/tr/2001/tr010405.htm

Shamsie, Y. (2000). *Engaging with civil society: Lessons from the OAS, FTAA and summits of the Americas.* Miami: North South Center.

Simmons, P. J. (1998). Learning to live with NGOs. *Foreign Policy, 112*, 82–96.

Soloway, J. A. (1999). Environmental trade barriers under NAFTA: The MMT fuel addition controversy. *Minnesota Journal of Global Trade, 8*, 55–95.

Standing Committee on Foreign Affairs and International Trade. (2001, June). *Report of the committee on balance, transparency and engagement after the Quebec Summit.* Ottawa: Government of Canada.

Summit of the Americas. (1998). *Santiago Declaration plan of action.* Santiago de Chile: OAS.

UNCTAD. (2001). *World investment report 2001: Promoting linkages.* Geneva: UNCTAD.

Union of International Associations. (1999). *Yearbook of international organizations.* Belgium, München: K. G. Saur.

Ward, H. (2001, February). *Governing multinationals: The role of foreign direct liability* (Briefing paper new series no. 18). London: Royal Institute of International Affairs Energy and Environment Programme.

World Bank. (2001a). *World Bank–civil society collaboration: Progress report for fiscal years 2000 and 2001.* Washington, DC: World Bank.

World Bank. (2001b). *Consultations with civil society—A sourcebook.* Washington, DC: World Bank.

World Bank. (2002, September 7). World Bank revises disclosure policy (Press release no. 2002/070/S). Washington, DC.

World Trade Organization (WTO). (1995). *Uruguay Round agreement establishing the World Trade Organization, Article V(2).* Geneva: World Trade Organization.

World Trade Organization. (1996). *Guidelines for arrangements on relations with non-governmental organizations: Decision adopted by the General Council* (WTO/L/162, 18). Geneva: World Trade Organization.

World Trade Organization. (2000a). *European communities—measures affecting asbestos and asbestos-containing products, communication from the appellate body* (WT/DS135/9 8 November). Geneva: World Trade Organization.

World Trade Organization. (2000b). *United States—Imposition of countervailing duties on certain hot-rolled lead and bismuth carbon steel products originating in the United Kingdom* (WT/DS138/AB/R 10 May). Geneva: World Trade Organization.

World Trade Organization (2001a). *Annual report: Overview of the state of play of WTO disputes—Addendum* (WT/DSB/26/Add.1). Geneva: World Trade Organization.

World Trade Organization. (2001b). *International trade statistics 2001.* Geneva: World Trade Organization.

CHAPTER 4

Cooperative Strategies in Environmental Nongovernmental Organizations

Jonathan P. Doh, William E. Newburry, and Hildy Teegen

Sharing resources among organizations through formal and informal cooperation and collaboration can produce benefits beyond what an individual organization can accomplish alone (Contractor & Lorange, 1988; Wasserman & Faust, 1994). Recent advances in technology have facilitated intra- and interorganizational communications, and these advances, coupled with increased recognition of societywide issues most actively addressed by nongovernmental, nonfirm actors, have broadened the range of organizations that might share in these benefits. Accordingly, interorganizational cooperation has increasingly come into play as a method for successfully managing organizations and their interactions with other entities within their environments, particularly environments characterized by turbulence and change. Nongovernmental organizations are one such organizational type that is especially influenced by these trends. However, as the purpose, organization, and governance of NGOs may differ from that of corporations, it seems probable that the benefits of cooperation may differ for these organizations.

The recognition of NGOs as influential actors is beginning to gain attention in the international relations field (Mathews, 1997; Simmons, 1998). Along with MNCs and international organizations, NGOs are increasingly mentioned as significant players in global affairs (Keck & Sikkink, 1998). Using their networks of members, NGOs play an important role in collecting and disseminating information, as well as working with national governments, international organizations, and other nonstate actors, including MNCs (Ottaway, 2001). However, defining and measuring NGO influence, particularly as reflected in cooperative and collaborative activities, is an understudied area.

In this chapter we focus specifically on environmental NGOs (ENGOs) because they are particularly active in using cooperative strategies to achieve their objectives. Our focus concerns the ways in which ENGOs use these collaborative strategies to enhance their performance. As organizations inherently distinct from corporations and governments, we note six interrelated performance measurements particularly relevant to these ENGOs: (1) access to donated funds/success of development efforts, (2) species preservation/ biodiversity sustainability, (3) standard setting/modeling of best practices associated with the ENGO, (4) land acquisition and/or protection through restrictive covenants and easements, (5) garnering favorable public opinion (as evidenced through successful ballot initiatives, for instance), and (6) legislative performance (nationally and internationally through treaties on trade, the environment, etc.). We contend that ENGOs can improve performance along these six dimensions through their use of cooperative strategies.

In this chapter, we describe and classify the inter- and intraorganizational cooperative ventures that are used by ENGOs in their efforts to enhance their performance. Using a contingency approach defined by the dimensions of (1) cooperative orientation (inside versus outside the organization) and (2) cooperative goal focus (internal versus external), we provide illustrations of these network effects in order to generalize how and when such benefits are more or less significant. For convenience, in this discussion we use the terms "cooperation" and "collaboration" synonymously, realizing that these two terms may have different meanings to different audiences. We argue ENGOs use networks to cooperate and collaborate, although other connections and associations among these concepts could be argued. Specifically, we explore a complex and interwoven series of intraorganizational and interorganizational cooperative ventures concerning a large environmental organization: the World Wide Fund for Nature/World Wildlife Fund (WWF). The World Wide Fund for Nature (WWF–International), a global environmental organization, its large U.S. affiliate, the World Wildlife Fund (WFF–US), and the international association of national country WWF offices collaborate and cooperate among each other and with other public and private organizations on a range of projects, activities, and initiatives. We highlight examples of cooperative activities relevant to WWF to illustrate the benefits that correspond to the four contingencies we propose. We conclude with a discussion of the implications of our theoretical framework and illustrations, along with some suggestions for future research.

A FRAMEWORK FOR UNDERSTANDING ENVIRONMENTAL NGO COOPERATION

There has been increasing research interest in environmental management (Reinhardt & Vieotor, 1996). This research has argued for consideration of nonhuman nature as a legitimate managerial stakeholder (Starik, 1995), outlined the competitive benefits of corporate environmental management practices (Hart, 1997), and described the range of environmental practices that companies can follow (Stead & Stead, 2000). Other researchers have examined the specifics of environmental advocacy within companies, focusing on the antecedents of championing episodes (Andersson & Bateman, 2000). In addition, limited research has explored the dynamics of voluntary environmental agreements, generally between corporations and governments (Delmas & Terlaak, 2001) and the potential for cooperative initiatives between corporations and NGOs (Doh, this volume; Teegen, this volume). However, there has been very little research based upon established perspectives on organizational cooperation, and even less effort directed toward exploration of such cooperation among ENGOs themselves.

In this chapter we specifically address environmental nongovernmental organizations because they are particularly active in organizing, developing, and exploiting internal and external networks. We believe ENGOs serve as a useful prototype for examination of other NGOs whose primary activities are related to advocacy and championing (Andersson & Bateman, 2000).

A Contingency Model of NGO Cooperation

Figure 4.1 presents a contingency model of how different types of NGO networks may be used to pursue various goals based upon two dimensions: the focus of network connections (e.g., within or between organizations) and the focus of the network goal (e.g., internal or external to the NGO). Based upon these quadrants, cooperative strategies can be classified into four different types: internal positioning, outside champion, unified internal front, and multiple front influence. It should be noted, however, that these four categories represent archetypes, and that any given cooperative venture might focus on internal and external goals and/or connections within or across organizations. Thus, it is possible for such ventures to simultaneously occupy multiple spaces within the boxes.

Figure 4.1
NGO Cooperative Ventures: Cooperative Goal Focus and Cooperative Connection Focus

Cooperative Goal Focus

	Internal	External
Within	Internal Positioning	Unified Internal Front
Between	Outside Champion	Multiple Front Influence

Cooperative Connection Focus

Although it is recognized that cooperation can occur at multiple levels of analysis, Figure 4.1 focuses upon cooperative strategies and activities involving organizations and/or significant groups (e.g., departments) within organizations. This analysis level is chosen in line with the focus of this chapter upon organizational goals (including the goals of major organizational subgroups). While individuals are recognized as also being important to achieving organizational and major group goals, individuals are only addressed herein to the extent that they represent a larger group. We use the term "sub-NGO" to refer to divisions or departments within an overall organization. While the four quadrants will be subsequently discussed in detail at a broad level, we recognize that not all cooperative activities are the same. We argue that appropriate and effective utilization of cooperative strategies by NGOs requires a contingency approach involving a simultaneous consideration of internal and external goals and within- and between-organization connections.

Internal Positioning Cooperation

The upper left quadrant of Figure 4.1 proposes that some cooperative strategies address goals that are primarily internal to an organization based upon cooperation among primarily internal subgroups of people. Within many organizations these internal groups are referred to as departments. However, other group names may also be used. Within these cooperative spheres, two or more groups within a given NGO may align their efforts in order to achieve a common goal. At times these spheres may be used to ensure the relative dominance of certain groups over others in an organization, geared toward ensuring those groups' survival, the primacy of their goals within the overall organization, and/or decision-making autonomy owing to prestige or proven credibility. Particularly in organizations with scarce resources, maintaining internal power bases could help groups within an organization obtain necessary resources to pursue specific group goals. As large NGOs often simultaneously pursue multiple projects, funding for one group's project may only come at the expense of another group's project funding. Moreover, in recessionary periods, small departments may wish to pool their efforts to ensure survival. For example, in the current, post-9/11 donor environment, some NGOs that are not involved in disaster relief have been forced to consolidate activities and rationalize their operations to survive severe shortfalls in donations.

It is most likely that NGO divisions, offices, and the like utilizing internal positioning cooperation do so to leverage reciprocity (Cialdini, 1993). Reciprocity works like logrolling. By tapping or incorporating other offices into an initiative that they may not be directly associated with, the organizing office can reasonably expect those included offices to "return the favor" and include that office in other initiatives in the future. As an extension, when NGOs rationalize operations by allowing certain divisions to become specialists in certain matters, the rule of reciprocity in the cooperative scheme allows all members to share (reciprocally) in the cost savings and deepening of expertise associated with specialist offices.

The rule of liking (Cialdini, 1993) is also invoked for internal cooperation. Support for another office's initiatives is more probable when another office "likes" an office. Liking has been shown to correlate empirically with (1) repeated interaction and (2) similarity (Cialdini, 1993). Thus, offices within the NGO may garner influence over other offices owing to their past dealings with another office. Those past dealings are the stuff of reputation and trust building which grease the wheels of eased interaction and information flow. Similarity gives ground to internal positioning cooperative activities linked in natural ways, such as among the offices representing migration patterns that share common bird species, albeit at different times of the year. By leveraging these "natural affinities" among divisions or offices of an NGO, otherwise limited resources, such as technical staff with advanced degrees, can be most efficiently mobilized within the organization. Blalock (1989) notes that efficient mobilization is a key determinant of an entity's power. Hence, we would assert that when pursing internal goals, sub-NGOs use internally focused cooperation to vie for position and garner support in relation to other internal sub-NGOs by leveraging the desire of those with whom they cooperate for reciprocation and liking, and by more efficiently deploying the organization's limited resources.

Outside Champion Cooperation

In addition to forming internal alliances to pursue internal goals, it is also suggested that groups within NGOs sometimes align with significant outside organizations to strengthen their position vis-à-vis other internal groups. For example, the research arm of an ENGO may solicit a grant from a well-known company to form a specialized center of study. This type of center may give the department additional legitimacy and clout when compared to other departments within the ENGO. Thus, sometimes the best way to gain power within an organization is to solicit backing from an outside champion. Although some researchers have described and documented "championing episodes" within private organizations, we describe a championing process (e.g., Andersson & Bateman, 2000) in which an important external organization gives one department external legitimacy that another department might not possess.

By using relationships with external organizations, internal divisions can wield more influence internally. The influence rule of authority (Cialdini, 1993) relates to this type of cooperative benefit. The outside organization serves to "vouch" or legitimate the activities and interests of the internal division in terms of technical, legislative, and/or funding approvals. When the outside cooperative connection is unique or rare (i.e., a structural hole is bridged [Burt, 1997]), the additional influence rule of scarcity is used by the sub-NGO division to garner more influence internally.

Clearly these outside champions provide internal NGO divisions with resources of various forms, including prestige or reputation and funding. Thus, according to Blalock (1989), these internal divisions gain power through the broader resource base they have available through their outside champions. We would therefore expect that when pursing internal goals, sub-NGOs use externally focused cooperative ventures to gain external validation via an outside champion.

Unified Front Cooperation

While the preceding examples focus on internal organizational goals, it is also recognized that NGOs utilize cooperative activities to pursue objectives that are primarily external to the organization. While many NGOs are made up of individual departments that may not see eye to eye on every issue; when addressing external goals that benefit the entire organization, it can be beneficial to present a unified front to the outside world. From a different vantage, NGOs may also receive inquiries from outside organizations to partner or collaborate. In order to ensure that one subunit of an NGO is not played off another subunit, it could be of benefit to align with other organizational units to present a coordinated front.

The coordination of activities among the divisions of the NGO allows the overall NGO to be influential, owing to the desire to maintain a consistent and even message (Cialdini, 1993). By agreeing to certain partnering guidelines, for instance, these divisions can be assured that their overall negotiation posture vis-à-vis outside organizations will be enhanced: They will portray a monolithicism that will obviate attempts by outsiders to "divide and conquer" the organization by leveraging different policies and goals of the various divisions within the NGO.

Furthermore, by uniting all (or many) divisions within an NGO along a standard policy guideline, for instance, the NGO can more effectively deploy its limited resources (Blalock, 1989). This is the basic "strength in numbers" argument and incorporates experience curve effects that call for volume in practice to achieve learning benefits. Therefore, we expect that when pursing external goals, NGOs use internal cooperation to demonstrate a unified front.

Multiple Front Influence Cooperation

The final quadrant of Figure 4.1 addresses the type of cooperative activities that might be most visible to persons outside an organization. This quadrant focuses on the fact that not all NGOs have the same capabilities. Thus, to solve some external problems, obtaining assistance from other organizations can be highly desirable. For example, while individual environmental organizations may be technically equipped to argue for passage of the Global Climate Change Treaty, formation of a coalition that reflects an even broader representation of environmental and even other interests would provide for a more effective voice. In this way the ENGO cooperates with external partners to leverage the influence that comes with enhanced reputations and legitimacy resulting from greater support across the NGO community. By linking and uniting the opinions and policies of diverse organizations on an issue or project, NGOs are able to more convincingly persuade others of their ideas. This persuasiveness is particularly acute for issues relevant to many ENGOs—those in which the definitive answers are unclear or ambiguous or where uncertainty reins (Tesser, Campbell, & Mickler, 1983).

These multiple-front influences gain power through both enhanced resource access and more efficient resource mobilization (Blalock, 1989). Here resources are enhanced not only in absolute scale terms as in the case of the outside champion cooperative ventures but, more important, in terms of the diversity of resources represented by these multiple front influence cooperative venture participants. The diversity of these network participants provides further opportunities for specialization beyond what are possible within the internal positioning networks, resulting in enhanced efficiency in the mobilization of the network's efficiency. Hence, we suggest that when pursuing external goals NGOs use external cooperation to demonstrate a multiple front, ensuring a comprehensive attack by utilizing the influence rule of social proof. These multiple front cooperative ventures allow participants to enjoy access to wide-ranging resources, and to more efficiently employ such resources, enhancing their individual and collective power and influence.

ENVIRONMENTAL NGO COOPERATION AT WWF

In this section we present brief illustrations of the types of intra- and interorganizational collaborative ventures described already. The examples provided here serve to illustrate the four contingent collaborative venture types we argue to be relevant for ENGOs, and as such provide a template for future research and testing in this area. We selected the World Wide Fund for Nature/World Wildlife Fund because of its long history and well-developed internal and external network relationships.

In 1961 the entire natural world seemed to be under siege. A limited number of organizations, such as IUCN (the International Union for Conservation of Nature and Natural Resources) and the Conservation Foundation (CF), were trying to meet conservation needs, but they were all short of funds. In that year, a small but influential group of Europeans—scientists, naturalists, and business and political leaders—founded World Wildlife Fund (WWF, 2001a). On September 11, 1961, World Wildlife Fund was legally formed and soon set up shop at IUCN's headquarters in Morges, Switzerland. H.R.H. Prince Bernhard of the Netherlands became its first president. H.R.H. Prince Philip, the Duke of Edinburgh, became president of the British National Appeal, the first national organization in the World Wildlife Fund family (WWF, 2001a).

The second national organization to be formed was World Wildlife Fund, Inc., the U.S. entity. Incorporated in the District of Columbia on December 1, 1961, WWF named Dwight D. Eisenhower its president of honor. In 1980 the IUCN, with critical support from WWF and the United Nations Environment Program, developed the World Conservation Strategy as a vehicle to articulate and share this vision. In 1985 World Wildlife Fund formally affiliated with the Conservation Foundation (WWF, 2001a). From 1985 until 1990 WWF and CF remained legally distinct corporations, although with identical boards of directors. In February 1990 the board of directors voted unanimously to consolidate the two organizations. The resulting corporation, World Wildlife Fund and the Conservation Foundation, Inc., came into existence on July 2, 1990. In October 1991 the board voted unanimously to change the name of the corporation to World Wildlife Fund, Inc. The new name became effective on December 4, 1991 (WWF, 2001a).

The forty-year evolution of World Wildlife Fund has entailed organizational changes in terms of WWF's relationship with the range of stakeholders that constitute the "the international WWF network." Although WWF in the United States is an independent organization, it plays an increasingly important role in the worldwide conservation program of the WWF network. A memorandum of understanding (MOU) signed in 1992 and revised in 1994 and 1998 by WWF-US and WWF–International, reflects a comprehensive agreement on planning and implementation of activities of the WWF network. Central to the MOU is the "'team approach,' which builds on the work of the country teams representing WWF–International, WWF–US, and other concerned national organizations (NOs) in the WWF network. The MOU also provides for greater representation of WWF–US and other NOs in the WWF network's decision-making bodies" (WWF, 2001a, p. 225).

In addition to the internal network cooperation, WWF has effectively developed a number of external network systems at various levels and with a range of actors. What follows are four interesting initiatives that rely on internal or external networks sponsored by WWF–US or WWF–International and typify the four contingent network archetypes we propose. Figure 4.2 presents an illustration of the range of inter- and intraorganizational cooperative activities described in this section.

Internal Positioning Cooperation: The Wloclawek Dam Technical Expert Team

The WWF–Poland office recently concluded a year-long study concerning the fate of the Wloclawek Dam on the Vistula river in Poland. This dam's safety had been eroded over time, and WWF–

Figure 4.2
Representatives' Cooperative Ventures of the World Wildlife Fund
(WWF–US) and Worldwide Fund for Nature (WWF–International)

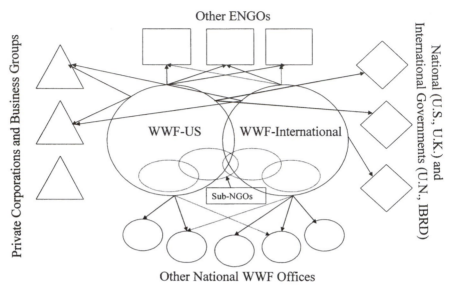

Other ENGOs

Private Corporations and Business Groups

WWF-US   WWF-International

Sub-NGOs

National (U.S., U.K.) and International Governments (U.N., IBRD)

Other National WWF Offices

Poland gathered a team of experts on hydrotechnical construction, hydrology, economy, regional development, power industry, and ecology in order to assess the economic, social, and environmental consequences of the various considered options, including decommissioning the dam and dam modernization (WWF, 2001d).

This technical expert network instituted by the WWF–Poland helped this office with its internal (WWF) audience in two important ways. By developing a multicriteria methodology pertinent to an actual dam case, the learning and resulting policy recommendations could serve as internal standards within the broader organization. Thus, the Poland office could be looked to for technical expertise on such matters in Argentina, where WWF interests concern the fate of the Yacyreta Dam, which is proposed to be raised some 83 meters (WWF, 2001c).

This standard setting and modeling could be further promoted within the broader organization through the Five-Point Plan to Save the World's Water proposed by the WWF Living Waters Programme presented at the International Conference on Freshwater held in Bonn, Germany, in December 2001 (WWF, 2001f). Since dams policy is one of the key elements of the plan, the WWF–Poland office's technical network surrounding this issue could become an important resource for the overall organization, enhancing the WWF–Poland office's stature in the overall WWF organization.

To summarize, WWF–Poland, by assembling a technical expertise network to provide assessments of possible solutions for the Wloclawek Dam on the Vistula River, can wield more influence surrounding overall WWF policy on rivers and dams. When referred to for all subsequent dam-related issues confronting the worldwide organization, the WWF–Poland office can be expected to demand reciprocity in resource exchange: their proven, relevant technical expertise in exchange for other valuable resources. Similarly, through repeated exchange with other members of the WWF organization, the WWF–Poland office may be more "liked" by other members, and thus be more convincing in its influence attempts. Finally, by linking various viewpoints in their technical team, the WWF–Poland office was able to provide solutions assessments much more efficiently than through a single-pronged approach to assessment.

Outside Champion Cooperation: The Global 200

WWF scientists have identified more than 200 outstanding terrestrial, freshwater, and marine habitats. The central concept of the Global 200 is to conserve the broadest variety of the world's habitats (WWF, 2001c). Using the Global 200 as a guide, WWF believes that the broadest varieties of the world's species can be saved. WWF has used its network relationships with the conservation science community to publish a number of widely reviewed research articles, and has partnered with *National Geographic* and the Ford Foundation to put a map of the Global 200 in every primary school in the country.

Thus, the Global 200 project networks the scientist core of WWF with their technical counterparts elsewhere. This network of peer review in scholarly journals provides WWF scientists with legitimacy within the WWF organization, and through membership in these scholarly networks, the WWF scientists can readily access the collected learning of the network's previous research efforts surrounding various habitats. *National Geographic* and the Ford Foundation both provide sources of authority and prestige to further the scientists' influence within the organization. Access to school classrooms is a unique resource that these partners can provide, and thus networking with these organizations further provides the scientists in WWF with influence, owing to scarcity.

Unified Front Cooperation:
Arctic National Wildlife Refuge

Using its national network of members, WWF initiated a campaign to keep the Arctic National Wildlife Refuge closed to oil exploration. Over 20,000 postcards from WWF members in key states were be delivered to members of Congress from Tennessee, Illinois, Pennsylvania, Ohio, Missouri, Georgia, Indiana, Louisiana, and Florida on Capitol Hill (WWF, 2001a). The postcards asked members of Congress to "please vote to protect the Arctic National Wildlife Refuge for future generations of people and wildlife." "Americans love our parks and wild lands, and they don't want to see our greatest wildlife refuge sacrificed in the search for more oil," said Brooks Yeager, vice president of the Global Threats Program at the World Wildlife Fund. "They also know there are better solutions for our energy security."

This network uses the WWF membership in various regions of the United States to send a monolithic message to Congress. This unified front relies on the influence rule of consistency (we all believe the same thing) and allows for an effective deployment of limited resources by using a procedure for unifying the voices of the membership in an impactful way without unduly burdening any individual member.

Multiple Front Influence Cooperation:
The Conservation Biodiversity Support Program

The Biodiversity Support Program (BSP) was an initiative funded by the U.S. Agency for International Development (USAID; a government agency) and a consortium consisting of the World Wildlife Fund, the Nature Conservancy, and World Resources Institute (WWF, 2001b). As such, it represented an active network comprising other ENGOs, WWF national offices, and a government agency. With more than $80 million in USAID funding over the years, BSP has pioneered the way conservation is practiced around the world (WWF, 2001a). This includes supporting local, and often impoverished, communities to manage their own natural resources sustainably. Emphasizing stakeholder participation, the program integrates conservation with social and economic development in hundreds of projects in sixty-five countries. Projects undertaken by BSP and its partners over the years have ranged from studies to understand the impact of climate change to programs to train local communities in watershed management and sustainable fishing practices (WWF, 2001b).

This network has been effective by using the influence rule of social proof and diverse interests coalescing to promote a common agenda in support of biodiversity. Furthermore, the various resources of the network members (financial, technical, reputational, etc.) have resulted in a powerful group that has produced measurable benefits for biodiversity conservation. A certain degree of specialization has also been employed, wherein the parties are given primary responsibility for design, administration, and monitoring of certain activities within the broad network.

CONCLUSIONS AND IMPLICATIONS

Throughout this chapter we have argued that nongovernmental organizations and in particular environmental nongovernmental organizations are increasingly important organizational forms that interact in environments with corporations, governments, and society. Yet the nature and quality of these interactions are not well understood. To shed light on this gap in our understanding, we described how and why an NGO and its respective subunits (divisions, offices, etc.) form cooperative relationships both within the NGO and between the NGO and other organizations. These relationships are directed toward efforts to share resources and to gain leverage for influence and power and are utilized to achieve internally and externally oriented goals.

Based on illustrations from various collaborations concerning the World Wildlife Fund/World Wide Fund for Nature, an internationally recognized ENGO, we find evidence supporting our general proposition that a contingency approach is needed to understand how and when benefits from cooperation may accrue to network members. In particular, we propose four distinct (although not necessarily mutually exclusive) contingency conditions dimensionalized by the orientation of the cooperative connection (within NGO versus between NGO and other organizations) and the focus of the collaborative venture's goals (internal or external to the NGO).

Furthermore, we find in our case illustrations support for distinctions in how influence and power are garnered in each of the contingent conditions. In the internal positioning cooperative venture formed within NGOs and geared to internal goals such as increased or sustained project funding in budgeting decisions, internal prestige, and decision-making authority, the influence rules of reciprocity and liking predominate in providing members with leverage. Furthermore, these ventures enhance resource mobilization efficiency through rationalization and sharing of resources among members.

In the outside champion cooperative ventures formed between a division of the NGO with external organizations oriented to similar internal goals as those for the internal positioning collaborative venture, the influence rules of authority and scarcity appear to best explain the venture member's leverage internally. By joining forces with an external entity, the division can also enhance its power internally by marshalling its venture partners' resources: financial, reputational, technical, and otherwise.

United front cooperative ventures are formed internally by the NGO and are oriented to external goals common to most ENGOs: funding and donations, species preservation and biodiversity, technical or scientific standard setting, land protection, garnering favorable public opinion, and legislative performance domestically and internationally. In these ventures, members use the influence rule of consistency to enhance the credibility of their claims. Furthermore, as a united front with the appearance of monolithicism, these ventures can more effectively deploy their limited internal resources.

The final collaborative venture archetype we propose, the multiple front cooperative venture, relies on ventures formed between the NGO and other organizations. These ventures call on social proof to influence others. Resources as a whole are enhanced by sheer scale, but also in terms of diversity, allowing for specialization and potential efficiency in mobilization gains.

We note that NGOs, and ENGOs in particular, gauge performance in ways distinct from corporations and governments, and our framework speaks to using various networks in order to enhance performance. Thus, we conclude that overall NGO performance can be enhanced by participation in these four types of collaborative ventures. We leave for future work a more detailed examination of the specific metrics for assessing internal and external performance for NGOs.

We recognize that our framework focuses heavily on benefits provided by membership in the four archetypes we propose. We understand that cooperation involves costs (monitoring, bureaucratic costs, strategic inflexibility, etc.) that need to be addressed in making normative judgments about participating in any of the four cooperation archetypes. Future work in the area will address the performance implications for NGOs from membership in these four types of cooperation and will thus necessarily incorporate both the benefits (as captured in the concepts of influence and power) and the costs of cooperative participation.

We have provided initial evidence in support of our typology, using examples of cooperative ventures from a single ENGO and its various internal and external relationships. To generalize from our typology, further work can examine this framework for other ENGOs as well as for other types of NGOs. Finally, we note that the four archetypes we present are not mutually exclusive in practice. A given network may involve activities geared simultaneously to internal and external goals, for instance. In future work an assessment of the interactions and in fact the possibility of dynamic progression from one network type to another would be warranted.

REFERENCES

Andersson, L., & Batemen, T. (2000). Individual environmental initiative: Championing environmental issues in U.S. business organizations. *Academy of Management Journal, 43,* 548–571.

Blalock, H. M. (1989). *Power and conflict: Toward a general theory.* London: Sage.

Burt, R. S. (1997). The contingent values of social capital. *Administrative Science Quarterly, 42,* 339–365.

Cialdini, R. B. (1993). *Influence: Science and practice.* New York: Harper Collins.

Contractor, F. J., & Lorange, P. (Eds.). (1988). *Cooperative strategies in international business.* Lexington, MA: Lexington Books.

Delmas, M. A., & Terlaak, A. K. (2001). A framework for analyzing environmental voluntary agreements. *California Management Review, 43* (3), 44–63.

Hart, S. (1997, May). Beyond greening: Strategies for a sustainable world. *Harvard Business Review,* pp. 67–76.

Keck, M. E., & Sikkink, K. (1998). *Activists beyond borders: Advocacy networks in international politics.* Ithaca, NY: Cornell University Press.

Mathews, J. T. (1997). Power shift. *Foreign Affairs, 76,* 50–66.

Ottaway, M. (2001). Corporatism goes global: International organizations, nongovernmental organization networks, and transnational business. *Global Governance, 7,* 265–292.

Reinhardt, F., & Vieotor, R.H.K. (1996). *Business management and the natural environment: Cases and text.* Cincinnati, OH: Southwestern.

Simmons, P. J. (1998). Learning to live with NGOs. *Foreign Policy, 112,* 82–96.

Starik, M. (1995). Should trees have managerial standing? Toward stakeholder status for nonhuman nature. *Journal of Business Ethics, 14,* 207–218.

Stead, E. & Stead, J. G. (2000). *Management for a small planet: Strategic decision making for the environment.* London: Sage.

Tesser, A., Campbell, J. & Mickler, S. (1983). The role of social pressure, attention to the stimulus, and self-doubt in conformity. *European Journal of Social Psychology, 13,* 217–233.

Wasserman, S., & Faust, K. (1994). *Social network analysis: Methods and applications.* Cambridge: Cambridge University Press.

World Wildlife Fund (WWF). (2001a). *About WWF: History of WWF.* Retrieved March 10, 2001, from http://www.worldwildlife.org/defaultsection.cfm?sectionid=15&newspaperid=15&contentid=68

World Wildlife Fund. (2001b). *Conservation leaders honor extraordinary global partnership.* Retrieved March 12, 2001, from http://wwfus.org/climate/climate.cfm?sectionid=189&newspaperid=16

World Wildlife Fund. (2001c). *Global 2000.* Retrieved March 10, 2001, from http://wwfus.org/global200/spaces.cfm

World Wildlife Fund. (2001d). *Living waters campaign.* Retrieved March 10, 2001, from http://panda.org/livingwaters/PR_Wloclawek.html.

World Wildlife Fund. (2001e). *Silent flood.* Retrieved April 12, 2002, from http://www.panda.org/livingwaters/flooding.cfm.

World Wildlife Fund. (2001f). *WWF launches five-point plan to save the world's water.* Retrieved April 23, 2001, from http://www.panda.org/news/press/news.cfm?id=2609

World Wildlife Fund. (2001g). *WWF members tell Congress: Save the arctic national wildlife refuge.* Retrieved April 20, 2001, from http://wwfus.org/news/headline.cfm?newsid=290

CHAPTER 5

Prospects for NGO Collaboration with Multinational Enterprises

A. Rani Parker

Nongovernmental organizations are growing at rapid rates and forming alliances that have increased their size, influence, and scope of interests. NGOs are nonprofit organizations that operate within or across political boundaries and are often driven by a mission that expresses the desire to help populations that are perceived as disadvantaged. Widely characterized by their diversity in size, scope, and focus, they have also generated a great deal of attention because of their growing number, size, and influence. In spite of their typically small size relative to multinational enterprises (MNEs) and governments, the visibility of NGOs has increased substantially with unprecedented opportunities for communication, networking, and organizing made possible through globalization.

Yet indicators of development present a compelling and bleak picture of the position of people who do not benefit from "global" prosperity. According to the World Bank (2001b), nearly half the world's population today lives on less than $2 per day and a fifth (1.2 billion people) live on less than $1 per day. In South Asia, nearly half the population (43.5%) lives on less than $1 per day. Since the 1960s the average income in the richest twenty countries has doubled to thirty-seven times the average in the poorest twenty countries. Such figures indicate that the net effect of globalization is that some people are extraordinarily wealthy while more than half the world's population are left far behind, not a particularly good report for NGO and other efforts to eradicate poverty and promote equity.

Globalization is associated with the growth and power of MNEs. In addition, globalization has resulted in the perception that MNE power and influence are affecting all aspects of economic, social, and political lives, and growing in ways that simultaneously connect distant peoples as well as alienate those for whom the promises of globalization appear unattainable. Globalization has meant that regulatory power is increasingly ceded to intergovernmental bodies that are dominated by the more powerful states. Increasingly the rules of society, especially as they pertain to the regulation of MNEs, are being established at intergovernmental fora where some states are dominant and the negotiating entities are principally states and MNEs.

The visibility of NGOs occurs in two principal ways, each focusing on a different type of NGO. First, the more public focus has to do with actions by advocacy-oriented NGOs (ANGOs) lobbying for policy change such as in the arrangements that constitute the WTO. As Deslauriers and Kotschwar (this volume) and Kobrin (1998) both note, one casualty of such action was the Multilateral Agreement on Investments. Ironically, many of the core elements of the MAI had already been negotiated into bilateral agreements favoring the more powerful states (Kobrin, 1997; Ramamurti, 2001). A second source of increased visibility stems from the accumulated assessments challenging operational NGOs (ONGOs) that had previously been believed to be above reproach. These NGOs are organizations like Save the Children that provide humanitarian services and relief in conflict areas. The distinguishing features of these two types of NGOs, as well as an emerging "hybrid" type of NGO (HNGO), are discussed in greater detail later. All three types of NGOs are experiencing a period of success through growth as well as struggles associated with change, while they are also subject to great visibility as well as public scrutiny.

This chapter addresses two fundamental questions associated with NGOs: Are NGOs destined to remain as adversaries to MNEs, and is there space for peaceful collaboration and within the bounds of what issues? Recognizing the diversity of NGOs, three types of NGOs are first delineated: ONGOs, ANGOs, and HNGOs. A review of the three types of NGOs reveals distinctly different approaches to convincing MNEs to act with greater social responsibility. A discussion then follows on the challenges faced by NGOs and implications for collaboration with MNEs. In particular, NGOs' capacity to respond to public scrutiny, to deal with growth, and to clarify identities and accountability in ways that build on NGOs' expertise and credibility are discussed. Finally, the chapter concludes with some of the ways that MNEs have dealt with social responsibility independent of NGOs as well as arising from cooperative and conflictive relationships with NGOs. NGO literature focuses much of the discussion on intersectoral relationships within the framework of a three-sector society—government, business, and civil society—and the failure of government to fulfill its social contract to the public (Heap, 2000). The MNE literature focuses more on the state and its power to regulate within its borders (Kobrin, 1997) and through multilateral agreements (Ramamurti, 2001). In their study of globalization of firms, markets, and regulation in thirteen industries, Braithwaite and Drahos (2000) found that "no one actor appears as master of the world. [Instead,] webs of influence" constituted by multiple parties are required to influence the process of globalization.

In spite of the rhetoric about NGOs, they appear low on the scale of influences that affect MNEs, requiring them to collaborate with other forces (Braithwaite & Drahos, 2000; Moser, 2000). Business Partners for Development, a World Bank initiative that promotes partnerships between business, government and civil society, provides the following rationale that is often expressed by government agencies: collaboration is first an "option because other approaches have been tried and have failed," and second because of the "growing power and influence of business in shaping the future" (World Bank, 2001a). It is no surprise that resources at many levels are shifting to focus more on encouraging intersectoral alliances between MNEs, governments, and NGOs. The focus of this chapter concerns the relationship between MNEs and NGOs only.

NGO TYPES

The diversity of NGOs is represented in an entire lexicon of acronyms that have come into existence differentiating the various types. In this chapter I am primarily concerned with one subset of NGOs, namely, those engaged in international development and poverty relief. Their unifying characteristic is their humanitarian basis for action, usually focused on a single issue (e.g., poverty), a group presumed to be vulnerable (e.g., children), or the provision of services (e.g., literacy training). In this chapter NGO refers to international NGOs; that is, those that either operate internationally or advocate through international networks. The term NGO in this chapter does not include NGOs that operate exclusively at the local level, although it may include such an NGO when it acts as part of an international coalition. The definition of NGOs can be amazingly diverse, sometimes including even international associations of professions lobbying for their professional interests. The U.S. Agency for International Development's initiative on intersectoral collaboration uses a definition that even includes universities as NGOs. The observations here refer to the perspective of the author, whose experience is largely in the operational and hybrid spheres of NGO management.

Operational NGOs

Operational NGOs grew out of humanitarian considerations based on principles of neutrality, independence, and a commitment to help people regardless of their affiliation. Early examples are the British Anti-Slavery Society and the Red Cross. After World War II, there was an expansion through the formation of organizations such as CARE that aimed to help war-affected peoples, continuing the emphasis on "nonpolitical" humanitarian assistance.

The operational nature of these NGOs has resulted in their presence in the form of "field offices" in many countries, which operate much like wholly owned subsidiaries in business, as well as a range of other relationships that create different sets of obligations between two or more parties. In part because of their broad infrastructure, operational NGOs tend to be particularly good at delivering social services in many parts of the world. Their humanitarian services grew significantly during the post-Soviet increase in intrastate conflict.

ONGOs are similar to MNEs in at least three important ways. First, their vast experience at the grassroots level gives them expertise in making decisions about when and how to enter a country, taking into consideration not only the needs of the people but also the local political and legal environment, as well as the possibilities for sustained funding. The large ONGOs make sophisticated assessments of their comparative advantage within a context (often during political crises) and are experienced in making decisions about when to exit. They are usually linked to large networks (through a variety of different relationships) that are held together by a combination of formal funding and informal social controls. They have excellent knowledge about conditions on the ground, what is possible and what is not and are able to operate across the cultural and technological variations represented by many countries. They access populations with services that neither businesses nor local governments are able or willing to deliver. In addition, the big ONGOs are able to handle budgets of several hundred million dollars per year and monitor them in dozens of countries with different financial realities.

Second, the constant tension between standardization and localization has become prominent as the demands on ONGOs have increased significantly. Although foreign assistance has been declining for some time, the funding share directed to ONGOs has been increasing. ONGOs that focus on helping those who fall through the cracks of safety networks are discovering that if they are to implement their programs on the large scale required by large funding, they need models that can apply across countries and regions and that accommodate a vast diversity of physical conditions, cultural practices, and competing needs. Whether such generic models exist for development work is debated. Achieving economies of scale through standardization while responding to local needs at the same time continues to present a major challenge to ONGOs in defining what they have to offer, not unlike similar tensions faced by MNEs.

Third, in the same way that MNEs are criticized for their ethics, increasingly ONGOs have become the subject of scrutiny by scholars and journalists who have questioned every aspect of their work and even their claims to their identity. On both the MNE and ONGO sides there is the perception that they are misunderstood and that the analyses of their critics are not sufficiently rigorous or that they are not fully aware of the complexities involved. Yet unlike their ANGO counterparts, operational ONGOs remain reluctant to engage with MNEs beyond fund-raising to carry out their work. They tend to be conflict-averse, claiming a high moral ground, and often deal in the business of what they perceive to be absolute goods such as saving children or feeding the hungry. Their view of the world includes the successes of development, which are conceived in notions such as greater literacy, longer lifespan, more children immunized, greater access to information, or building capacities for self-development.

Today, the so-called Big Eight NGOs are all international alliances dominated by ONGOs. ONGOs have received their share of criticism, of which the most relevant to their potential relationships with MNEs has to do with identity and accountability.

Advocacy NGOs

In contrast to ONGO neutrality and fear of confrontation, ANGOs act out of a sense of betrayal concerning an implicit social contract with government to monitor and regulate MNEs with the public interest as the central concern. They are motivated by the size and scale of MNE influence and apparent power. They see the power MNEs hold through access to very large financial, technical, and environmental resources. That the revenue of the world's top five corporations alone is more than double the GDP of the 100 poorest countries together strikes them as an indicator of the unequal power relations between the business community and the representation of public interest through governments (Utting, 2000). A compelling case for growing MNE power and the inability of NGOs and governments to keep up is made by Matthews (1997) through her analysis of increasingly large and fast financial transactions of MNEs.

Although not distinguished as such, much of the action by NGOs, such as the protests at the meetings of the World Trade Organization and subsequent meetings of intergovernmental agencies, were the result of action by ANGOs. Their persistent and vocal presence at several major U.N. conferences and more recently at intergovernmental meetings gives them the appearance of size and capacity to be feared.

Perhaps the most obvious feature of ANGOs is that, unlike their ONGO counterparts, they are not behemoths weighted down by long-term investments in offices and staff in various parts of the world. Communications technology has made it possible for them to exist with few staff, and through electronic linkages to maintain vast and loose networks of groups with many different interests. Their capacity to call upon forces within these networks to draw attention to an issue or to disrupt a process that is perceived to be undemocratic (or in some other way contrary to a set of values they espouse) has been demonstrated with some consistency in recent years.

Assessment of ANGOs poses unique difficulties, since the diversity of each coalition makes it difficult to know who should be held accountable for what over time. The ANGOs are so well known that MNEs sometimes believe that apart from their professional associations, all NGOs are ANGOs.

Individuals in business and in the NGO community consistently recognize the important role of ANGOs in highlighting issues, but express concern about the viability of their approach. Indeed, a major concern about ANGOs in the NGO community appears to be that MNEs will assume that all NGOs are like the ANGOs. Other issues that arise with MNEs have to do with the accuracy of the data and analysis of ANGOs and charges from their targets (business and government) of their inability to come up with solutions. Some MNEs have also noted the ANGO preference to take on a monitoring (and thus potentially antagonistic) role rather than a collaborative role with MNEs when changes are made.

While such a reaction may seem uncooperative, the skills and capacities in identifying issues and monitoring are substantial, and the choice to build on those as an organizational focus need not be negatively viewed. Some ANGOs, such as Global Exchange, do a very thorough job of monitoring and keeping the interested public informed about progress among MNEs. Their recent report, "Still Waiting for Nike to Do It," is an example of how corporate executives can be held accountable (in the same ways that governments have been in the past) to their own standards for change (Connor, 2001). ANGOs tend to advocate for independent monitoring and certification, and even those programs have been questioned. A recent *New York Times* article reported that a major auditing firm, Price Waterhouse Coopers, which does more than 6,000 factory inspections a year (including for Nike) "glossed over problems of freedom of association, overlooked serious violations of health and safety standards, and failed to report common problems in wages and hours" (Greenhouse, 2000). ANGOs do not just report the bad news. Global Exchange reported the case of the Chocolate Manufacturers Association when it "accepted responsibility for child labor practices on cocoa farms" and agreed to "work with lawmakers, growers and unions to eliminate child slavery and other exploitation" (Chatterjee, 2001).

ANGOs are discussed because they appear to play a critical role in paving the path for, if not directly taking up, cooperative relationships with MNEs. Criticisms of their analyses must be considered in light of the very different perspectives on the world that MNEs and ANGOs analyze.

The Hybrid NGO

A third category that warrants attention is the hybrid NGO. The hybrid types are important because implicit in the way they are organizing and operating is the notion that they can act as a countervailing force that is capable of influencing markets and even representing the public trust when there is the perception that the state has fallen short of its obligations toward the public at large. The HNGO may also be a product of experience with humanitarian assistance in areas of conflict. Whereas the principle of feeding everyone regardless of political affiliation had been the norm in the past, increasingly HNGOs are becoming aware that by feeding criminals (as in Rwandan refugee camps) HNGOs may be perpetuating criminal activity and further damaging the position of the victims. The need for more complex normative analyses cannot be ignored, but the solutions have not been easily forthcoming.

The HNGO represents a potential set of points on a conceptual continuum between the traditionally apolitical ONGO and the more public political activist ANGO. Perhaps the most visible indicator of the significance of this hybrid breed of NGOs is the high degree of sophistication among them with respect to MNEs. It is difficult to find any of the leadership in this group taking categorical positions about MNEs. They recognize the vast range of possibilities and the diversity among MNEs, and tend to hold fairly sophisticated perspectives on the complexities associated with NGO–MNE relationships. These HNGOs are able to take strategic advantage of their own vast networks internationally. The opportunity for specialization and breadth, from community-level programming to international advocacy, can be especially significant for the large HNGOs with international affiliates. Oxfam International, often considered one of the Big Eight in access to large humanitarian assistance budgets, represents an exemplary case. Its humanitarian assistance programs on the ground give it knowledge of the hard realities. It puts forth a sophisticated and public strategy toward MNEs that is coordinated across the members of the Oxfam family. Oxfam America has become very much an ANGO. It wrote a scathing critique of Pfizer regarding HIV/AIDS drug pricing and supply in the developing world, yet acknowledges another corporate giant, Starbucks Coffee, for purchasing and selling Fair Trade coffee, which guarantees a "living wage" to producers. The wage is now double the market rate in the coffee industry.

Some of the other larger HNGOs, such as CARE and Save the Children, sometimes act as advocates, although their principal functions are operational. By drawing upon international affiliates who may be essentially ANGOs they are able to take political positions on some issues. The example of American Save the Children (SC/USA) is informative because although it is principally an ONGO, it is part of a network of affiliates that includes ANGOs such as the Swedish Save the Children. Where an issue concerning the human rights of children is concerned, SC/USA is able to take a high profile as an advocate by benefiting from the analysis and organizational capacity of its partners, and in turn contribute legitimacy through its on-the-ground operational experience. The international alliance of Save the Children organizations successfully advocated for and pushed states to ratify and be held accountable (through international monitoring mechanisms) for the Convention on the Rights of the Child, a treaty ratified by all U.N. members except the United States and Somalia.

Also of interest are the smaller and younger HNGOs and the ways in which they are flexible in the dynamic global context while retaining a strong sense of identity. An excellent example is Pact, which works in only sixteen countries with an annual budget of about $20 million, in contrast to CARE's annual budget of approximately $400 million. Pact conducts extensive research that permits it to assess potential partners regarding impact and risk. The result of the research is a final risk–impact score. According to Pact's CEO, Sarah Newhall (2002), "We believe that businesses and communities working together are a powerful engine for social and economic change."

With respect to decisions about which businesses Pact will work with, she adds, "In the end it is a subjective judgment that is made, but it is done with the information gathered in the due diligence process, especially the risk–impact analysis."

The distinct differences between the highly political ANGO and the "apolitical" ONGO are not always distinct, with the new NGO powers to be found in the hybrids that are able to retain depth of knowledge and experience through community-level programs, as well as breadth through economic, social, and political analysis and advocacy at the transnational level. When an alliance of NGOs operates as a HNGO, it acquires practice working in partnership among its members, sometimes depending on less or more powerful organizations within the alliance. As successes are increasingly documented through such cooperation, HNGOs are learning to respect and value the different agendas of NGOs with different ideological positions, different priorities, and different understandings of acceptable bottom lines. HNGOs now constitute a strategic entry point for MNEs because they have already constructed the foundations for relationships that recognize interdependence and where mutual respect can be found in different priorities and thresholds. However, the critical element of ideological solidarity remains among organizations comprising an NGO alliance that is not likely to exist between an NGO and an MNE.

CHALLENGES FACED BY NGOs

As NGOs become more prominent on the international scene, they have also become a legitimate topic for increased scrutiny. As a whole, NGOs have not fared well under the microscope of journalists and researchers (Fowler, 2000a; Maren, 1997). Unfortunately, the NGO record on sustainability (i.e., the capacity of local people and institutions to carry on the work previously supported by NGOs after funds have been used up) is not widely studied and the evidence that does exist indicates that it is not very good (Edwards, 2000). These assessments have focused on ONGO legitimacy as representatives of the poor (Holloway, 1998; Abramson, 1999), the lack of transparency in their operations (Fowler, 2000a, their increasing dependence on foreign aid (Fowler, 2000a; Wilkinson, 1998; Krut, 1997), and their apparent lack of accountability (Ghai, 1999; Malhotra, 2000). The ONGO agenda of partnerships is also criticized as one that promotes dominance of the North and efforts to sustain ONGOs themselves under the guise of solidarity (Fowler, 2000a; Edwards, 2000). One of the more outspoken and well-respected critics, Alan Fowler, argues that an important assumption about NGOs that "the forces that create poverty, exclusion and injustice exist only in governments, public policies and market institutions" is false. In the conclusion to a detailed study of NGOs, Fowler (2000a) states, "The civil arena contains roots of power differences that are used to perpetuate poverty and exclusion."

Some of the questions raised by the critics and that remain in debate even within and among NGOs are fundamental. What is the role of NGOs in a globalized world? How are apolitical and political positions balanced? What is a realistic assessment of the types of influence an NGO could assert or would want to? How does the NGO place itself in a world of powerful MNEs and the existence of increasingly capable local NGOs? How nongovernmental (i.e., independent) are NGOs when they are increasingly dependent on governments for funding? What is the impact of contracting for services rather than drawing on their unique knowledge and experience at the grassroots level? Who does the NGO represent and what is the basis for that legitimacy? Are there principles of operation? Are there values? What are they?

How NGOs choose to respond to these questions will determine the future role of NGOs as agents of influence in the change process. If the criticisms continue to grow without visible response, NGOs may begin to lose their credibility in ways that reduce their value as potential partners, which could end in their gradual disappearance. If the opportunities presented by globalization are tempered by NGO withdrawal into more conservative, protective positions rather than in rethinking their conceptual and operational frameworks, they may disappear from the global scene anyway, simply by having become irrelevant. Some critics have called this a period of "anxiety" for NGOs, anxiety rooted in the questioning of NGOs' fundamental claims to the moral high ground (Edwards, Hulme, & Wallace, 1999; Fowler, 1998). At the least the combined forces of great financial and programmatic possibilities concurrent with the questioning of NGO credibility have put NGOs in a period of transition. To the extent that human need will always provide a space for charity, it is difficult to imagine the disappearance of the charitable work of ONGOs. On the other hand, if NGOs desire to help people in the long run to escape dependence on charity and to help themselves, then clearly a sound understanding of the forces of change and strategies to influence the direction of change become important. If the charity alone route is taken, the opportunities for a significant role in influencing the direction of change and representing the interests of marginalized groups will have faded. Two core issues are raised that together have a direct bearing on the likelihood that an NGO would and could engage with an MNE constructively. The principal challenge of reformulating or reaffirming NGO identity is explored through the experience of NGOs with partnerships. Pressures arising from financial growth and increasing visibility are addressed as a second critical issue.

Experience of Partnerships

Perhaps the most visible identification of NGOs is their claim to moral high ground (over MNEs, for instance) associated with their focus on the weak and needy. The question of NGO identity is impossible to ignore, yet is rarely the explicit topic of discussions about NGOs. NGOs are notorious for claiming the moral high ground and, rightly or wrongly, have been granted it by the public in many northern countries. NGOs often fear being corrupted and coopted by business; they often fear trusting businesses. NGO leadership often believes its claims to truth. There is the perspective that MNEs and NGOs are so different that they will never be able to work together. NGOs fear that their ideological and financial missions are so different from those of MNEs as to render them irreconcilable. Some even argue that the maintenance of separate paths for NGOs and businesses is healthy and assures the presence of both self-interest (through MNEs) and group interest (through NGOs). Can businesses with profit as their bottom line work with NGOs for whom ending poverty may be the bottom line? Apart from the question of whether the stated mission is indeed the bottom line, what will an NGO do or not do to assure alignment with its bottom line? With respect to MNEs, very few NGOs even have policies concerning the rules of engagement beyond fundraising.

NGOs have long preached the importance of recognizing all stakeholders and valuing all interests, even those of the poorest. To NGOs, partnerships represent the expression of solidarity based on a common vision and shared principles and goals. The clear and dominant motivation for NGOs to approach MNEs, however, is funding, not partnership in the sense of solidarity. There is the perception that MNEs have access to great resources. This view is not unique to NGOs. Utting (2000) of The United Nations Research Institute for Social Development (UNRISD) argues that in part the U.N. overtures to MNEs are a consequence of tight funding within the United Nations and the perception of greater financial resources among MNEs. As the instances of relationships between NGOs and MNEs grow, they are being documented by a number of governmental and nongovernmental sources (Heap, 2000; Zadek, 2001), and that has generated a greater comfort level and confidence to approach MNEs. Shirley Buzzard (1999), president of Corporate Community Invest-

ment Services, which coordinates a network of NGOs interested in
learning how to work effectively with MNEs, states that the combined forces of "funding needs of NGOs, an awareness of the bottom
line benefits of social investments on the business side, and the realization on the part of NGOs of the possibility of non-philanthropic,
strategic relationships with MNEs" explain growing NGO interest
in MNE relationships.

One of the obvious consequences of the globalized world is exposure wherein nothing is hidden. Like MNEs, NGOs are encumbered
by traditions of dominance and privilege. Ignoring that history under the pretense of being beyond human fallacy by ignoring its institutions (some that continue to reinforce oppression and domination)
serves only to cloud the progress that has taken place. In addition to
their strengths, NGOs' acknowledgment of their own flawed history,
exemplified by disconnects between practice and theory, for instance,
could in the long term strengthen the NGO position in negotiations
with MNEs by giving sharper focus to the overarching goals of the
NGO. NGOs are trapping themselves by claiming "rightness" and moral
authority. As one businessperson in fall 2001 pointed out in a confidential interview, "The arrogance factor is not confined to the business
sector. One of the indicators of arrogance within NGOs is how poor
they are at partnerships among themselves because of their arrogance about the rightness of what they do. The warts we bring as
human beings are carried not only to businesses but also into NGOs."

The predominantly funding nature of NGO partnerships among
themselves and with donors sets the basis for the tendency on the
part of NGOs to view relationships in hierarchic terms in which the
donor is dominant. Ken Giunta (2001), vice president of InterAction,
an association of 165 American NGOs engaged in humanitarian assistance, observes that NGO "fears arise from the mentality that they
are the subservient partner because they are often not able to differentiate between working with an MNE as a partner and being a
grantee. NGOs also tend to undervalue their contributions to these
partnerships, not fully appreciating and defining their comparative
advantage." The history of NGO experience with partnerships can
be very revealing in understanding at least in part the fears they
experience. In spite of the unequal nature of NGO partnerships, there
is a belief among NGOs that their partnerships (albeit with highly
unequal, far smaller, and financially dependent organizations) are
an expression of solidarity. There is the sense that it has to do with
joining forces to achieve a common goal that is linked to a shared
ideology. That these partnerships have been soundly criticized by
many as relationships of dominance does not change the NGO perspective that it simply brings its resources to bear on the promotion
of shared goals. However, historically NGOs have not been required

to deal with other private forces of power (like themselves) operating within the work environments where they are often the single dominant external forces. Potentially there are fears associated with being the subservient partner. There are also doubts about the existence of shared goals or ideology. For their part, MNEs are not seeking or expecting full solidarity with NGOs. Both MNEs and NGOs may need to recognize the space where there is mutual need with different and perhaps even opposing goals.

The previously quoted MNE response from a fall 2001 confidential interview continued by discussing NGO feelings of being subservient: "Yes, NGOs are inferior from a resource dimension, but superior, at least they claim to be superior on the moral dimension, [but this is] not well deserved." NGOs may not be willing to risk a relationship with a partner who may have more power, as they have been the holders of power in the (poor) countries where they have worked throughout much of the history of international development. But a close analysis of the situation may reveal that NGOs can wield a great deal of power if they could reach clarity about who they are and what they represent.

Northern NGO insecurity can be understood in part through relationships with their southern partners. It is useful to distinguish between northern NGOs (NNGOs), which work in developing countries and are mostly North American and West European, and southern NGOs (SNGOs), which are mostly Asian, African, and Latin American. The former Soviet Union and Central and East European countries are grouped among the SNGOs because they tend to rely on funding channeled through NNGOs and to be highly dependent on foreign aid. A recent inquiry into southern perspectives on development conducted by INTRAC (International NGO Training and Research Centre) revealed that while there is much rhetoric about partnerships and enhancing civil society, a majority of development funds are in fact channeled through semicontractual arrangements for service delivery—not what one would expect to see based on the rhetoric or spirit of partnerships (Fowler, 2000b). At a seminar of the World Summit for Social Development, northern attitudes toward southern NGOs were characterized as "a mixture of sensationalism and romanticism designed to provoke feelings of guilt and charity" (Krut, 1997). The INTRAC study, as well as Edwards and Sen (2000), found that there is increased competition for funds, with northern NGOs positioning themselves in their countries of operation to compete against southern (local) NGOs for revenue transfers from decentralized public services.

If most NGOs do not believe they have an identity problem, they are acutely aware of the criticisms concerning funding, accountability, representation, and transparency. NGOs believe they are transparent and accountable. Large amounts of funding do not come without a price. NGOs are accorded moral authority, but they are also subject to great expectations. They are expected to empower the weakest and most disadvantaged segments of society, to offer low-cost services in the most difficult circumstances, where even local governments are not able, and to qualitatively improve the lives of the poor and disadvantaged. That the governmental share of ONGO funding continues to rise may be one indicator that ONGOs are able to demonstrate results that impress their donors. Edwards and Sen (2000) argue that continued funding of northern ONGOs has more to do with perceptions of weakness in southern NGOs than in particular strengths of northern ONGOs. A separate and deeper inquiry is required as to why these perceptions of Southern NGO underdevelopment persists among both NGOs and the governmental and private donor communities. Fowler's (1998) study concluded that ultimately partnerships among NGOs reflected northern dominance. He cites the tendency of northern NGOs "to behave in paternal ways when holding the purse strings, [and] in-built bias and overvaluing of Northern ONGOs' development approaches and policies."

Financial Pressures

NGOs have begun to resemble governments due to increasing dependency on government and foreign aid as funding sources—an increase from 30 percent to 60 percent of revenues in the last ten years (Fowler, 2000a). This dependency is fueled by significant increases in funds channeled through NGOs in spite of overall reductions in foreign aid (Fowler, 200a). Disbursements to NGOs from OECD members increased from $12.9 million in 1970 to $1 billion on 1996. The 1998 OECD survey of 3,000 NGOs revealed that 43 percent of their revenues came from government sources, 41 percent from private sources, and 16 percent from investment income (Wilkinson, 1998). Their increasing dependence on governmental funding has not gone unnoticed by NGOs. Major initiatives are under way in the big NGOs to diversify funding sources in order to reduce overdependence on one donor.

It is difficult to estimate the exact amounts that ONGOs receive as a group. Northern ONGOs may receive funds directly for development work, for humanitarian relief, as tied aid, or as contractors or subcontractors. Estimates for 1997 range from $12 to $15 billion dispensed by northern ONGOs (Fowler, 2000a; Wilkinson, 1998). There also appears to be a steady increase in direct funding to southern NGOs by many donors, although the amounts remain very small in comparison to funding channeled through NNGOs. For example, direct funding from the Danish International Development Agency to SNGOs increased from $1.5 million in 1980 to $42 million by 1993 (Wilkinson, 1998). Members of InterAction are estimated to receive approximately $3 billion a year in private funds (InterAction, 2001).

Within NGOs, both programmatic and organizational consequences follow from this trend. Programmatically, ONGOs are becoming more inclined to follow the money and focus more on service delivery and to seek large contracts rather than mobilize communities for action. Allocation of resources for this purpose has created its own set of controversies within and outside the ONGO community. Competing for contracts has required different human resources and systems capacities than ONGOs have traditionally housed, requiring in turn the additional allocation of resources. Organizational resources are also increasingly shifted to support specialized and narrow technical capacities in service delivery where the largest funds are available. The effects of the growing NGO–donor–government relationship are widely felt within ONGOs through changes in language and self-expression, and in the substantial influence that ONGOs have on their "partners" (i.e., local NGOs). With respect to MNE engagement, this trend is significant because the needs of the (government) contractor become pressing and "real" (tangible, concrete), while the potential for MNE relationships remains in the abstract.

Even in the instances where it might be to their advantage to seek out MNE partners, NGOs may choose not to because many of them are what Ely and Myerson (1999) call monocultural organizations, which they define in part as Organizations that

are typically created by and for a relatively homogeneous group of people—not for all men, but for particular kinds of men: straight, middle, and upper-middle class men, who tend to be white and from industrialized countries of the world. As a result, accepted ways of doing work—framing tasks, communicating ideas, building teams, reaching goals and leading—tend to reflect and support an even narrower set of experiences and life situations. . . . This keeps marginal many groups who are outside the "mainstream"—women, people of color, people from non-industrialized countries, poor and working-class people. In both subtle and not so subtle ways, the organization systematically ignores, dismisses, or otherwise devalues the knowledge and perspectives that are often important and competitively relevant, but that may deviate from accepted "wisdom" that has traditionally prevailed. These are the forces that create what are essentially "mono-cultural" organizations.

One argument NGOs have made to seek out and accept large amounts of government funds is that they believe that growth in dollar terms will represent greater influence and opportunities for quality programs. There is some evidence that "big" in money terms does indeed mean more funding. An OECD survey of 3000 European NGOs found that in 1997, 90 percent of all EU funding to NGOs went to only 20 percent of NGOs, the large ones (Wilkinson, 1998). However, more money and influence with governmental donors has not necessarily resulted in more influence on behalf of the disadvantaged. There is also no evidence that more money is correlated with higher quality. Some, such as American Oxfam (as distinct from Oxfam International, the HNGO) and the American Friends Service Committee, are well known for high-quality work in spite of their relative small size.

The significance of the dollar dependencies created by NGO reliance on government funds lies in the reinforcement of a paradigm of philanthropic relationships. These relationships are hierarchical, with the donor at the top defining the parameters within which the discourse on development may take place. Technocratic aggregation to demonstrate "concrete" results can reduce the work of NGOs to meaningless statements, such as that they "touch" a certain number of people (Fowler, 2000a). The tendency of NGOs to adopt the assessment frameworks provided by their largest single donors, usually governmental aid agencies, and actually apply these frameworks across the board to all their work (including programs not funded with government resources) is among the most visible influences of government on the full spectrum of the work of nongovernmental organizations. Thus, "results" for nongovernmental organizations become defined by governments. Finally, pressure from government and many forces within NGOs to become more "businesslike" has generated both conceptual and operational issues related to identity. At the conceptual level, when visible factors such as efficiency or profit become extremely important, it is easy to lose sight of their instrumentality, especially when the overarching goal may be somewhat abstract, such as human development or the realization of human rights. Resistance to the business model (usually understood as one where results are quantified and there is a high reliance on dollars in assessment of value) is often based in the fear that the fundamentally human core of the development business becomes instrumental to achievement of the goal of efficiency rather than the understanding of efficiency as an instrument to facilitate the achievement of human development. This distortion is in part the effect of pressures to be more businesslike and a consequence of not having a clear identity at the core of the organization.

At the operational level, NGOs in the pursuit of greater efficiency have sought guidance from the corporate sector and adapted "reengineered" guidelines from their governmental donors. Many

NGOs count among their directors representatives from business. The result has been a series of shifting approaches and restructuring processes that may not be appropriate for NGOs. Unlike the clear monetary bottom line of business, an NGO's bottom line may be described within the spectrum that spans a commitment to help the poor to an interest in obtaining personal power. Both extremes are felt very personally throughout an organization and neither accommodates very easily to bureaucratization. While businesses may also face adjustment problems due to growth, their bottom line measured in dollars is able to provide concrete and measurable clarity that personal commitments and interests do not. Whatever the reason, the effect is that businesses generally do not provide a good model for NGOs to emulate.

One interpretation of a business perspective means that NGOs simply focus on economic development and let people make their own choices about priorities for spending their income. Thus, social services will become a local choice of people with private means. The logic of that would argue simply for the "living wage" models often advocated for by ANGOs. In many respects the changes within NGOs toward greater awareness of business possibilities may be reflected in this trend. Nevertheless, it remains hotly debated. According to a typical MNE perspective, a business approach requires "products and buyers" of the products. For NGOs, that means there must be a donor or individual members to fund their work. Some argue that the idea comes first and the right donor is sought out, but the easier route is to respond to the donors. The latter potentially creates an inherent conflict of interest with respect to the clients of NGOs (usually people who are disadvantaged in some definable way), whose interests may not be the same as those of the donors. The knowledge that the NGO brings from its experience on the ground becomes irrelevant or at best subservient to donor interests, which may have more to do with visibility, large-scale impact, and national or local politics. In this context the fact that NGOs are increasingly relying on governments to fund their work becomes extremely important because accompanying that shift is the transference of that culture and its preferences in terms of what is good development, as well as how progress and success are defined and measured.

The perception of lack of transparency of NGO results is often the consequence of requirements by the aid system that frame success in terms of discrete projects or programs, rather than as an overall system where a number of projects (sometimes seemingly unrelated) together determine the ultimate impact on the population they aim to affect. This is exacerbated by the motives that drive foreign aid at the governmental level, where the development rhetoric often boils down to aid preferences based on political and economic interests of the donor countries. Although the short-term service-delivery approach meets the needs of politicians running for office every few years, it also emphasizes short-term results and does not allow for the commitment of resources for monitoring long-term impact.

It is not surprising, then, that evidence is not easily forthcoming when questions are posed concerning long-term impact. Underlying the question of accountability is the perception by some that NGOs operate with impunity. In reality, NGOs are accountable to a number of different types of audiences that, depending on the size of the NGO, could include the whole spectrum from public officials to private corporations to individuals who may not understand development. However there is now no mechanism that ensures an NGO's accountability to the people it claims to serve. This situation is linked to the hierarchical relationships around which foreign assistance is constructed, which place the final recipient at the bottom of the hierarchy with no feedback loop to the source, the taxpayer. Local NGOs in some sense can be said to be accountable because they are not as easily able as international NGOs to simply leave the scene when funds run out.

THE EXPERIENCE OF COLLABORATION

That NGOs are facing a difficult period in the realms of their traditional work has boded ill for engagement with MNEs. The positive side of transitions has generated a mass of creative responses, particularly from the younger and more flexible hybrid NGOs. Documentation of these experiences has helped legitimize such endeavors of cooperation and collaboration. MNEs have become socially responsible in at least three ways, each with different motivations, but with converging self-interests of both the MNEs and the NGOs. These are instances where

- the MNE is socially responsible as a fundamental business imperative, usually through the commitment of leadership.
- the MNE takes up assistance from NGOs to help it be socially responsible as a fundamental business imperative.
- the MNE is forced to take up social responsibility because of adversarial NGO action directed against it.

The Socially Responsible MNE

Some MNEs have been socially responsible from inception and as a central part of their identity. Perhaps best known of this type is

The Body Shop. In this type of business, leadership has a view of the world in which business is an important institution sharing responsibility for the creation of wealth and poverty. These MNEs, out of their own social awareness, aim to be socially responsible and take action accordingly. Recognition that being socially responsible has a direct and positive effect on one of their largest investments and resource needs, their workforce, is one driver of business social responsibility.

Not all such MNEs have benefited. Some have learned the hard lessons of development, including that the best of intentions is not sufficient and may even hinder desired outcomes. The case of Ben and Jerry's Ice Cream is most instructive. The company conducted a social audit, which revealed that suppliers of nuts were living in terrible conditions, exploited by middlemen. Ben and Jerry's immediately moved to make changes in its sourcing strategies; but rather than being credited with conducting an audit and making changes, the company was criticized for permitting the problems, although those problems were discovered through the company's own initiative. Businesses do not always get the benefit of the doubt when NGOs are involved. The Body Shop faced a similar fate when it discovered that some of its products were tested on animals. When its social impact studies revealed that the company was inadvertently engaging in practices it opposed, the climate of opposition led to criticism of these companies rather than recognition of their positive initiative and assistance with fixing the problems.

It is not clear whether involvement of an NGO in this matter would have improved conditions for Ben and Jerry's or The Body Shop. In some respects the debate has become so polarized that emotions are high. Categorical positions are formed about MNEs being "bad," and they in turn take away incentives for those MNEs that recognize their social responsibility to act positively. Some MNEs may choose legitimately to practice socially responsible behaviors without NGOs. There is great potential for this model, but it requires open-mindedness in the NGO community. The combination of adversarial NGO attitudes and regulation of MNE activities that emphasize the promotion of MNE parent-country interests through bilateral arrangements (Ramamurti, 2001) serves as a disincentive to undertake socially responsible business practices in host countries. ANGOs, ONGOs, and HNGOs have questioned MNE abilities to self-monitor. Private standards, such as SA8000 for labor, are rarely applied in any systematic and verifiable way by MNEs. But MNEs point out rightly that NGOs themselves are self-regulated and indeed that MNEs are subject to far greater regulation than NGOs. As Braithwaite and Drahos (2000) found, although MNEs may actually face disincentives for social responsibility from the perspective of government regulation, a number of examples of MNE initiatives that respect the rights of the people in whose communities they work indicate the greater complexity of forces at work in influencing MNE decision making about core business practices.

NGOs as Catalysts of Business Social Responsibility

Much as NGOs are seeing the potential for different types of relationships with MNEs, MNEs are seeing the bottom-line benefits of social responsibility. Collaboration between NGOs (who knew the situation on the ground), international organizations (that had influence and financial resources), as well as the Bangladesh Garment Manufacturers Association (that sought efficient ways to produce) resulted in the removal of child labor from garment factories along with compensation for the loss of income to the working child's family and education opportunities for the child. In addition, the agreement stopped the entry of more children into garment-factory work.

Partnerships with NGOs who share mutual interests can help MNEs establish credibility as good corporate citizens. Starbucks Coffee Company has a history of linking with NGO work that can be traced back to its early days when it was a much smaller business. Starbucks vice president Sue Mecklenburg says, "NGOs can be valuable in extending the reach of our company to areas where we have interests but no expertise or in-country presence." Through its collaboration with Conservation International, Starbucks has provided technical assistance to improve the quality of coffee of small coffee farmers and helped make a source of affordable credit available to them. According to Mecklenburg, Starbucks is contemplating a new line of sustainably grown coffees that would be a product of the evolving relationship with Conservation International.

A more common approach is the use of an NGO simply to deliver social services, often in communities where the MNE is engaged in its own activities. In these instances, NGOs would be contractors, and the potential for reliable quality delivery is high. Even Fowler (2000a), in spite of his many criticisms of NGOs, notes that they are very good at delivering outputs. NGOs can develop and conduct their own due diligence processes, like the one used by Pact, or use the guidance provided by the U.S. Agency for International Development's Global Development Alliance. This type of MNE–NGO alliance needs to be monitored over time, as it may continue for many years without any change at all to the business practices of the MNE while the MNE continues to use the name of the NGO to garner credibility.

Business Social Responsibility Due to NGO Pressure

There have been many cases where an MNE engages in practices that violate human rights and its violations are brought to public attention through an ANGO. The power of this type of action has increased substantially with MNE reliance on branding. Opposition to practices in one factory could damage sales of multiple products under the same brand name. In instances of adversarial action, the MNE realizes it has to act but is not willing to collaborate with the ANGO (network) to find a solution, or the ANGO is not willing to negotiate. One vice president of a large multinational cited confidentially in October 2001 the case of an ANGO that was so opposed to a business that after adversarial action it refused to work with that business to find a solution. After a great deal of effort on the part of the business, the ANGO and the MNE are beginning to cooperate. This situation is a dangerous one when MNEs are not aware that there are different types of NGOs and that there is a range of ideologies among both ONGOs and ANGOs. Indeed, when they think that all NGOs are antagonist and uncooperative ANGOs, they are not willing to engage with any NGO.

Among the best known of these types of cases is Shell in Ogoniland, Nigeria. The company faced seemingly intractable problems and eventually hired an individual who had previously worked with NGOs to establish and lead their community-development initiative in Nigeria. Since that experience the MNE has also taken on a broader strategy of forming a number of alliances with NGOs in many different parts of the world. ANGOs claim a lot more examples of this type, but they are difficult to document and attribute causality. MNEs are reluctant to explain their actions, especially any changes in business practice as a direct consequence of adversarial ANGO action.

The impetus for change in this model is the ANGO (or network of NGOs) that takes adversarial action to pressure MNEs into action. If this is what is required for (positive) change to occur, then funding of ANGOs should become a major responsibility of both governmental and private donor agencies. Promoting the growth and diversity of ANGOs further becomes a very important responsibility of public and private donors, as does the creation of appropriate performance standards.

If the NGO is wise, it will not simply accept a check and sell its services at cost (plus standard overhead). It will instead negotiate for a long-term relationship that involves mutual learning and assistance and protection of its credibility, which will include pricing the value of its name. Well-established ONGOs like CARE or Save the Children may hold very high "brand" value, and pricing these brands in explicit terms could substantially change the cost of NGO services. At present there are no accepted standards for such pricing, and lessons from MNEs may be relevant and important in this area.

The issue of the possibilities for solidarity or identification of common goals is ultimately peripheral. It is clear that the central interests of NGOs are ideological and financial interests tend to be secondary. The core interests of MNEs are financial and their secondary goals include social responsibility. Making this difference explicit removes the need for ideological solidarity or anything like it. Rather, clear intentions can generate honest expectations and replace the atmosphere of suspicion with one of mutual respect and understanding.

Therein lies the challenge to the NGO–MNE relationship. Is it possible to recognize the different goals as equally valid, to the point of being able to develop actions that can be jointly agreed upon to solve shared problems? Successful examples reveal that mutual respect is the foundation of learning about each other, and that, in turn, helps the relationship to evolve from small to big, from shallow to deep. Dr. Shirley Buzzard (1999) notes that one of biggest challenges for NGOs is to learn to respect the profit goal as the motivator of an MNE. Rather than conceiving it as an antecedent, mutual respect may very well be what is achieved following a set of joint activities, even where the motivations of each party may have been different. Things change when people work together and the essential humanity of others is difficult to ignore in close quarters.

CONCLUSIONS

If NGOs could redefine and become explicit to themselves about their identities, there is no reason to exclude the possibility of developing strategic alliances with MNEs. NGO–MNE relationships would require that NGOs learn the culture and language of MNEs. One "business" benefit from such a route is that NGOs could begin to price not only their services but also their "brand." But good pricing will require a clear sense of who they are, whom they represent, and what they offer, in terms of both product and image.

It is difficult to argue that NGOs are any more or less corrupt than other organizations. NGOs would certainly argue that they are accountable to a variety of donors and that they meet all legal requirements for transparency. The overreliance of some NGOs, especially ONGOs in the development arena, on government funds and the need for diversity of funding sources is one of the forces pushing NGOs to consider increased engagement with MNEs. The discussion about becoming more businesslike requires considerable thought, and the variations within this need to be identified. Is it possible for an NGO to retain its mission and values, and even its less-tangible development goals, such as helping build self-esteem, and yet learn how to speak the language of business as a means to affect business practice to achieve the NGO's own goals? If so, then would it not also be possible for an MNE to retain its different mission and values and yet learn how to work with NGOs to attain the MNEs goals?

Academics and practitioners who have studied NGO–MNE alliances have put forth frameworks and principles (Austin, 2000; Buzzard, 1999). NGO experience reveals that the path to cooperation is highly complex and dynamic. Mutual respect for different ultimate goals needs to be developed, first within and between the individuals making contact, and over time through organizational systems and cultures. Although the focus here has been very much on ONGOs, the questions of clarity about identity, history, and accountability may be equally applicable to MNEs. To avoid perceptions of being disengenuous, MNEs claiming social responsibility should strive to be honest and comfortable with the overriding goal of profit, even in conversations with NGOs. Dishonesty in efforts to represent altruism that does not exist, although it may very well be desired, will create the foundations for distrust and reinforce negative attitudes about MNEs.

NGOs that take adversarial actions against MNEs are important because they highlight key problems and force action. They may need to temper that with more rigorous analysis, care with "facts," and learning how to collaborate with or at least provide options to MNEs so that their actions lead to constructive change rather than increased and unresolvable animosity. ONGOs are uniquely positioned by their culture and history to relate to issues faced by MNEs, and their history of reconciliation rather than conflict opens opportunities for cooperation with MNEs. Not unlike their MNE counterparts, the leadership of ONGOs can be arrogant. Either party may question the ethics of the other, but the evidence is clear that perceptions of questionable ethical practices persist on both sides, and the claim to the moral high ground by NGOs (or the claim to more sophisticated analysis by MNEs) does not necessarily mean that their work may not also result in inequity and exclusion. The question of certainty about the rightness of their positions does appear to be an issue that clearly constrains both sides in any potential relationship.

REFERENCES

Abramson, D. M. (1999). A critical look at NGOs and civil society as means to an end in Uzbekistan. *Human Organization, 58,* 240–250.

Anonymous, (2001). Confidential interview with *Fortune* 500 executive, November 19.

Austin, J. E. (2000). *The collaboration challenge.* San Francisco: Jossey-Bass.

Braithwaite, J., & Drahos, P. (2000). *Global business regulation* (Parts 1 and 3). Cambridge: Cambridge University Press.

Buzzard, S. (1999). *Partnerships with business: A practical guide for non-profit organizations.* Washington, DC: USAID.

Chatterjee, S. (2001). *Chocolate industry to help end child slavery.* San Francisco, CA: Global Exchange.

Connor, T. (2001). *Still waiting for Nike to do it.* San Francisco, CA: Global Exchange.

Edwards, M. (2000). *NGO rights and responsibilities: A new deal for global governance.* London: Foreign Policy Centre.

Edwards, M., Hulme, D. A., & Wallace, T. (1999). NGOs in a global future: Marrying local delivery to worldwide leverage. *Public Administration and Development, 2,* 117–136.

Edwards, M., & Sen, G. (2000). *NGOs, social change and the transformation of human relationships: A 21st century civic agenda.* Retrieved November 19, 2001, from http://www.futurepositive.org/social.pdf

Ely, R., & Myerson, D. (1999). *Integrating gender into a broader diversity lens in organizational diagnosis and intervention* (Unpublished working paper). Simmons College Graduate School of Management.

Fowler, A. (1998). Authentic NGDO partnerships in the new policy agenda for international aid: Dead end or light ahead. *Development and Change, 29,* 137–159.

Fowler, A. (2000a). *Civil society, NGDOs and social development: Changing the rules of the game* (unpublished manuscript), Geneva.

Fowler, A. (2000b). *Partnerships: Negotiating relationships.* Oxford: INTRAC.

Ghai, D. (1999). *International Civil Society: An Assessment* (unpublished manuscript). Geneva.

Giunta, Kenneth (2001). Personal phone interview with author, October 23.

Greenhouse, S. (2000, September 28). Report says global accounting firm overlooks factory abuses. *New York Times,* p. A12.

Heap, S. (2000). *NGOs Engaging with Business.* Oxford: INTRAC.

Holloway, R. (1998). NGOs: Losing the moral high ground? *UN Chronicle, 35,* 93–94.

InterAction. (2001, June 6). Annual Report. Retrieved November 19, 2001, from http://InterAction.org/files.cgi/479_Annualreport2001.pdf

Keck, M., & Sikkink, K. (1998). *Activists beyond borders: Advocacy networks in international politics.* Ithaca, NY: Cornell University Press.

Kobrin, S. J. (1997). Political perspectives in international business. In B. Toyne & D. Nigh (Eds.), *International business: An emerging vision* (pp. 238–291). Columbia: University of South Carolina Press.

Kobrin, S. J. (1998). The MAI and the clash of globalizations. *Foreign Policy, 112*, 97–109.

Krut, R. (1997). *Globalization and civil society: NGO influence in international decision-making* (monograph). Geneva: UNRISD.

Malhotra, K. (2000). NGOs without aid: Beyond the global soup kitchen. *Third World Quarterly, 21*, 655–668.

Maren, M. (1997). *The road to hell: The ravaging effects of foreign aid and international charity.* New York: Free Press.

Matthews, J. T. (1997). Power shift. *Foreign Affairs, 76*, 50–66.

Moser, T. (2000). MNCs and sustainable business practice: The case of the Colombian and Peruvian petroleum industries. *World Development, 29*, (2), 291–309.

Newhall, S. (2002). Role of MNCs in international development (panelist commentary). First International Development Forum, The George Washington University, Washington, DC, Febraury 1, 2002.

Ramamurti, R. (2001). The obsolescing "bargaining model"? MNC–host developing country relations revisited. *Journal of International Business Studies, 32*, 23–39.

Salamon, L. (1994). The rise of the nonprofit sector. *Foreign Affairs, 73*, 109–122.

UNCTAD. (2000). *World investment report 2000: Cross-border mergers and acquisitions and development.* Geneva: UNCTAD.

Utting, P. (2000). *Visible hands: Taking responsibility for social development.* Geneva: U.N. Research Institute for Social Development.

Wilkinson, R. (1998). *Institutional funding trends.* London: Save the Children/UK.

World Bank. (2001a). *Endearing myths, enduring truths.* Washington, DC: World Bank.

World Bank. (2001b). *World development report 2000/2001.* Washington, DC: World Bank.

Zadek, S. (2001). *The civil corporation.* London: Earthscan.

CHAPTER 6

Business–Government–NGO Bargaining in International, Multilateral Clean Development Mechanism Projects in the Wake of Kyoto

Hildy Teegen

In this chapter I use a negotiation framework to model and assess the roles and interactions of businesses, governments, and NGOs in "Clean Development Mechanism" (CDM) projects. I describe an illustrative case to demonstrate how such a framework is useful to understanding these negotiation exchanges between parties in these three sectors. The Clean Development Mechanism is an initiative under the 1997 Kyoto Protocol, stemming from the 1992 U.N. Framework Convention on Climate Change (UNFCCC). CDM projects are designed to bring together various interested parties in creating and implementing carbon sequestration or carbon emissions reductions throughout the world. I argue here that international nongovernmental organizations (INGOs) play vital roles in the development and administration of these projects; without their participation, governments and business would likely forego the many benefits available from participation in a CDM project.

This chapter is organized as follows. The first section will address the broad negotiation context: climate change, the Kyoto Protocol, and the Clean Development Mechanism. This discussion of the context will be followed by an overview of a negotiation framework that will be useful in understanding the roles and interactions of the parties involved in the CDM project. The illustrative CDM case will then be introduced and discussed in terms of each party's interests and the terms of the negotiated deal. The critical role of the INGO will be highlighted and a discussion of differences among the parties will be addressed in terms of joint value creation in the CDM project. In the final section I present conclusions from this examination.

THE NEGOTIATION CONTEXT

Climate change is an area of growing scientific and public policy concern throughout the world. Although the rate and causes of change are not universally accepted, the preponderance of global sentiment concurs that the increasing concentrations of greenhouse gases in the atmosphere are increasingly trapping more sunlight and heat and thus beginning to alter the planet's climate (IPCC, 2001). Since all members of all nations of the world largely share the global atmosphere, discussions concerning climate change are inherently supranational in character (Teegen, 2002). The organizing entity for the bulk of such discussions is the 1997 Kyoto Protocol of the U.N. Framework Convention on Climate Change.

The Kyoto Protocol

Of particular relevance to this chapter is the Kyoto Protocol, a significant product of the third "Conference of the Parties" (COP-3) meeting of nations under the UNFCCC in 1997. The Kyoto Protocol was the first to stipulate quantitative targets for carbon emissions reductions by ratifying countries, using 1990 national emissions as a base year for reduction calculations. The requirements under the Kyoto Protocol will not be put into force until at least fifty-five countries representing 55 percent of the developed countries' carbon emissions ratify the protocol (Peacock, 2002). As of summer 2002, the prospects for full adoption of the Kyoto Protocol are tenuous. The European countries have been leading the charge for full ratification, with nearly every EU member planning on ratifying by summer 2002. The principal areas of continued disagreement over full ratification of the protocol are (1) supplementarity, (2) sinks, (3) compliance, and (4) funding (International Institute for Sustainable Development, 2000). North–South (industrialized nations–developing nations) debates feature as prominent challenges to these disagreements, but the European Union–United States split has been even more pervasive over the past two years of negotiations over the finer details.

There are a few ways that an Annex 1 (developed) country can meet its targets: (1) by reducing emissions at the source, (2) carbon sinks on its own territory to offset emissions, (3) purchasing/trading carbon credits with other countries, (4) Joint Implementation projects with other Annex 1 countries, which may involve technology transfers, assisting in more efficient production processes abroad, or creating carbon or forest sinks, and (5) Clean Development Mechanism projects that may be in the form of energy conservation (with technology transfers, assisting with wind energy, increasing cement plant efficiencies, etc.) or through forest or carbon sinks. The United States and practically every other country in the world has signed and ratified the UNFCCC, and a majority of countries have signed but have not ratified the Kyoto Protocol. The UNFCCC itself is widely accepted and is itself not under negotiation. It is the Kyoto Protocol to the convention that is still being negotiated. Most of the details have been worked out and agreed to over the past five years, but some significant finer details still remain, and many of these details have to deal with the CDM.

"Supplementarity" refers to the idea that any progress made in reducing carbon emissions should be gauged relative to a reliable quantitative baseline (Bailey, Begg, Jackson, & Parkinson, 2003). Similarly, any funding required for such carbon emissions reductions should not displace current funding for other similar projects within a country or abroad. A technical challenge on accurate baseline measurements as well as full accounting for all impacts of proposed projects to reduce emissions create doubts about the likelihood for including the supplementarity requirement in an operational protocol. Boundary issues also emerge in the supplementarity debate: Producers in one nation may make production technology choices that reduce emissions within their nation while implying either upstream or downstream increases of emissions outside their nation. How these transnational impacts will be addressed is a limitation of the proposed provisions of the protocol.

Sinks are areas of forested or vegetated lands that are protected from logging or other activities that destroy vegetation. By cutting timber, carbon trapped within the trees and in the soils below is released into the atmosphere. Through reforestation or protection of vulnerable forested areas, carbon remains trapped in the vegetation itself and in the soils as well, creating a carbon sink. There are two main factions in the sinks dispute. The "natural solution" faction claims that the polluting industry should be at liberty to benefit from sink creation and protection to offset otherwise productive activities that are deemed harmful to the atmosphere. The "technological replacement" faction argues that although benefits from carbon sink creation and protection may be valuable, polluting industries (and nations) should be required to make necessary technological investments in clean (or at least cleaner) methods of production (Burnett, 1997). This faction views sinks as sources of potential incremental gain above and beyond cleaner and more efficient technologies being required.

Compliance with the emissions reductions requirements is another sticking point; nations have expressed concerns about the trustworthiness of other countries in self-reporting emissions. A polluting nation, it is argued, has significant incentive to misstate its reduction performance. Even where a nation can be trusted to report emissions reductions honestly, due to technological limitations and the costs of measuring and gathering these data (which will be significant), nations may not be equally capable of self-monitoring emissions reductions. In this case a supranational monitoring body has been proposed, which leads to concerns about national sovereignty as well as influence peddling and logrolling by powerful nations in these supranational venues, akin to concerns raised about developing nations' abilities to effectively negotiate with multinational enterprises from powerful nations (Ramamurti, 2001). Even where a nonpolitical and universally acceptable supranational body can be composed for monitoring, reliance on local players for data and interpretation will be required, due to the enormity of this monitoring task.

Funding for emissions reductions is at the heart of the North–South debate pertaining to the Kyoto Protocol. Developing nations (organized as the G-77) argue that the industrialized world was able to achieve its significant economic development in an environment where natural resources (often located in developing nations) were wantonly exploited in environmentally harmful production processes resulting in atmospheric degradation. They argue that their current attempts at economic development are hampered by heightened restrictions on production, and thus their development will be retarded under the provisions of the Kyoto Protocol. Although the Kyoto Protocol only requires Annex 1 countries to reduce emissions, others should attempt to reduce emissions. Nonetheless, developing countries argue that economic growth could require increased emissions, thus limits to their growth may be provisioned under Kyoto. At a minimum, the industrialized nations should be (and are) required to achieve more rigorous reductions relative to 1990 baselines (least developed countries [LDCs] are largely expected to attempt to meet 1990 baselines; industrialized countries are largely required to reduce below 1990 baselines). Furthermore, they argue, the industrialized nations should shoulder a large proportion of the financial burden for achieving global carbon emissions reductions, owing both to their greater financial capacity as well as to recognize the cumulative environmental costs of their previous development efforts. Despite continued difficulties in reaching consensus around these four remaining areas, significant progress is being made in practical ways to further the goals laid out in the Kyoto Protocol.

Clear examples of such progress take the form of Clean Development Mechanism projects throughout the world.

Clean Development Mechanism (CDM)

In 1995, the UNFCC initiated a program entitled "Activities Implemented Jointly" (AIJ) whereby firms, businesses, and nongovernmental organizations could join forces to pilot projects that would reduce or eliminate carbon emissions. Under the 1997 Kyoto Protocol the program was extended in a subsequent pilot phase known as the Clean Development Mechanism intended for projects involving developed and developing country partners. These projects are voluntary arrangements that require the approval of national secretariats associated with the UNFCCC/CDM program. The two stated goals for CDM are (1) sustainable development in the host country and (2) helping Annex 1 countries meet their emissions reductions targets through these offsets.

The CDM program was initiated to promote prototype collaborative projects between and among diverse parties spanning public, private, and "third" or nongovernmental sectors. The projects are to serve as data sources for developing standards and methods for measuring carbon emissions reductions and for monitoring projects. The program explicitly anticipates the potential development of a carbon credit trading mechanism whereby emissions reductions and eliminations will be certified and traded like any other commodity in world markets. The creation of a global carbon-trading mechanism would provide a viable monetization (conversion to economic value) of carbon emissions reductions (in the form of offsets or credits) through market-based trading within and across national borders.

Carbon credits trading, put simply, will allow firms, governments, individuals, NGOs—any entity with legal ownership privileges—to purchase credits to offset carbon emissions or to sell credits to generate income. As a first pass, nations could be allocated carbon credits or permits based upon emissions targets agreed to globally. Individual firms (and other entities) within nations could then be allocated carbon credits or permits to emit carbon into the atmosphere. Should an individual firm, nation, or other entity find that its competitive strategies or economic-development goals require production with emissions that exceed their permitted level, these entities will have the option to purchase carbon credits from other parties within their country or from abroad. Similarly, firms (and other entities) within nations that introduce cleaner technologies or reforest other areas (creating carbon sinks) will provide a net decrease in carbon emissions, thus generating carbon credits that can be sold to others. The 2001 Marrakech Conference of the Parties (COP) eliminated the preservation of forested areas (carbon sequestration) as a legitimate CDM tool. The price for these carbon credits will thus fluctuate according to the laws of supply and demand for this tradable good.

Economists have long held that our global economic system gains from trade. Such gains from trade could extend to the arena of carbon emissions reduction. By allowing parties to trade carbon credits, those countries (or other entities) with higher marginal costs of reducing emissions will be better off purchasing credits from countries (or other entities) with lower marginal costs of reducing emissions. These credit sellers will benefit from these sales, resulting in a net gain to the system, an "expanded pie" in negotiation parlance. This purely economic argument, however, ignores important political disagreements over the "moral" use of credits trading in reducing carbon emissions, as discussed earlier.

Although the CDM program envisions an ultimate resolution to the carbon credit trading issue, under the existing pilot phase of the program, no country, firm, or organization is guaranteed any sort of credits for carbon emissions reductions owing to the CDM. Thus, involvement by a party is contingent on an understanding that no promise of any future carbon credit will be granted. This being said, many participants anticipate favorable treatment for pilot CDM participants should such a trading scheme become fully implemented, and their involvement may represent speculation on such positive impacts at a later date. Also, through early involvement in a CDM project these participants will have gained important experience in these projects that will position them well for future projects that may have tradable credits attached.

The CDM has several requirements of its pilot projects. All such projects reside in a geographical location governed by a sovereign nation. As such, a principal requirement of CDM is for the proposing entities to have established a host country buy-in for the program. This buy-in is represented at a minimum by the country's secretariat approving the project; often further involvement of national agencies is seen in CDM projects, including monitoring by relevant government ministries. The proposed projects must incorporate specific measures to reduce or to sequester greenhouse gases, as well as develop baseline measurements on conditions prior to the project's initiation. In so doing, the project can provide specific measurements on the supplemental impact of the project.

Supplementarity, addressed as additionality, must also be shown for the project, in terms of both greenhouse gas emissions and funding. There must be a demonstrable net reduction in carbon emissions and funds invested for these projects. Leakage is a key concern here, where gains in the principal project may create second-order losses elsewhere. Those losses must be tracked, monitored, and incorporated into the overall accounting for the project. A further requirement for CDM projects is that a full assessment of nongreenhouse gas impacts from the proposed project is required. These impacts may be positive, negative, or neutral in nature, but must be delineated and, where possible, quantified or monetized. Examples of such nongreenhouse gas impacts from a CDM project may include impacts on biodiversity and migration patterns or on employment opportunities for rural poor, spillover effects on related industries, and tourism opportunities.

THE NEGOTIATION FRAMEWORK

Negotiations are inherently about seeking resolution to real or perceived conflicts about resources, information, values, and so on between and among individuals and organizations. Thus, negotiations are often distinguished by the parties involved, including how many there are and their relationships with each other (Raiffa, 1982; Fisher & Ury, 1991). Following this, a key consideration in analyzing a negotiation concerns the identification of the relevant parties. For the purposes of our organizing framework, "parties" are defined in a manner similar to stakeholders, one of the theoretical foci of Chapter 1 of this volume (Mitchell, Agle, & Wood, 1997), (1) as individuals or entities who have a stake in the outcome of the negotiation, (2) those who have some degree of power to impact, affect, or control the outcome of the negotiation, and (3) when an entity is composed of various individuals, they are relatively monolithic in their interests. Where groups are divided along interest lines, separate parties should be recognized that espouse those interests. It is important to note here that a time dimension plays a role in deciding which individuals or entities warrant characterization as parties to a given negotiation. At a given point in time, certain individuals or entities may not fulfill the requirements for inclusion as parties, yet reasonable expectations about their future fulfillment might call for their inclusion as "expected" parties. A full negotiation analysis calls for casting a wide net, thereby identifying all potentially relevant parties. This wide net approach should not be mistaken for a "kitchen sink" approach, however, whereby any and all individuals or entities are called parties without regard to the previously cited qualifying conditions.

By clearly identifying the parties to the negotiation, an assessment of the substantive issues in the negotiation can be addressed. Parties negotiate to promote their interests. Interests are those underlying needs and desires that parties hope to satisfy by participating in a given negotiation. They are distinct from positions which are merely the stated stances of negotiating parties—those things that parties say they want from their counterparts in the negotiation (Fisher & Ury, 1991). Interests can take many forms: tangible–intangible; quantitative–qualitative; immediate–long term; and so on. All negotiators simultaneously pursue a panoply of interests in a particular negotiation. Most parties do not reasonably expect to be able to fully satisfy all of their various interests in a given negotiation; there is a strong norm toward give-and-take and reciprocity inherent in most negotiations (Cialdini, 1982). Not all pursued interests are equivalent in importance to the negotiating party, either. Each interest has a certain "valence" to that party. The relative valences of interests form an internal exchange rate whereby a party might then know how to trade interests off through negotiation in order to (ideally) optimize satisfaction of their interests.

The interests for each party, and their relative valences, combine in a negotiation to define loose boundaries around the substantive issues to be resolved. A party will be reluctant to agree to, and/or subsequently adhere to, the conditions of a negotiated settlement if they do not satisfy the primary interests that spurred the party's involvement in the negotiation in the first place. Thus, knowledge of each party's interests, and those interests' valences, define the first test condition for a viable negotiation settlement: At least the primary interests of all parties to a negotiation must be met in the terms of the settlement or at least one of the parties will not agree to the deal.

Parties with their various interests do not enter into negotiations from a vacuum. Indeed, many parties will enter into a negotiation having previously considered alternative solutions to satisfy their interests. When valid alternatives exist for one or several of the parties to a negotiation, a tightening of the boundaries around the terms of potentially viable settlements results. The acronym term BATNA (Best Alternative To a Negotiated Agreement) is instructive here. No party can reasonably be expected to agree to a settlement that is inferior (in terms of satisfying interests) to an alternative that the party has available elsewhere (Fisher & Ury, 1991). By understanding each party's BATNA, a second test for viability on a negotiation settlement obtains: The negotiation settlement must be (perceived to be) superior to all parties' respective BATNAs.

The success of a given negotiation depends on the parties' ability to accurately assess the interests and alternatives of all parties. In so doing, the parties seek to expand a viable zone of agreement in an attempt to maximize each party's interest satisfaction. A viable zone of agreement exists where the parties' interests are sufficiently compatible. The colloquial expression "expanding the pie" reflects this concept of broadening wherever possible the viable zone of agreement.

I now focus on the specific case of the Rio Bravo project—a Clean Development Mechanism project in Belize, Central America—and use the framework to guide the analysis of this negotiation.

THE RIO BRAVO CLEAN DEVELOPMENT MECHANISM PROJECT

The Rio Bravo Conservation and Management Area is the site of one of the first Clean Development Mechanism projects, initiated in October 1995 in the northwestern corner of Belize in Central America. The project protects acreage representing 4 percent of Belize's landmass (260,000 acres) which is home to 392 species of birds, 200 species of trees, 70 species of mammals (including the jaguar), and 12 endangered animal species (Programme for Belize, 2002). The site is also significant in historic, cultural, and archaeological terms, pertaining principally to Mayan settlements in the area. The CDM project in the Rio Bravo Conservation and Management area protects existing forest resources from nonsustainable timbering practices (although such preservation no longer qualifies under the Marrakech COP of 2001) and has extensively replanted in areas where traditional slash-and-burn agriculture coupled with large-scale timbering had depleted the forest stock. These efforts are expected to reduce, avoid, or mitigate 2.4 million metric tons of carbon during the forty-year life of the CDM project, 700,000 metric tons of which will qualify under the CDM (The Nature Conservancy, 2002). Approximately half the land is managed as a nature preserve, while the other half is used for economic purposes that are compatible with environmental sustainability, such as the harvesting of thatch, chicle, and agroforestry (Programme for Belize, 2002).

The Parties to the Negotiation

When the Rio Bravo CDM project was negotiated prior to its inception in fall of 1995, parties representing the following groups were involved: businesses (largely energy providers and suppliers to the energy industry), national governments (Belize, United States), a local environmental NGO (LNGO), and international NGOs. The following section identifies the various parties reflected in these groups along with the interests they pursued in negotiating this CDM project.

Business

One of the industries most vulnerable to criticism for environmental degradation is that pertaining to energy and power production and distribution. Utilities in the United States have traditionally relied on "dirty" feedstocks, principally coal, in producing electricity. A natural by-product of their service provision is carbon emissions into the atmosphere. Despite restrictions on such emissions stipulated in the Clean Air Act in the United States, many utility companies throughout the nation are making further efforts to mitigate the impact of their processes on the environment. Some of these efforts are reactions to consumer demands and the activities of advocacy NGOs, while others reflect adherence to core principles of the firms (see Adams, this volume).

The energy companies involved in the Rio Bravo project are WEPCO (a Milwaukee, Wisconsin–based utility), Detroit Energy, Cinergy Services, PacifiCorp, and Suncor Energy. Subsequently, Utilitree purchased 50 percent of WEPCO's project interest. Together these firms contributed $5.6 million to fund this CDM project. In exchange for this substantial investment, these firms sought to satisfy five main interests.

Perhaps the most important interest for these firms is the potential value of carbon offsets or credits that would be generated by this CDM project. Recall that under the pilot provisions of the CDM program under the Kyoto Protocol, no guarantee of offsets is provided. However, this project is anticipated to equate to 700,000 million metric tons of carbon offsets over its forty-year life. Despite the explicit lack of guarantees about offset provision, participants believe that there is some option value in participating in early CDM projects should a viable global trading market be created and offsets be granted to the investing partners in CDM projects. The wisdom of such a stance lies in the likelihood that should the Kyoto Protocol (or a variant) be ratified by the threshold 55 percent of industrial pollution countries—including the United States—provisions both further limiting these utility companies from emitting carbon into the atmosphere and creating a trading mechanism for carbon offsets will be adopted. Thus, the option value of potential carbon offsets from this CDM project serves as a future hedge against emissions restrictions for these firms.

As mentioned earlier, these energy companies also benefit from the public relations value of participating as founding investors in one of the first CDM projects globally. Through their financial investment, these firms can point to demonstrable involvement in providing environmental solutions to concerned customers, investors, regulators, and the public at large. This value extends to these businesses' interactions with policy makers at home. No fewer than eight federal departments and agencies in the United States are involved with CDM project approval (the Department of State, Environmental Protection Agency, Department of Energy, Agency for International Development, Department of Agriculture, Department of Commerce, Department of the Interior, and the Treasury Department). Furthermore, high-profile projects, such as the U.S. federal Climate Change Challenge program, provide opportunities for firms to demonstrate to agencies their commitment to environmental protection. In this way, businesses participating in CDM projects gain a seat at the table with agencies that can impact their future operating latitude and treatment by regulators, positioning the businesses as partners versus a more typical adversarial role.

The CDM projects involve significant technology transfers and envision technological innovations that may provide market development opportunities for businesses that provide services for or relate to the energy sector. Participating energy businesses seeking to diversify their product–market portfolios may benefit from new opportunities found in the CDM project. Finally, these participating firms are largely domestic in their operations and outlook. This CDM project gives them a conduit to learn about foreign markets. In addition, because of the cross-sector nature of CDM projects, these firms can learn to work better in partnership with potentially competing firms, NGOs, and governments.

Local Government

Governments are charged with promoting and protecting the interests of their citizens, both at home and abroad. At the national level, concerns such as education, health, and safety are paramount. Protecting and preserving national resources also comes under a local government's purview. Developing nations like Belize face a particularly daunting set of circumstances in providing needed services, promoting development, and protecting resources. A condition for approval of a CDM project is demonstrated local government support for the project, and so local government interests must be adequately addressed in a CDM project.

In particular, local governments such as those in Belize have various and at times conflicting interests that they pursue. Economic development, as evidenced by employment creation, economic diversification (away from monocrop or extractive raw materials exports and into more value-added industries, such as ecotourism and sustainable silviculture), and access to clean, renewable energy sources is a goal shared by all developing nations, which strive to foster an economic system that can provide for citizens beyond basic subsistence levels.

These governments also seek to protect their resource endowments, natural, heritage or historic, and others. Protection of these endowments for use and enjoyment by future generations is difficult for nations straining under pressures today; forfeiting benefits for future citizens who do not participate in the current political process becomes a tempting solution for many pressing problems governments must address. As has been argued elsewhere (Teegen, 2002), the public good nature of resource protection is also responsible for some governmental reticence in outlaying scarce capital. When a government such as that of Belize spends money to protect its forests, the citizens of the world indirectly benefit from the carbon sequestration benefits. Yet the world citizen beneficiaries of cleaner air may not proportionately contribute the funds necessary for such protection. In this way a poor country of the South, Belize, is called upon to subsidize a benefit for rich countries of the North.

Developing nations like Belize also actively seek out infusions of technology. With lower rates of internal technological innovation, these nations depend on transfers from abroad. CDM projects require a wide array of technologies for successful implementation addressing silviculture, drainage, pest management, and the like. Of obvious benefit to the project's goals, these technologies once adapted to the Belizean context can also provide spillover benefits to related industry and operators in the country as the technologies are diffused throughout the nation.

In addition to technology, Belize is a nation that lacks sufficient internal capital to fund the development of the economy. It relies on investment from abroad to support economic growth. Where the country can participate in a program that attracts needed investment from abroad, it gains immediately with the capital infusion and it gains subsequently through increased visibility within the investor community. In the particular area of funding to promote environmental protection, establishing large tracts of land under protection serves as a magnet to attract further investment in protection, as critical mass plays a role in effective protection.

Finally, as is the case with all nations, Belize must be concerned with questions of sovereignty and self-determination. Although as a nation it relies on individuals, organizations, and governments of other nations, it must ensure that its involvement with these other entities does not deny its pursuit of legitimate national interests.

Investor Firm Government

The government of the investor firms (the United States for all but one Canadian firm in this CDM project) also has important interests that must be incorporated into the CDM project. The United States prides itself on technological leadership in a variety of fields. By promoting involvement of U.S.-based firms (and NGOs) in CDM projects abroad, the government promotes the diffusion of U.S. technology in promising new areas and markets. By diffusing rapidly throughout the world, U.S. technology will become the standard in a given field, such as silviculture, ensuring a competitive advantage for U.S. technologies for years to come.

By promoting U.S. involvement in CDM projects, the United States can also claim some moral authority in the environmental protection game. As discussed previously, nations of the North like the United States have borne the brunt of criticisms leveled by the South on the inequities owing to historic resource depletion and environmental degradation by the North, for the benefit of the North. It is argued that those inequities should be redressed by the North's now bearing a compensatory burden in ensuring global clean air while not depriving the South of the means to progress economically. U.S. firm and NGO involvement in CDM projects can thus be pointed to as "burden sharing" by the United States in protecting the global environment.

The United States also has "special" interests in the Western Hemisphere owing to potential linkages between environmental protection projects and programs and trade, security, immigration, and other regional matters. By having firms and NGOs with important roles in projects in the region, the United States gains sympathetic eyes and ears on the ground in these nations to provide information and support for other U.S. government initiatives that may be linked. This involvement in other nations, however, may erode host countries' sense of sovereignty, raising important foreign policy concerns.

International Nongovernmental Organizations

In the case of the Rio Bravo CDM project, the principal INGO is the Nature Conservancy (TNC), based in Arlington, Virginia. Founded in 1951, its primary mission, under the motto "Saving the Last Great Places," concerns the preservation of plants, animals, and natural communities to promote biodiversity through a variety of means, including placing sensitive lands under protective easements and engaging in scientific programs for improvements in environmental protection. It is an international organization in that its membership and work efforts take place globally: Nearly 100 million acres have been protected worldwide owing to TNC projects. This INGO attributes its success in environmental protection to three key tenets of its operating philosophy. These tenets include a commitment to

1. work closely with communities, businesses, and individuals in their conservation efforts.
2. rely on proven science to ensure tangible results for conservation.
3. utilize a nonconfrontational approach to "saving the last great places."

Like all NGOs, TNC must utilize limited resources efficiently. It must compete with other environmentally focused NGOs in attracting donor funding. Future funding is at least partially dependent upon TNC's ability to demonstrate effective utilization of those funds. To enhance its effectiveness, it invests in science to ensure appropriate expenditures in terms of overall preservation efforts, and it leverages its financial, operational, and technical resources through partnering with other organizations to achieve common goals. For instance, in the Rio Bravo project, protection of this vast acreage of forested land required purchases that were funded by the CDM project's corporate partners, mitigating the requisite financial outlays for TNC.

This INGO also explicitly incorporates local nongovernmental organization partners into its global projects. In so doing, TNC is able to tap into the skill base and connections of each LNGO without having to duplicate those efforts and administrative functions in each area of the world where it operates. A second benefit of leveraging each LNGO's resources is to broaden support for local activities: The LNGO serves as the INGO's conduit to information in the area and allows the INGO to avoid concerns about "not-invented-here" solutions to environmental problems that are inherently unique to each venue. Thus, partnering with LNGOs improves the INGO's legitimacy with local audiences as well as in circles globally that are concerned with responses that are appropriate to local contexts; such issues are typical in North–South debates.

In order to attract donors, resource-rich partners, and capable employees, TNC is also interested in establishing a global reputation for various aspects of environmental protection. The use of protective covenants and easements and the purchase of development rights exemplifies areas in which TNC has become recognized in the United States as a technical (and operational) leader. Similarly, by serving as an organizing entity, or a broker of sorts for an early CDM project such as Rio Bravo, TNC could hope for similar standard-setting recognition as a leading organization for involvement in this high-potential environmental protection model in the future. Once a reputation as a key leader organization in a CDM project is established, garnering support from national governments, local organizations, and businesses is eased in the future.

Of particular benefit to TNC is the establishment of some degree of "ownership" of the greenhouse gas (GHG) emissions question within environmental circles. An organizational mission of biodiversity preservation is broad; the specific challenges to biodiversity and overall environmental protection afforded by leading GHG projects puts a finer point on the organization's efforts and carves out a specialist niche for competing (for donor dollars, overall legitimacy, etc.) against other international nongovernmental organizations involved in the broad area of environmental protection. Among the U.S. INGO community, TNC could be recognized as the most committed and most experienced NGO in terms of implementing carbon sequestration projects abroad.

Local Nongovernmental Organizations

The Programme for Belize (PfB), a local environmental organization in Belize, has an overall mission similar to that of its INGO counterpart, although its efforts are focused exclusively on protecting natural resources in Belize for the primary benefit of the citizens of that nation.

As an NGO in a developing country, finding funding for its intended protection projects is an awesome task. As such, where this LNGO can access resources from other organizations, and particularly from sources outside its national boundaries, it greatly improves its own prospects for fulfilling its mission and thus ensuring its future viability as an organization in the country.

Because of a paucity of resources, LNGOs like the Programme for Belize often lag behind their INGO counterparts in terms of technical, operational, and administrative capacity for engaging in large-scale environmental projects. A relatively small organization like the PfB cannot hope to compete in terms of relevant scientific discovery concerning, for instance, erosion control in replanted acreage, against large international organizations. Thus, through participating in a CDM project this LNGO can access resources from business partners abroad and from their INGO partner, allowing them to more quickly or more viably protect the environment at a scale and scope that alone would be impossible.

Despite the LNGO's need for resources that CDM partners from abroad can provide, typically these organizations are the best suited to recognizing the limits and opportunities for environmental protection in the local venue. Knowledge of indigenous groups, economic development models; and the local political landscape is critical for the effective design, implementation, and functioning of any environmental protection program. The LNGO is privy to such information, and thus will likely insist that it take a leading role in the CDM project to ensure that its knowledge is credited and utilized for a successful project.

Given the need for outside resources, coupled with the scientific reality that favors massing environmental protection areas for biodiversity protection (versus geographical scattering that does not reflect the natural habitat boundaries needed for species sustenance), LNGOs have an interest in proving their worth as local partners to the others involved in the CDM project such that they might be included in any future CDM activities of the INGO and business partners. Similarly, by working with these outside groups, the LNGO gets direct access to organizations and the resources that they represent that they otherwise could not hope to access owing to informational, visibility, or reputation limitations.

Having described the parties to the Rio Bravo Clean Development Mechanism project and their various interests, we now describe the "deal," the defining aspects of the CDM project that resulted from the negotiation between and among these parties. Since the CDM project is ongoing, it is presumed that the conditions for solution viability (meeting principal interests of all parties, better than or equal to each party's best alternative) were met in producing this CDM project.

The Rio Bravo Clean Development Mechanism Project: Negotiation Result

This CDM project uses millions of dollars from the business partners to purchase at-risk forested acreage and to replant barren or underutilized acreage in the conservation management area. In exchange for these financial outlays, the energy-company business partners were likely to earn a large share of any potential offset or carbon credits that this project may be granted in the future. The value of these speculative offsets is uncertain, but these business interests presume some value for their participation, either as an option value on the credits or in terms of public relations value.

The government of Belize ensures that sensitive lands in the nation are protected, earning international recognition as a partner in global conservation. By protecting a significant proportion of its land mass, Belize becomes a more attractive target for future conservation initiatives, with positive spillovers in terms of economic development and diversification. The country already faces stiff competition in seeking to host more CDM projects, as Costa Rica and other

Central American neighbors are positioning themselves as optimal host countries for such projects.

The U.S. government retains some credibility and leverage in Kyoto negotiations via the EPA's U.S. Initiative on the Clean Development Mechanism and via the involvement in the CDM project by a U.S.-based organization, the Nature Conservancy, as well as the U.S.-based business partners. Positive examples of U.S. involvement in environmental protection are important to an administration that has eschewed extensive involvement or adoption of comprehensive environmental protection, to noted international criticism. The U.S. government agencies also gain experience and expertise as facilitators of such projects, providing them with greater capabilities and efficiencies for future work.

The INGO that has contributed seed money, initial partner identification and brokering, technical expertise, capacity building, and some level of monitoring and oversight receives, in exchange, a leadership position (and attendant credit) for this CDM project. Its limited financial resources are leveraged to protect a significant "great place" in Belize and furthermore to build its reputation as the leading NGO on carbon sequestration projects, a potentially massive business to be in, depending on how the final details of Kyoto are worked out.

The LNGO that implements and reports on daily monitoring of the project receives and makes use of various resources contributed by the partner organizations in creating a sustainable project to protect the invaluable natural resources of Belize, for the direct benefit of the citizens of Belize.

The community of nations and interests, as represented through national delegations to the Kyoto negotiations, gains the insight and experience from a concrete Clean Development Mechanism project, knowledge that can be disseminated to other areas for improving the global environment.

This negotiated solution was made possible only through the specific involvement of an INGO. Here I describe the critical roles of the INGO in facilitating the formation of this particular CDM project partnership. These roles can likely transcend this particular example to other CDM projects, and arguably to partnerships pertaining to a wide array of issues.

The Critical Roles of INGOs

Using the Rio Bravo CDM case as our guide, it is evident that there are several areas in which the involvement of an INGO—in this case the Nature Conservancy—was critical in ensuring a viable CDM partnership. To pull together the resources represented by the various parties to this negotiation requires significant time and effort. The INGO, through previous dealings in the environmental sector with business and governmental and other nongovernmental organizations, can reduce the transactions costs associated with project-team formation. TNC could provide information, both technical and relational, to all the parties involved concerning the venue and the underlying environmental science for the project. In fact, it has already successfully undertaken similar initiatives though its main business of land purchases and conservation and though the brokering of international debt-for-nature swaps in Belize in the past (with PfB and the Belize government) and elsewhere in Latin America. It had developed contacts with the various partners to bring them more quickly and smoothly on board than could any of the other partners alone. Finally, through its interactions in the various worlds represented by the other parties, the INGO could readily identify and broker differences among the parties. Its organization is somewhat similar to each of the other partners' organizations in ways that allow them to be perceived as neutral, or as natural mediators between the other parties (Teegen, 2002). Later I discuss how these differences were the fount of joint-value creation in the CDM project.

The INGO could also reduce the transaction costs associated with each partner organization's ensuring against opportunistic acts by the other partners in the CDM project. The INGO provides a tangible vehicle to future CDM project involvement, either in Belize or elsewhere, to increase the stakes for compliance for all the parties. It also serves as a link to external audiences where "bad behavior" by one partner in the CDM team could be quickly exposed across the globe. Thus, the stakes for noncompliance with the agreed-upon CDM project terms are significantly raised by the INGO's involvement.

In its broker capacity, the INGO can facilitate successful settlement of a negotiation by creating or enlarging a zone of agreement. It can accomplish this through providing side payments to one or more parties negotiating a CDM project. For instance, should the LNGO find that the terms of a proposed CDM project do not fully satisfy its interest of access to technical capacity or improvements, the INGO could offer to provide technical training without expectation of recompense from the LNGO in order to get the LNGO on board with the focal CDM project. A dissatisfied business partner could be offered access to involvement in a cobranding opportunity with the INGO outside the scope of the CDM project to improve the overall benefits it receives and thus gain its buy-in with the CDM project.

The INGO's involvement across national boundaries gives it some supranational credibility to ensure a voice for the CDM project and its goals in global venues (Teegen, 2002). It can legitimately argue that its mission transcends the local parochial interests of national governments or even locally based NGOs, or the profit-seeking motivations (negatively) attributed to businesses in critique of their involvement in such projects. This improved credibility can be critical in garnering supranational approval for the project (by the CDM executive board and the Conference of Parties).

Differences Create Joint Value

As indicated previously, in their role as deal brokers, INGOs like the Nature Conservancy can recognize where differences between relevant parties reflect potential opportunities to create joint value. It is commonly presumed that differences (in interests, perspectives, etc.) among negotiating parties create friction and stumbling blocks to successful resolution of issues faced by the parties. However, not all differing interests are truly competitive in nature, wherein should one party achieve its interest, it can do so only at the expense of another party's interest. In fact, many differences reflect compatible or complementary differences among parties. These compatibilities are the raw materials that brokers like INGOs can use to craft solutions that are beneficial for all parties concerned.

One area of compatible differences among parties concerns priorities. Recall that although all parties have a variety of interests that they are pursuing, the valences of these interests vary. Thus, by effectively identifying not only the interests, but also their relative importance, INGOs can recognize opportunities for logrolling, whereby one party achieves a high-order interest while trading off a low-order interest, and another party makes a concomitant trade-off. The INGO's involvement allows these parties to safely express these valences so that they can be used for creating a mutually satisfying outcome.

Time frames are also typical areas that differ among parties. Where one party requires immediate results (bowing to reelection pressure in an upcoming year, or to a fickle investor community that demands quick financial returns), another party may be willing to invest in a potentially larger future gain in exchange for benefits today (e.g., the payoff to future generations of investments in seedling planting would of necessity be longer term). Again, here INGOs can help to identify these time frame complementarities.

Particular to these CDM projects is the potential value of offsets or carbon credits. Each party in this CDM project has different ideas about these credits: whether or when credits will be granted for participation in this project, whether or when a viable trading mechanism will be enacted globally, the future value of such offsets (in financial and strategic terms), the mechanism for credits distribution (allocation versus auction), the fiscal implications (taxation, etc.), and the probabilities for each (relating to the certain versus speculative valuation of this "option"). In the structuring of the CDM partnership, the INGO plays an important role in incorporating potential offsets or credits into the compensation arrangement in the future for the participating parties. Knowledge of each party's likely perceptions and thus stance on the offsets issue is an important way for the INGO to broker a successful CDM project.

CONCLUSIONS AND FUTURE DIRECTIONS

A negotiation framework provides a useful lens for analyzing the interactions among governments, businesses, and NGOs in the environmental sphere. The particular setting of Clean Development Mechanism projects under the Kyoto Protocol is one where such multisector negotiations are required by design.

In this chapter, I have highlighted the specific case of the Rio Bravo Clean Development Mechanism project in northwest Belize to illustrate the utility of a negotiation framework. The various sector parties are identified as are their interests in the CDM negotiation. I describe the CDM solution and highlight the critical role of the international NGO, the Nature Conservancy.

In future work it will be useful to examine other intersectoral negotiations to gauge the relative importance of an INGO in brokering viable settlements. Examining a series of CDM projects would be a promising start in order to identify the conditions under which INGO involvement promotes solutions that are beneficial to all parties involved. Investigating related projects that lack an INGO broker as "null hypotheses" cases would allow for some degree of testing the importance of these international third-sector players in CDM projects and related large-scale projects in the environmental sector, as well as in other areas germane to NGOs, such as poverty alleviation and human rights.

REFERENCES

Bailey, P., Begg, K. G., Jackson, T., & Parkinson, S. D. (2003). Constructing joint implementation project emission reductions: Searching for baselines. *Global Environmental Change*, forthcoming.

Burnett, J. (1997). Costa Rica pioneers market-based conservation strategies. *Sustainable Development Reporting Project* (October 15). Retrieved November 19.2002, from http://lanic.utexas.edu/project/sdrp/conservation.html

Cialdini, R. B. (1982). *Influence: How and why people agree to things.* New York: Morrow.

Fisher, R., & Ury, W. (1991). *Getting to yes: Negotiating agreement without giving in* (B. Patton, Ed.). New York: Penguin Books.

Intergovernmental Panel on Climate Change (IPCC) Working Group I. (2001). *Climate change 2001: The scientific basis.* Cambridge: Cambridge University Press.

International Institute for Sustainable Development (2000). *The framework convention on climate change overview.* Retrieved May 16, 2002, from http://www.iisd.org/trade/fccc.htm#elements

Mitchell, R. K., Agle, B. R., & Wood, D. J. (1997). Toward a theory of stakeholder identification and salience: Defining the principle of who and what really counts. *Academy of Management Review, 22*, 853–886.

The Nature Conservancy. (2002). Retrieved May 25, 2002, from http://www.tnc.org

Peacock, M. (2002, 8 March). Britain says Bush climate change plan too little. Reuters News Service.

Programme for Belize. (2002). Retrieved May 25, 2002, from http://www.pfbelize.org

Raiffa, H. (1982). *The art and science of negotiation.* Cambridge: Belknap Press of Harvard University Press.

Ramamurti, R. (2001). The obsolescing 'bargaining model'? MNC–host developing country relations revisited. *Journal of International Business Studies, 32*, 23–39.

Teegen, H. (2002, March 23). *NGOs as global institutions: Their impact on MNEs and governments.* Presentation to the third annual International Business Research Forum, Institute for Global Management Studies, Temple University, Philadelphia, PA.

CHAPTER 7

Corporate Strategy, Government Regulatory Policy, and NGO Activism: The Case of Genetically Modified Crops

Edward Soule

The 1993 market launch of bovine somatotropin (BST) provided visible evidence of Monsanto's transition from producer of industrial chemicals to a "life sciences" organization. Although BST has endured trenchant criticism, it pales in comparison to the hostility directed at two genetically modified crop varieties (GMOs) introduced to the market in 1997. These products prompted a response by environmental NGOs that threatened the commercial viability of GM crops and Monsanto's biotechnology strategy. While several factors typically account for conflicts between corporations and environmental NGOs, the interaction of two conditions deserve special attention in this case: risk assessment of novel technology and the unusual structure of commercial food markets. It will be argued that these factors conspired to produce profound differences in the way different groups framed the risks and benefits of GM technology, differences that could not be overcome through conventional marketing or public relations techniques or through better stakeholder management. By viewing this dispute through the theoretical lens of framing, this chapter provides some tentative recommendations on how the introduction of similar technology under similar conditions might be reframed to diminish future controversies.

In the first section of this chapter, I provide some background on Monsanto and its entry into agricultural biotechnology. A brief overview of the GM crop industry will follow. Next is a discussion of the controversy, with special emphasis on the regulatory environments in the two principal venues: the United States and the European Union. This discussion rehearses the relevant technical aspects of transgenic crop technology including the environmental and human health risks. In this section, I also address the NGO–activist role in this controversy. Following the discussion of the controversy setting, I review the relevant extant literature on intractable conflict and framing within such conflicts. The particular case of Monsanto will be mapped to this literature in order to form recommendations for contending with similar controversies with NGOs.

BACKDROP TO THE CONTROVERSY

Monsanto and Its Entry into Life Sciences

Throughout the 1980s, after eighty years in various commodity and specialty chemical businesses, Monsanto made significant investments in agricultural biotechnology research (e.g., plant genomics) and purchased the pharmaceutical and food additive maker, G. D. Searle. In 1993 the firm's first commercial application of biotechnology was released: Bovine somatotropin (marketed under the trade name Posilac®) increased the milk production of dairy cows. Coincidentally, Robert Shapiro was appointed chief executive officer that same year. In the succeeding four years, Shapiro radically transformed Monsanto through a series of acquisitions (e.g., Calgene, Inc., Asgrow Agronomics, Monsoy, and DEKALB Genetics) and divestitures, including the 1997 spin-off of the nonagricultural chemical businesses in the newly created Solutia, Inc.

These and other such transactions gave rise to an organization fundamentally different from the industrial chemical company of years past. The new Monsanto was dubbed a "life sciences" company to emphasize its technical competencies in human health and nutrition, with product goals ranging from plants (agricultural productivity) to people (pharmaceuticals). The spirit of this newly conceived strategy is captured by the firm's new moniker: "Food, Health, Hope."

In hindsight, Monsanto's self-styled "life sciences" strategy might have been ill conceived. Novartis AG, the Swiss attempt to marry animal and plant sciences, recently divested its crop protection and seed businesses. Commenting on their decision to sever the pharmaceutical from the agricultural businesses, Norvartis management said, "As the synergies between Pharmaceuticals and Agribusiness proved marginal, we determined that the potential benefits of a life science business do not outweigh its complexities" (Novartis, 2000, p. 24). Interestingly, the divested businesses of Novartis were combined with similar ones of AstraZenecca (the Anglo-Swedish attempt at creating a life sciences company) to create Syngenta. In October 2001, Aventis, the French–German attempt at life sciences, agreed to sell its agricultural businesses to Bayer, A.G.

Whatever defects there may have been in Monsanto's strategy were exacerbated by the extraordinary costs of bringing it about. The series of acquisitions saddled the company with a punishing burden of debt service. According to documents filed with the Securities and Exchange Commission, Monsanto's long-term debt totaled $1.979 billion and stockholders' equity amounted to $4.04 billion on December 31, 1997 (Monsanto, 1998). A year later, long-term debt had soared to $6.259 billion, while equity had only increased to $4.986 billion. This increase in financial leverage removed any margin for error in executing Monsanto's new strategy and put a premium on the speed with which new products were brought to market. When product delays and other unforeseen developments occurred, Monsanto became vulnerable to a hostile takeover. In response, management sought a friendly merger; first an unsuccessful one with American Home Products in 1998 and then a successful one that was completed with Pharmacia & Upjohn on April 3, 2000. In October 2000, 15 percent of the shares of a newly constituted Monsanto were taken public.

In its most recent incarnation as a publicly traded firm, Monsanto has been shorn of everything but its agricultural businesses. Accordingly, it adopted a scaled-down corporate vision ("Abundant Food and a Healthy Environment") and mission (to assist food producers to "Meet the world's growing food and fiber needs, conserve natural resources, and improve the environment"). These humanitarian-sounding aspirations were incorporated in a business plan based on Monsanto's leadership in agricultural productivity (e.g., herbicides and hybrid seeds) and plant genomics. Genomic technology was first commercialized in 1997 with two categories of genetically engineered traits: resistance to insect predation (e.g., Bollgard® cotton, Maisgard® corn, and NewLeaf® potatoes) and resistance to broad-spectrum glyphosate herbicides (e.g., Roundup Ready® corn, soybeans, canola, and cotton). Pest-protected crop varieties are attractive to growers because they reduce the need to apply expensive pesticides. Herbicide resistance is attractive because it makes possible the use of broad-spectrum herbicides after the crop has germinated.

The Commercialization of GM Crops

Agricultural biotechnology has made commercial inroads that are both stunning and disappointing. On the one hand, after only five years of commercial production, genetically modified crops were planted to 109 million acres worldwide in 2000 (James, 2000), 90 percent of which were produced by Monsanto (Monsanto, 2000b). Despite fairly rapid dissemination of these products, geographical adoption has been grossly uneven. Growers in the United States embraced them, planting 75 million acres to GM varieties in 1998 that yielded over 40 percent of domestic cotton, soybeans, and corn acreage (Fernandez-Cornejo & McBride, 2000, p. 12). But these plantings represented 69 percent of worldwide GM cultivation, with (in declining order) Argentina, Canada, and China ranking far behind. Although worldwide biotech plantings increased 11 percent in 2000, virtually all of that growth came from developing countries. Plantings in the developed world stalled to a 2 percent increase (Monsanto, 2000b). Plantings of some varieties actually decreased, corn and potatoes in particular.

Such irregular adoption of a commodity product is curious at best, since early adopters (growers) report near universal satisfaction, as is the case with agricultural biotechnology (Biotechbasics, 2001). This anomaly can be traced ultimately to resistance to GM technology in the European Union.

Discrepant Environments: Regulation and NGO Involvement in Europe and the United States

Spurred on by activists' claims of environmental and human health risks, European regulators threw up roadblocks to the widespread adoption of GM crop technology and the importation of GM foods. Early in 1999, after years of hesitantly approving only a handful of GM crop applications, several EU member states announced their refusal to participate in the regulatory approval process, creating a de facto moratorium on new product approvals ever since. A recent EU directive (2001/18/EC OJ L 106 of April 17, 2001) is intended to relieve this impasse, but it is premature to determine its impact. The problem is not limited to the dearth of GM crop cultivation in Europe where in 1999 transgenic crops accounted for only 0.03 percent of all the cultivated acreage in the European Union (CECDGA, 2000). The EU resistance to GM foods affects growers in other countries, whose harvest is intended for export to the European Union. Simply put, EU resistance has the potential to cripple the growth of GM crop varieties anywhere in the world.

The EU resistance is related to the environmental risks associated with GM crops. Specifically, the technology introduces three different categories of environmental hazard that in one way or another imperil agrodiversity and sustainable food production. The first is a worry that a genetically engineered trait such as protection against pest predation will harm nontarget species (e.g., monarch butterflies instead of corn borers). Reduced populations of nontarget species could upset the regulatory mechanisms that naturally constrain pest populations. The second worry is the risk that, through cross-pollination, wild relatives of the cultivated crop will inherit the genetically modified trait ("gene flow"). The concern here is that a modified wild relative becomes a so-called super-weed by virtue of the advantage conferred by the GM trait. Third is the possibility that the pests targeted by the genetic modification will evolve resistance to the protective feature (e.g., *Bt*), making them impervious to conventional controls and undermining other pest-management efforts.

Any of these risks are cause for prohibiting the commercialization of GM crops, and no amount of research or testing can prove their environmental safety. No less of a passionate advocate of agricultural biotechnology than Monsanto CEO Robert Shapiro warned,

When you start talking about large-scale introduction of dramatic traits in combination with each other, you are dealing with systems that are so complicated that no one can effectively model them. You can start with running field trials, just as when you introduce a new drug you run clinical trials to see if people really keel over. But, just as the human body is a subtle and complicated thing, it may be that only one time in a million some side effect happens. (Specter, 2000, p. 67)

But these risks should not be exaggerated. For one, a great deal of research, testing, and government oversight precedes the release of new GM crops. As McHughen (2000, p. 159) explains, "Compared with similar products from conventional technologies, GMOs are highly regulated." And Charles (2001, p. 309), no advocate for agribiotech, says, "Indeed, if the standards governing genetic engineering were applied to the rest of agriculture, much food production would have been banned long ago." In the United States, GM plants are subject to the Coordinated Regulatory Framework for the Regulation of Biotechnology, administered by the Food and Drug Administration, the Environmental Protection Agency, and the U.S. Department of Agriculture. For purposes of this discussion it is important to note that this regulatory protocol identifies and considers each of the three categories of environmental risk with respect to each plant that is approved for commercialization. It is also relevant that the efficacy of this protocol has undergone two extensive reviews in recent years, once in terms of its overall scope (National Research Council, 2000) and once with an emphasis on the crucial permitting process under the Department of Agriculture's Animal and Plant Health Inspection Service (National Research Council, 2002). In both cases recommendations were made to improve the system but serious weaknesses were not identified. Similarly stringent protocols exist in the United Kingdom and in most other European countries.

Moreover, it should be borne in mind that extant agricultural practices are not particularly friendly to the environment. Implicit in the regulatory approval of a GM crop is the belief that its environmental risks are acceptable in light of some more environmentally pernicious practice that it replaces. For instance, regulators concluded that the possibility of diminished agrodiversity from cultivating pest-protected GM crops was preferable to the destructive effects of chemical pesticides on agrodiversity, surface and subsurface water, wildlife, and so forth. As a "replacement technology," GMOs are evaluated in light of status quo conditions and as substitutes for what are sometimes more environmentally harmful agricultural practices. I discuss the reasonableness of this regulatory methodology elsewhere (Soule, 2000).

GM technology also raises two human health concerns. One is the possibility of allergic reactions to any proteins contained in the GM plant that are not present in the unmodified variety. Second, some have raised concerns over the "pesticide" (e.g., *Bt*) contained in the plant tissue that is subsequently consumed. To address these concerns, U.S. regulators have adopted a "substantial equivalence" test, whereby food products derived from genetically modified plants must behave in a way that is physiologically identical to that of their unmodified cousins in terms of toxicity and allergenicity. Substantial equivalence is the food safety analog to the "bioequivalence" standard in the pharmaceutical industry (Hatch–Waxman Act, 1984). This protocol licenses generic drugs on the basis of their chemical composition and does not require the extensive clinical trials that the original pharmaceutical was subjected to.

Notwithstanding this regulatory structure and similarly rigorous ones in the European Union, GM technology has faced savage criticism. Such criticism has been waged internationally, but as was not the case in the United States, Canada, Argentina, and elsewhere, it gained legislative and regulatory traction in the European Union. Initially leveled on the basis of environmental risks, some of the most strident opposition claims that GM foods are dangerous to eat. These claims have persisted without regard to the widespread cultivation of GM crops and the consumption of GM foods without incident. Quite to the contrary, there are good reasons to believe that GM crops have reduced the use of environmentally unfriendly pesticides and have increased the adoption of conservation tillage. While firm comparative data from an unbiased source is hard to obtain, it is difficult to understand why U.S. growers would bear the higher cost of GM seeds were it not for reduced costs of other production factors. Notwithstanding the lack of evidence—ecological or physiological—GM crops and food products have been subjected to onerous regulatory and trade restrictions. For instance, the Cartagena Protocols on Biosafety (Conference, 2000) single out GM seeds for special embargo authority without risk of suffering from unfair trade sanctions. Perhaps most important, the fears, which were originally directed at regulators, were redirected to consumer markets, where some food processing, retailing, and restaurant firms have rejected GM crops as potential food ingredients.

This baffling result is captured succinctly in the sentiment of David Byrne (2001), European commissioner for health and consumer protection, that "there is an irrational fear of GM food in the EU." Whether this fear is irrational or not does not change the fact that EU resistance to GM crops and food products poses a monumental obstacle to Monsanto's strategic direction.

FRAMING OF DISPUTES: THEORETICAL UNDERPINNINGS

Framing is a process wherein we communicate to our audience an appropriate context or "field of vision" for understanding our messages (Follett, 1942; Tannen, 1986; Bateson, 1972) and for defining a situation (Goffman, 1974). But frames are jointly developed, as both the sender and the receiver of communications provide input to the framing of a message, thus creating shared meanings (McLeod, Pan & Rucinski, 1989). Frames of reference are influenced by past events, individual intentions, the perceived importance of a given situation, and what values are related to the situation (Bateson, 1972), and so actors may find that their frames diverge. Framing of a dispute involves issues definition as well as the relevant actors in a controversy (Bacharach & Lawler, 1981; Putnam, Wilson, Waltman, & Turner, 1986). Even where actors share understanding of a situation, however, they may remain opposed (Putnam & Holmer, 1992).

In their review of theory surrounding framing, Linda Putnam and Majia Holmer (1992) identify main schools of thought concerning the study of frames in conflict situations. Included is the *cognitive heuristics approach*, with precursors in prospect and behavioral decision theories (Raiffa, 1982; Tversky & Kahneman, 1981; Bazerman, 1983). They identify several important characteristics of framing associated with this school, including perceptions of loss–gain, anchoring (reference points) for frames, overconfidence, and isolation of issues.

Loss–gain framing relates to actors' increased willingness to accept solutions when they are framed as potential gains versus a reluctance to accept solutions when they are framed as potential losses (Neale & Bazerman, 1985). Individuals with gain frames tend to be more concessionary, perceive outcomes as fairer, and avoid conflict escalation more than those with loss frames (Neale & Bazerman, 1985, Schurr, 1987). Bontempo (1990) finds that the scope of issues in a dispute interacts with positive–negative frames and outcomes. Positively framed disputes are resolved more satisfactorily when they are single agenda-disputes, whereas negatively framed disputes are resolved more satisfactorily when they are multiple-agenda disputes.

Related to loss–gain framing is the concept of a reference point or anchor. Anchors define an issue as a gain or a loss, and tend to remain constant despite disconfirming information acquired subsequently (Einhorn & Hogarth, 1978; Huber & Neale, 1986). How an individual frames a situation is also related to overconfidence biases (Neale & Bazerman, 1985). Northcraft and Neale (1986) discuss the availability of information—the ease with which information is accessed and perceived as concrete or definite. More available information impacts one's confidence and thus one's framing of a situation to a greater extent than less available information. Gain–loss frames may be misconstrued due to an isolation effect (Tversky & Kahneman, 1981). Individuals may not consider all options or all facets of an option in framing a situation, thus biasing their interpretation. A final point concerning gain–loss framing concerns the interactions of individuals employing these distinct frames. Research has shown individuals to be more cooperative when their opponents employ positive as opposed to negative frames (Putnam & Holmer, 1992).

Another school, that of issue development, is also included in this review (Putnam & Holmer, 1992), based largely on the work of Putnam and various collaborators. This school posits that frames can change ("reframing") such that underlying disputes are transformed. Here again, the importance of information availability is invoked: Information is deemed important or relevant by the actors via their respective frames (Pinckley, 1990). By reframing a controversy, past anchors and issues are put up for question (Osiek, 1986), potentially allowing room for resolution of disputes (Pruitt, 1983). Similarly, reframing can impute more value for a range of options or attributes otherwise neglected through the isolation effect.

THE CONTROVERSY:
NGO AVERSION TO GM TECHNOLOGY

European resistance to GM crops and food products raises questions about the way Monsanto introduced its initial products. Indeed, the company's experience has been explained and criticized accordingly. After years of researching the regulatory, public policy, and managerial ethics of this episode (Soule, 2000; 2003), I find these explanations flawed as either accurate descriptions or useful guides for successfully navigating future controversies. In what follows I consider the most prominent of these accounts, beginning with the accusation that Monsanto management failed to adequately engage environmental NGOs as genuine stakeholders in the commercialization of GM technology. Then I consider whether Monsanto was the victim of nontariff trade restrictions. I will argue that neither of these explanations does justice to the complexity of this case. Following these accounts I address two other factors, risk assessment and market structure. I will argue that these factors provide the insight to fully understand Monsanto's experience and to propose realistic strategy alternatives.

Stakeholder Management

According to some, Monsanto's mishandling of environmental activists made them equal parts victim and culprit in the EU conflict (Eichenwald, Kolata, & Peterson, 2001). Others treat Monsanto as typical of the contemptuous management style that "exploits cheap labour or [is] indifferent to the environment [and then] arrogantly dismiss[es] their [activists'] concerns as irrational or minority views" (Soap-box, 2001). It is tempting to attribute this episode to such behavior, and Monsanto's foes can cite ample evidence for doing so. This interpretation suggests a failure in stakeholder management and implies that more effective stakeholder management would have produced a more favorable outcome. According to the dictum of stakeholder theory (Clarkson, 1991; 1995), Monsanto pursued a benignly "reactive" or a legally minimal "defensive" strategy instead of an "accommodative" or a "proactive" strategy that was called for.

How accurate is this description and how realistic are the suggested alternatives? First, it should be noted that the entire universe of NGOs concerned with environmental and food productivity issues did not oppose GM technology. Indeed, many of them, from the Rockefeller Foundation to scientific associations around the world, enthusiastically supported the technology. The most strident and what would prove to be the most effective criticism hailed from several environmental NGOs, first in Germany and then in England. Here again, it would be wrong to suggest that Monsanto ignored these groups. Indeed, in 1996 Monsanto executives went so far as to meet with Benedikt (Benny) Härlin, a member of Germany's Green Party, a representative to the European Parliament from 1984 to 1990, and perhaps the most influential anti-GMO force within Greenpeace, Germany (Charles, 2001, p. 209). It can be argued that Monsanto's reaction to Mr. Härlin's concerns was feeble, but it would be wrong to assume that they were not taken into account. Indeed, the traditional concerns of Greenpeace and other environmental NGOs should have been assuaged by Monsanto's EU strategy. Said another way, Monsanto's EU strategy, during the time the firm incurred the wrath of environmental protest, was accommodative of environmental interests. In April 1996 Monsanto received EU-wide approval to import raw and processed products containing Roundup Ready® soybeans, but the firm did not request permission to cultivate GM soybeans in Europe. Although subsequent applications were made (and approved) to cultivate GM crops in the European Union, these came two years after the firestorm of 1996.

Beyond this strategic accommodation of environmental concerns in the European Union, it is unclear what else could have been done to assuage the concerns of Monsanto's most vocal critics.

Consider the taxonomy of NGO organization types suggest by Ron Duchin (Krebs, 2001), as shown in Figure 7.1.

According to Duchin, pragmatic NGOs are candidates for rational discourse but dogmatic ones are not. It is arguable that Monsanto was confronting opposition of a dogmatic nature. Consider Jeremy Rifkin, described by Charles (2001, p. 26) as "more responsible than anyone else for awakening popular fears about the consequences of biotechnology." Rifkin says, "They've got it all wrong if they think the issue was arrogance or transparency. It's the product they're putting out and the environmental implication. Their problem wasn't presentation" (Pollack, 2000, p. C1).

Rifkin's comments suggest that engaging radical groups in rational discourse would not have changed the outcome of this episode. As further evidence of this possibility, consider the effort by German sociologist Wolfgang van den Daele to bring some modicum of consensus to the debate over GM crops. Beginning in 1990, van den Daele brought together members of the opposing sides, including Monsanto and other biotechnology firms, to engage in a process of "participatory assessment" (Charles, 2001, p. 102). A group of fifty representatives convened for several ten-day sessions of open interchange. Following this, a smaller representative group of GM pro-

Figure 7.1
Taxonomy of NGOs

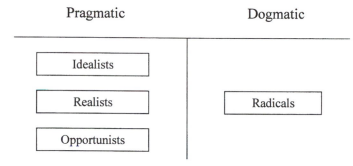

Developed from data in Krebs (2001).

ponents and environmentalist worked at bringing closure to the discussions. This process exemplified the ideal process for achieving social acceptance of new technology as described by von Wartburg and Liew (1999). But after two years the process broke down when the NGO faction abandoned the group. As explained by van den Daele, "Apparently it would have been difficult for them to declare explicitly that the conflict was not about risks but about social goals and political reforms, after they had committed themselves categorically to the rhetoric of risks and used it successfully in the mobilization of the public" (Charles, 2001, p. 107). That is, the environmentalists conceded that GM technology was safe in a scientific sense but refused to relent in their public opposition. According to van den Daele, the quarrel was irresolvable because it involved the "the whole structure of capitalistic societies" (Charles, 2001, p. 107).

This episode dramatizes the challenge faced by Monsanto management. While their behavior toward hostile NGOs was not exemplary, it is not clear that it mattered. This is particularly true with regard to a frequently heard demand for additional testing; a rallying cry of NGO proponents of what I describe as the "strong precautionary principle" (Soule, 2000, p. 316). Advocates of this dictum demand proof that GM crops are environmentally safe, and they reject evidence that GM crops have not demonstrated any harmful consequences as insufficient. Consequently, they criticize Monsanto for not having done more in the way of testing. For Monsanto to take these calls for further testing seriously assumes that the controversy could have been settled on the basis of science, but that was not likely to happen. As evidence, consider the responses of Lord Melchett, head of Greenpeace (UK) and one of the most ardent critics of Monsanto in questioning before the House of Lords:

Question 101: Lord Melchett, in relation to genetic modification, what do you object to and why?

Lord Melchett: My Lord Chairman, the fundamental objection is that there are unreliable and unpredictable risks.

Question 105: How far are you prepared to carry your objections to these developments?

Lord Melchett: I am happy to answer for Greenpeace. . . . Greenpeace opposes all releases to the environment of genetically modified organisms.

Question 107: Your opposition to the release of GMOs, that is an absolute and definite opposition? It is not one that is dependent on further scientific research or improved procedures being developed or any satisfaction you might get with regard to the safety or otherwise in the future?

Lord Melchett: It is a permanent and definite and complete opposition based on a view that there will always be major uncertainties. It is the nature of the technology, indeed it is the nature of science, that there will not be any absolute proof. No scientist would sit before your Lordships and claim that if they were a scientist at all. (Trewavas & Leaver, 2000)

The intransigence of this attitude prompted one of the original founders of Greenpeace to break ranks with the organization and publicly scold their stance on GM technology (AgBioWorld, 2002). It is highly unlikely that Monsanto could have prevailed in this controversy for another reason. While it is tempting to dismiss Monsanto's failure as one of arrogance or neglect, Turcotte and Pasquero (2001, p. 447) investigate a similar instance of what they dub "multistakeholder collaborative roundtables" (MCRs) and are "cautious about the real potential of MCRs to help solve complex collective problems like environmental issues." Apparently, these mechanisms provide small chance of changing this outcome, regardless of firms' skill in managing NGO stakeholders in their businesses. To suggest otherwise is to trivialize the opposition management confronted.

Americans in Europe

Another explanation offered for this episode and its unfortunate outcome claims that Monsanto suffered from nontariff trading barriers because it is a U.S. firm and therefore an outsider in the European Union. However, this explanation is inconsistent with other facts. For one, Monsanto did not have similar experiences in Canada, South America, or with the largest single U.S. agricultural export nation, Japan. Also, transgenetic seed technology is not the exclusive province of Monsanto. Other producers at the time, most notably Novartis (Swiss), Zeneca (British), AgrEvo (German), and Rhône-

Poulenc (French) shared a similarly adverse fate. The NGO hostility was focused on Monsanto, but it covered an entire industry, much of which was based in the European Union.

GM Technology and Risk Assessment

GM technology raises concerns that are not easily allayed by the scientific community (Fischoff, Nadai, & Fischoff, 2001). For one, the science is inordinately complicated and not subject to straight-forward demonstrations of safety. In particular, the environmental risks cannot be addressed ex ante by any laboratory or field experiments that would satisfy critics concerned about widespread cultivation over long periods of time. Consequently, critics of GM technology can discount virtually any scientific finding as inadequate. Moreover, the technology is so complex and seemingly powerful that it lends itself to fantastic but frightening mischaracterizations. Stories about Brazil nut genes inserted in soybeans and the widespread risks of severe allergic reactions or about fish genes being inserted into tomatoes persist in the public imagination. That such myths have obtained factlike status is testament to the ease with which genuine science can be obscured. In short, rational public discourse concerning the risks of GM technology is difficult. Therefore, public consensus concerning its safety and desirability is elusive at best.

Ideally, government regulators would intervene and resolve issues concerning environmental and food safety, but for regulation to work—for it to screen out genuinely dangerous products yet permit the exploitation of promising technology—the public must trust the regulatory process. The disparate experience of GM technology in the United States versus the European Union is directly related to different public attitudes toward food safety regulators in the two territories. Consider the variance between the underlying disposition of EU and U.S. citizens toward GM technology during a crucial period of time, a one-year period overlapping 1996 and 1997. In April 1996 Monsanto received EU-wide approval to import Roundup Ready® soybeans. In the fall of that year, as U.S. soybean exports began to arrive in European ports, protests erupted. Eurobarometer surveys at the time indicated that 22 percent of Europeans described themselves as supporters of GM food products but 30 percent described themselves as opponents. In contrast, 37 percent of Americans were in support of such food products while only 13 percent were opponents (Gaskell, Bauer, Durant, & Allum, 1999). A similar variance was found between European and American voters with respect to cultivating GM crops. Whereas 35 percent of Europeans supported and 18 percent opposed GM cultivation, 51 percent of U.S. respondents supported their cultivation while only 10 percent opposed it.

Why such a striking difference? Gaskell, et. al. (1999) isolate a startling difference in public trust in the relevant regulatory authorities: In 1996, only 4 percent of Europeans identified national regulators as their favored source for learning "the truth about genetically modified crops," slightly more than the food industry (1%), but considerably less than farming organizations (16%). But 23 percent of European respondents rated environmental organizations as the most reliable source of the truth about genetically modified crops, the highest score among all possible sources. Since environmental NGOs were waging protests against GM technology, it is not surprising that the EU public would process the risk as they did. The 1996 British announcement of a connection between mad cow disease in livestock and new variant Creutzfeldt–Jakob disease in humans did little to raise the stature of EU regulators.

In contrast, 90 percent of U.S. respondents in 1997 had confidence in USDA statements about biotechnology, with the FDA garnering the confidence of 84 percent (Gaskell et al., 1999). These findings do much more than explain the different reception GM technology received in the European Union as opposed to the United States. They also suggest that Monsanto encountered a much more difficult challenge in making its case to the European public than might be assumed. If 23 percent of Europeans were inclined to believe NGOs like Greenpeace, it is unrealistic to think that regulators of food and environmental safety, believed by a mere 5 percent, would make a difference. Rather, it is more realistic to expect public risk assessment to take the turn that it did.

Other factors peculiar to GM technology exacerbate the difficulty of portraying accurately the risks of GM technology. First, as discussed, GM technology is in great part a replacement technology; although it introduces environmental risks, it alleviates others. Statements about biodiversity risk should, ideally, be followed by the question, "Compared to what?" The environmental risks of GM plants are in most cases much more desirable than those associated with agrichemical pesticides, traditional cultivation techniques, and so forth. However, a replacement technology is vulnerable to being evaluated in isolation, particularly by a public whose attention has been focused on the risk side of the risk–reward ledger.

Second, few products provide the combination of risks that are claimed to be associated with GM technology: that it will degrade the environment and poison consumers. Other novel technologies bear risks of one variety or the other, but a combination of the two is particularly difficult to overcome. In cases where both risks are present (e.g., industrial discharges), it is rare that the substance in question is one intended for human consumption.

Third, GM technology is vulnerable to rhetorical abuses that can undermine consumer acceptance. For instance, it is a small step from genetic manipulation to charges of "playing God," as portrayed in a *New York Times Magazine* feature article (Pollan, 1998). Likewise, these techniques conjure dark images of eugenics, particularly in the European context. In a memorandum dated July 26, 2000, Jean Hudon, Earth Rainbow Network coordinator, conflates human and plant genomic research in the concept "The New Eugenics." In the same memorandum she refers to plant genomics as "techno-eugenics." Similarly, concepts of "genetic contamination," "Frankenfood," "biopiracy," and "terminator technology" have found their way into the GM vernacular. As evidence of this vulnerability, consider these elements from Monsanto's recently adopted pledge: "We will respect the religious, cultural and ethical concerns of people throughout the world by not using genes from animals or humans in products intended for food or feed. We affirm our commitment not to pursue technologies that result in sterile seeds. We will use alternatives to antibiotic-resistance genes to select for new traits as soon as the technology allows us to do so" (Monsanto, 2000a).

While ethics and social responsibility have been insinuated into most corporate missions, few firms have found it necessary to worry whether their products will insult religious or cultural norms. The mere mention of moving genes between animals and plants is jarring; likewise with technology that sterilizes living things. The idea of genetically based anti-biotic resistance is not the sort of information one normally encounters in a corporate annual report. Each of these statements is grist for a menacing rhetorical mill. Upon closer examination, after learning about the overlap between the plant and animal genome and the arguably valid reasons such movements could be made, these notions are not disturbing, but that examination is a tedious one that as von Wartburg and Liew (1999) point out, is not likely to overcome emotional caricatures of the technology.

The Structure of Food Markets

Biotechnology companies and their grower customers stand to reap whatever financial rewards GM technology may ultimately produce. Other benefits, such as sustainable agricultural methods or environmental safety, are too abstract and distant to register as tangible rewards to any particular consumer. The health risks of GM food products, genuine or not, are borne by individual consumers and, derivatively, by the companies that sell food products with GM ingredients. In order for the benefits of a novel product to serve as a genuine incentive to bear the costs of using or consuming it, the risks and the rewards should be focused (ideally) on a single consumer. Pharmaceutical drugs pose a known probability of serious and sometimes deadly side effects, yet consumers routinely accept this risk by virtue of the benefits of pharmacological therapies. At a minimum, consumers are presented with both sides of the risk–reward equation and can decide rationally whether the risks are worth taking. GM crops are different because the consumer taking the putative risk of consuming GM foods does not enjoy the benefits. The profit margins in agriculture production are so slim that any increased productivity from GM seeds is likely to remain with the grower or with Monsanto. Moreover, it is unrealistic to believe that were these gains to be passed on to food processors that consumers of processed foods would notice a material difference, much less ascribe it to its rightful source. GM technology presents consumers with perceived risks to their health with no clear benefit (see Figure 7.2).

This peculiar structure makes GM crops particularly vulnerable when activists urge food processors or restaurateurs to remove GM ingredients from the items on their shelves or on their menus. Simply put, these firms have no incentive to disagree and a significant incentive to accommodate. So when Greenpeace brought pressure to bear on Gerber to remove GM ingredients from its baby food products in July 1999, they did so, and H. J. Heinz soon followed suit. Rewe, a German retailer stopped selling food products with GM ingredients after two other European firms, Nestlé and Tegelmanns, were encouraged to do so. The list has grown considerably and the motivation is simple: Why bother to defend against claims of "GM contamination" when a priceless alternative is available? Lambrecht (2001, p. 12) relates a severe incident from the spring of 2001 when Greenpeace threatened to stage demonstrations at selected McDonald's restaurants in the United States unless the firm agreed to exclude GM ingredients from its menu. McDonald's instructed their french fry suppliers to curtail the use of GM potatoes, dealing Monsanto's NewLeaf® potato a fatal blow. Potatoes require a very concentrated use of pesticides; and, ironically, McDonald's acquiescence to the Greenpeace threat may have had undesirable environmental repercussions. But that is not a fight that McDonald's has any incentive to engage in and one they very much wanted to avoid.

The Gerber case is particularly poignant and illustrates graphically the extent of this problem. When Gerber decided to set, as they described it, the "gold standard" for their industry by producing GM-free baby food, their Swiss parent, Novatis, was competing with

Figure 7.2
Relationships among Key Stakeholders

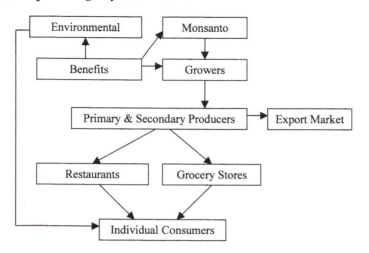

Monsanto in the GM seed business. As a result, the product of some
Novartis seed technology was being eschewed by its baby food sub-
sidiary. As irrational as this seems, it is perfectly reasonable at the
unit level that Gerber management was responsible for, and presum-
ably this decision made sense to managers whose responsibility
spanned the consolidated businesses. That Novartis had an incentive to intervene but did not illustrates how serious the threat of
NGO activism was taken. Likewise, it dramatizes the vulnerability
of GM technology to such campaigns.

This anomalous industry structure accounts for another obstacle
in gaining public acceptance of GM foods. In short, Monsanto lacked
the scale to contend with the outsized magnitude of the concern
over GM technology. The problem stems from the widespread uses
for soybeans and corn. Derivatives of these crops (e.g., oils and meal)
appear as ingredients in virtually every processed food product and
as feed for all varieties of livestock, so the potential audience concerned for the safety of GM technology is practically everyone. But
this outsized reach of GM products is particularly extraordinary when
viewed in relation to the size of biotechnology firms and their respective revenues and profits. This observation implies that it will
be daunting for these firms to influence public attitudes through
conventional means of advertising or public relations.

Most consumer goods companies do not confront similar mis-
matches in scale because, generally speaking, market size and penetration are closely correlated with firm size. Firms that have

penetrated significantly a broad consumer goods market tend to be large companies, and the lack of market share or a narrow niche market usually indicates small firm or business-unit size. Therefore, the magnitude of any given problem firms confront tends to correlate positively with the resources necessary to address it. Monsanto is anomalous because they are a relatively small firm whose products, and the problem they caused, affected the widest possible range of consumers—virtually anyone that consumes packaged food products. In contrast, consider two firms that have struggled with difficult product problems that affected a similarly broad range of potential consumers. In 2000, Johnson & Johnson (Tylenol) earned $4.8 billion of net income on $29 billion of revenue and Ford (Explorer) earned $5.4 billion on $170 billion of revenue. In comparison, Monsanto, with 90 percent of the worldwide agribiotech sales, earned $149 million on $5.5 billion of revenue ($3.5 billion in nonseed businesses) in 2000 (Grant & Crews, 2000). Another prominent competitor, the agrosciences division of Dow Chemical earned $212 million (before interest and taxes) on $2.3 billion of sales (Grant & Crews, 2000). Indeed, the entire worldwide market for seeds and agrichemicals totals only $40 billion (Grant & Crews, 2000), making it about the size of a single pharmaceutical company (e.g., Merck) but much less profitable. Consequently, it is not realistic to believe that Monsanto or even the combined agricultural biotech industry could muster the necessary resources to affect the attitudes of the consumer group materially impacted by GM technology.

THE GMO CONTROVERSY: FRAMING AND REFRAMING

The preceding discussion identified potential root causes of this controversy and argued that two, risk assessment and the structure of food markets, deserve consideration. Elements of these causes can be explained in terms of framing, and understanding this dispute in these terms provides a basis for recommendations on how such a dispute might have been reframed and thereby ameliorated or avoided.

Win–Loss Framing

Throughout the controversy, NGO rhetoric indicates a belief that wins for Monsanto equate to losses for humankind in the form of environmental degradation or human health risks. This zero-sum conceptualization creates conditions for entrenchment of positions and escalation of the conflict.

Anchoring to Immutable Reference Points

That GM crops are difficult-to-assess technological innovations creates a need for assessment of the technology relative to an understood standard or heuristic and reliance on third parties such as governmental regulators to ensure public health and safety. In this controversy, the GM technology introduced by Monsanto was contemporaneous with the vivid anchor of mad cow disease, which was believed not to be sufficiently guarded against by European government regulators. The graphic images of this tragedy, the portrayal of GM food as "Frankenfoods," the association of GM technology with eugenics, and similar images constituted a powerful "affect pool" from which consumers made judgments regarding the safety of GM foods.

Availability of Information

The complexity of the GM technology made it difficult for the public to assess its impact on society; the inability to "prove" safety confounds this difficulty. Since the technical and scientific evidence was difficult to grasp, it was not well attended to by the public in responding to this controversy. The peculiar structure of food markets provides only weak, indirect, and intangible incentives for consumers to risk consuming GM foods. This structure also presented an obstacle for Monsanto alone or the agricultural biotechnology industry working as a group to overcome through traditional public relations or advertising techniques.

Overconfidence

Growing public trust in NGOs, particularly in Europe, coupled with a decidedly radical bent taken by many NGOs active in this controversy created conditions for overconfidence among these players that was not matched by Monsanto. Indeed, Monsanto was constrained by law as to what it could say about these issues. Moral high ground, couched in rhetoric against playing god or sociobiological engineering, is easily attended to by most citizens and thus serves as an easy frame for assessing this controversy.

Isolation Effect

The GM products introduced by Monsanto are largely replacement technologies that reduce the need for and use of potentially harmful products such as herbicides. In this controversy, however, these GM products were presented and evaluated in isolation, without full consideration of the incremental benefits in addition to the incremental costs of this technology's introduction into the marketplace. The controversy was presented as a polarized dispute between Monsanto (and other GMO-producing firms) and NGOs. Yet NGOs were far from monolithic in this dispute: Many important NGO actors active in environmental and human health spheres did not join the public stance against the commercialization of GM products.

Single versus Multiple Agendas and Issues

This dispute was framed by the NGOs in a negative light. By starting with the single issue of environmental degradation (a single-agenda dispute) and transitioning into a two-agenda dispute by linking with the issue of human health, the NGOs were able to degrade the likely outcome for Monsanto.

Reframing the Dispute: Strategy Options for Monsanto

By withstanding the hostilities of 1996 while forging ahead with the approval process for Roundup Ready® soybeans, Monsanto was able to launch the product in the United States and prove its commercial viability and its environmental and health safety. Had they delayed regulatory permission to import the product into the European Union, it is doubtful whether U.S. growers, many of whom were targeting EU export channels, would have adopted the product. However, we now know that this success was limited; and although the international tide may eventually turn in favor of GM technology, its future is less than assured. Following are some strategic considerations designed to respond to the specific obstacles Monsanto encountered. This is not to suggest that these ideas should have been part of management thinking or that they would have fared any better. Rather, they are presented humbly as possible ways to overcome the sort of criticism posed by the radical NGOs in this dispute.

Generally speaking, these ideas are described in terms of reframing strategies because they would characterize the technology in different and less hostile terms. They involve changes in research emphasis and ultimately to the sequencing of product introductions. If successful, they would have been symbols of the positive potential of biotechnology and taken some of the steam out of the environmentalist boiler. They are typical of other successful launches of novel technology. For instance, public acceptance of electricity (originally referred to as lightning in a wire) was due in no small part to the friendliness of its initial application, exterior lighting, and the recognized fire hazard of kerosene lamps, the dominant technology it replaced. The very real risks of electric power were diminished by the way consumers framed the technology. Had the first application been the electric chair or some weapons technology, consumers may have been less inclined to permit "lightning" to course through the walls of their homes.

How, if at all, could GM technology have been framed differently so that it would not be vulnerable to hostile mischaracterization? First, consider that the organic food industry is a significant force in hobbling the public acceptance of GM crops in two important ways. First, environmental activists urge organic farming as a viable alternative to both GM crops and the agrichemical hazards they replace. But the organic food industry also leveraged environmental hostility toward GM crops by positioning organic food as an alternative; and in doing so, they furthered the impression that GM food is somehow adulterated or contaminated (True Food Network, 2003). Accordingly, the organic food industry represents a formidable obstacle to public acceptance of GM food, one that is nearly intractable at this time. Indeed, at the urging of organic food interests the recently released National Organic Program sponsored by the Agricultural Marketing Service of the USDA defines "organic" such that GM ingredients are forbidden (§ 205.2). The reasonableness of this distinction is scientifically dubious, but that is all the more reason to take seriously the political potency of the organic food industry and its unbridled hostility to GM foods.

Yet the hostility between organic and GM food is not rooted in nature and there is no prima facie reason why the organic food industry should be hostile toward GM technology. Organic foods are hybrids of something else, and many of them are brought about through crass technological means that preceded the precision of GM methods. By providing benefits to the organic food industry, Monsanto would have gone a long way to reframing the entire dispute. In short, if this hostility toward GM technology had been replaced with self-interested concern, this dispute might have turned out differently. Consider what Dr. Klaas Martens, an expert in organic farming and an industry advocate, has to say:

I can't talk for all organic farmers, but most of the ones that I know would rather not be involved in this controversy at all. . . . I believe that if the first transgenic seeds to be released had been something like a mosaic virus resistant Vinton 81 soybean [the mosaic virus is the biggest problem in the production of the special soybeans grown for the organic Japanese tofu market], rather than herbicide resistant crops, history may have taken a very different course. I believe that if such a crop [as the transgenic papaya] could be developed and offered to farmers . . . it would make many organic farmers in the US wish they were allowed to use it. It's not hard for organic farmers to reject products like roundup ready and BT because they don't serve any purpose on organic farms anyway.

Whether these ideas are practical or not is a question beyond the expertise of this writer, but the point being made bears consideration. While there is no way to tell whether this would have changed materially the outcome of this dispute, it would have gone a long way to reframing the technology in a more consumer-friendly fashion.

Monsanto's challenge in the European Union was not limited to the frightening images that were used to mischaracterize their products; the firm itself was demonized as a global bully intent on controlling the world's food supply and unconcerned with the environmental or human health damage it may cause in the process. Both assaults are unfair caricatures of reality, but their success is an indication that any reframing would only be successful if it carried a very high emotional appeal, a success that is far from certain.

What is assured is that Monsanto's vision about "Abundant Food and a Healthy Environment" and its mission of "Meeting the world's growing food and fiber needs," regardless of how well intended they might be, were grossly insufficient. Moreover, the products that were launched first, Roundup Ready® soybeans and *Bt* corn, provided benefits that were too indirect and complex to make sense of those sentiments in any tangible way. This problem was a repeat of Monsanto's earlier experience with BST. The case for BST is similar to any other instance of agricultural productivity: Posilac® increases the efficiency of milk production, thereby reducing the requisite size of dairy herds and their environmental footprint, reducing the costs of milk and milk products, and increasing the profits of a beleaguered dairy production industry. Not surprising, Posilac® is widely embraced by large dairy producers. But equally understandable, it is banned in the European Union, as are milk and meat products from cows treated with BST. This ban has persisted in the face of the product's safety (attested to by the regulatory agencies in thirty countries, the World Health Organization, and others), as well as findings that the product is humane (e.g., the EC's Committee for Veterinary Medical Products). But increasing the productivity of milk production, a product in chronic oversupply, is not likely to compete effectively in the public imagination with images of the dangers of cows treated with steroid-like hormones. In short, unless one owns a very large dairy herd, there is no reason to care and every reason to worry about feeding milk from hormone-enhanced cows to babies.

The vulnerability of Posilac®, the subsequent fates of *Bt* corn and Roundup Ready® soybeans, and the inability to affect public attitudes through conventional public relations and advertising techniques suggest that another approach was warranted. Consider the so-called golden rice, a modified beta carotene–enriched variety that overcomes vitamin-A deficiencies (VAD) in populations dependent upon rice for the majority of their nutritional needs. The World Health Organization estimates that 250 million people suffer from VAD-related disorders, from impaired vision to immune system function. In particular, WHO emphasizes that children are particularly susceptible to such inflictions, pointing out that nearly 500,000 go partially or totally blind each year as the result of inadequate micronutrients, vitamin A in particular. Agricultural biotechnology is well suited to contend with this scourge and, accordingly, the European Union and the Rockefeller Foundation funded the research of Ingo Potrykus (the Institute of Plant Sciences in Zurich) and Peter Beyer (the Centre for Applied Biosciences in Freiburg, Germany) to produce golden rice (Palevitz, 2001). They recently announced the availability of the first variety, which will be provided free of charge to Asian growers. Ironically, Monsanto research provided the basis for large portions of this work. Indeed, Monsanto research resulted in the first comprehensive map of the rice genome. Had Monsanto devoted resources to develop this product in the early stages of the development of GM technology—before the release of *Bt* corn, Roundup Ready® soybeans, or any other applications with no apparent humanitarian value—ascriptions like "Frankenfoods" might have struck many in the public as misplaced. By removing the isolation of one product from others with tangible benefits to society, Monsanto was robbed of the opportunity to anchor its entire GM product line with positive images.

It is worth noting that Monsanto ultimately did many of the things that would have contributed to this favorable image. For instance, the firm contributed their rice plant research to the International Rice Genome Sequencing Project. But they did so in April 2000, after GM technology had been framed negatively. This also occurred after their patent estate had served as an obstacle to humanitarian efforts of others. For instance, Potrykus and Beyer bemoan the need to obtain permission to use seventy patents, many held by Monsanto, to develop a product with unambiguous humanitarian value (Palevitz, 2001). By emphasizing biotech patents and by only exploiting those technologies with commercial value, Monsanto fell prey to the critical accounts of biotech as just another profit-making scheme. A product that demonstrably relieves human suffering without any profit motive would have gone a long way to counter that criticism.

Other such applications, like drought-resistant wheat and virus resistant sweet potatoes, offer significant benefits for African growers to make genuine progress toward self-sufficient food production. Monsanto and most other agricultural biotechnology firms have assisted these efforts by granting free access to their basic science discoveries to stimulate general research into plant genetics. For example, Monsanto's "working draft" of the rice genome sequence was contributed in April 2000 to the International Rice Genome Sequencing Project, a ten-member consortium of rice genome sequencing projects around the world, and is available free of charge to other researchers. These data are recognized as crucial to improved rice: its nutritional level; yields; and adaptability to seasons, climates, and soils. According to estimates by the International Rice Research Institute (2003), more than half of the world's population will depend on rice for their primary nutritional needs by 2020. Also, Monsanto has funded a nine-year research project with the Kenya Agricultural Research Institute (KARI) to develop a virus-resistant sweet potato. The key technological discovery, a coat protein responsible for the virus resistance, was donated to KARI, royalty free. These actions create opportunities for reframing by bringing other beneficiaries to the table who can lend credibility to Monsanto's claims of benefits to society.

Opportunities abound from framing GM technology in terms that comport with Monsanto's stated mission, but pointing to these applications as abstract possibilities while devoting resources to commercially valuable row crops simply stokes the suspicions of hostile NGOs and their plaint followers. Indeed, Monsanto has been described as part of the "bio-industrial complex" (Wheale & McNally, 1998). Such characterizations, of Monsanto and of the products they managed to produce, would have been difficult in the face of stunning humanitarian contributions.

CONCLUSION

Monsanto has faced a particularly daunting challenge to its strategic dominion over the commercialization of GM products, particularly in Europe. This challenge stems from the actions of radical NGOs, whose success in swaying public opinion in Europe has been formidable. The controversy is discussed in terms of the literature on framing, the context within which issues are conveyed and understood. With an understanding of the root causes of the contro-

versy in terms of framing dimensions, reframing suggestions are offered for firms facing similarly hostile interactions with NGOs. Given
the increased effectiveness of NGO organization and information
dissemination in recent years, corporations must proactively manage the framing of their concerns vis-à-vis a concerned public to
counter unfounded, unwarranted, and undesirable claims by NGO
activists. To do otherwise, to depend upon the merits of one's product or service winning out in the court of rational public opinion, is
dangerously naïve.

REFERENCES

AgBioWorld. (2002). *Greenpeace founder supports biotechnology: Moore
    criticizes colleagues for opposing golden rice.* Retrieved February 25,
    2002, from http://www.agbioworld.org/biotech_info/pr/moore.html
Bacharach, S. B., & Lawler, E. J. (1981). *Bargaining: Power, tactics, and out-
    comes.* San Francisco: Jossey Bass.
Bateson, G. (1972). *Steps to an ecology of mind.* New York: Ballantine.
Bazerman, M. H. (1983). A critical look at the rationality of negotiator judg-
    ment. *American Behavioral Scientist, 27,* 211–228.
Biotechbasics (Monsanto). (2001). *Biotech01 Introduction.* Retrieved Janu-
    ary 30, 2002, from http://www.biotechbasics.com/biotech01/
    intro.html
Bontempo, R. N. (1990). *Heuristics and negotiations: Effects of frame and
    agenda.* Paper presented at the annual meeting of the Academy of
    Management, San Francisco.
Byrne, D. (2001, October 9). *A European approach to food safety and GMOs.*
    Speech to the National Press Club, Washington D.C.
Commission of the European Communities, Directorate General for Agri-
    culture (CECDGA). (2000). *Economic impacts of genetically modi-
    fied crops on the agri-food sector: A first review.* Retrieved January
    30, 2002, from http://europa.eu.int/comm/agriculture/publi/gmo/
    summary.htm
Conference of the Parties to the Convention on Biological Diversity. (2000).
    *Cartagena Protocol on biosafety to the convention on biological di-
    versity,* pp 1–19. Report issued Montreal, January 24–28. Retrieved
    November 12, 2001, from http://www.binas.unido.org/binas/regula-
    tions/cartagena-protocol-en.pdf
Charles, D. (2001). *Lords of the harvest: Biotech, big money, and the future
    of food.* Cambridge, MA: Perseus.
Clarkson, M.B.E. (1991). Defining, evaluating, and managing corporate so-
    cial performance: The stakeholder management model. In L. E. Preston
    (Ed.), *Research in corporate social performance and policy* (vol. 12,
    pp. 331–358). Greenwich, CT: JAI Press.
Clarkson, M.B.E. (1995). A stakeholder framework for analyzing and evalu-
    ating corporate social performance. *Academy of Management Review,
    20,* 92–117.

Eichenwald, K., Kolata, G., & Peterson, M. (2001). Biotechnology food: From the lab to a debacle. *New York Times,* January 25, p. A1.

Einhorn, H. J., & Hogarth, R. M. (1978). Confidence in judgment: Persistence illusion of validity. *Psychological Reports, 85,* 395–416.

Fernandez-Cornejo, J., & McBride, W. (2000). Genetically engineered crops for pest management in U.S. agriculture. *Agricultural Economics Report, 786,* p. 12.

Fischoff, B., Nadai, A., & Fischoff, I. (2001). Investing in frankenfirms: Predicting socially unacceptable risks. *Journal of Psychology and Financial Markets, 2,* 100–111.

Follett, M. P. (1942). Constructive conflict. In H. C. Metcalf & L. Urwick (Eds.), *Dynamic administration: The collected papers of Mary Parker Follett.* New York: Harper & Brothers.

Gaskell, G, Bauer, M., Durant, J., & Allum, N.C. (1999). Worlds apart? The reception of genetically modified foods in Europe and the U.S. *Science, 285,* 384–387.

Goffman, E. (1974). *Frame analysis: An essay on the organization of experience.* New York: Harper & Row.

Grant, H., & Crews, T. (2000, May 31). *Monsanto financial/investment community presentation,* New York.

Huber, V. L., & Neale, M. A. (1986). Effects of cognitive heuristics and goals on negotiator performance and subsequent goal setting. *Organizational Behavior and Human Decision Processes, 38,* 342–365.

Hudon, J. (2000) *Memorandum, July 26.* Retrieved February 28, 2002, from http://www.cybernaute.com/earthconcert2000/GMOUpdate26.htm

James, C. (2000). Global status of commercialized transgenic crops: 2000. In *International Service for the Acquisition of Agri-biotech Applications 21-2000.* Retrieved January 30, 2002, from http://www.isaaa.org/publications/briefs/Brief_21.htm

Krebs, C. (2001, January). Industrialized activism? Modern protesters have turned idealism into an institution. *AgriMarketing,* 43–45.

Lambrecht, B. (2001). *Dinner at the new gene café: How genetic engineering is changing what we eat, how we live, and the global politics of food.* New York: St. Martin's Press.

Martens, K. (2001, January 1) Email messages from Klaus Ammann.

McLeod, J. M., Pan, Z., & Rucinski, D. M. (1989, May). *Framing a complex issue: A case of social construction of meaning.* Paper presented at the annual meeting of the International Communication Association, San Francisco.

McHughen, A. (2000). *Pandora's picnic basket: The potential and hazards of genetically modified foods.* New York: Oxford University Press.

Monsanto. (1998). *Annual report 1998 summary.* Retrieved November 17, 2002, from http://www.corporate-ir.net/ireyelir-site.zhtml?hcke/=MON&script=700

Monsanto (2000a). *About us.* Retrieved November 19, 2001, from http://www.monsanto.com/monsanto/about_us/monsanto_pledge/default.htm

Monsanto (2000b). *Plant biotechnology.* Retrieved November 19, 2001, from http://www.monsanto.cp,,pmsamtp/content/media/bio/BioCrp Rpt2000.pdf

National Research Council. (2000). *Modified pest-protected plants: Science and regulation.* Washington, DC: National Academy Press.

National Research Council. (2002). Environmental effects of transgenic plants: The scope and adequacy of regulation. Washington, DC: National Academy Press.

Neale, M. A., & Bazerman, M. H. (1985). The effects of framing and negotiator overconfidence on bargaining behavior. *Academy of Management Journal, 28*, 34–49.

Northcraft, G. B., & Neale, M. A. (1986). Opportunity costs and the framing of resource allocation decisions. *Organizational Behavior and Human Decision Processes, 37*, 348–356.

Novartis. (2000). Novartis operational review 2000. Retrieved November 18, 2001, from http://www.pharma.ch.novartis.com/d/presse/finanzen/oprevoo-g.pdf

Osiek, C. (1986). *Beyond anger.* Boston: Paulist Press.

Palevitz, B. (2001). Untitled. *The Scientist, 15*, 8.

Pinckley, R. L. (1990). Dimensions of conflict frame: Disputant interpretations of conflict. *Journal of Applied Psychology, 75*, 117–126.

Pollack, A. (2000, November 28). Companies seek looser rules on labeling genetically altered seed. *New York Times*, p. C1.

Pollan, M. (1998, October 25). Playing god in the garden. *New York Times Magazine*, pp. 44–92.

Pruitt, D. G. (1983). Integrative agreements: Nature and antecedents. In M. H. Bazerman & R. J. Lewicki (Eds.), *Negotiation in organizations.* Newbury Park, CA: Sage.

Putnam, L. L., & Holmer, M. (1992). Framing, reframing and issue development. In L. L. Putnam & M. E. Roloff, (Eds.), *Communication and negotiation.* Newbury Park, CA: Sage.

Putnam, L. L., Wilson, S. R., Waltman, M. S., & Turner, D. (1986). The evolution of case arguments in teachers' bargaining. *Journal of the American Forensic Association, 23*, 63–81.

Raiffa, H. (1982). The art and science of negotiation. Cambridge, MA: Belknap Press of Harvard University Press.

Schurr, P. H. (1987). Effects of gain and loss decision frames on risky purchase negotiations. *Journal of Applied Psychology, 72*, 351–358.

Soap-box salesman. (2001). *The Economist*, October 13, p. 38.

Soule, E. (2000). Assessing the precautionary principle. *Public Affairs Quarterly, 14*, 309–328.

Soule, E. (2003). *Reasons to regulate: Morality and market intervention.* Lanham, MD: Rowman & Littlefield (forthcoming).

Specter, M. (2000, April 10). The pharmageddon riddle. *The New Yorker*, pp. 58–71.

Tannen, D. (1986). *Framing and reframing: That's not what I meant!* New York: William Morrow.

Trewavas, A., & Leaver, C. (2001). Is opposition to GM crops science or politics? An investigation into the arguments that GM crops pose a particular threat to the environment. *EMBO Reports, 2*, 455–459.

True Food Network. (2003). *Food fight: The truth about GMOs.* Retrieved February 16, 2003, from http://www.truefoodnow.org./resources.html

Turcotte, M.-F., & Pasquero, J. (2001). The paradox of multistakeholder roundtables. *Journal of Applied Behavioral Sciences, 37*, 447–464.

Tversky, A., & Kahneman, D. (1981). The framing of decisions and the psychology of choice. *Science, 211*, 453–458.

von Wartburg, W., & Liew, J. (1999). *Gene technology and social acceptance*. Lanham, MD: University Press of America.

Wheale, P., & McNally, R. (1998). The social management of genetic engineering: An introduction. In P. Wheale, R. von Schomberg, & P. Glasner (Eds.), *The social management of genetic engineering*. Brookfield, VT: Ashgate.

CHAPTER 8

From Boycotts to Global Partnership: NGOs, the Private Sector, and the Struggle to Protect the World's Forests

Joseph Domask

This chapter explores the changes in the responses to environmental degradation over the past fifteen years or so by examining the role that NGOs have played in responding to the crisis of global deforestation in the past and how NGOs have responded more recently in light of broader global political and economic trends. In the first section, I review the emergence of the global forest crisis in the 1980s and with it the emergence of various types of NGO responses to the crisis. In light of the some of the broader shifts in the world economy and changing roles of governments, NGOs, and the private sector, the latter section of this chapter explores the emergence of a unique voluntary forest certification system that resulted from NGO–business collaboration and has since further enabled and facilitated historically unprecedented collaboration between NGOs and business entities of all sizes and types. While this chapter is primarily focused on NGO–business relations, both antagonistic and synergistic, I also discuss the ways in which governments are or are not involved in NGO-business collaboration in the realm of forest certification.

The history of deforestation and NGO responses over the past two decades is largely analogous to the history of environmental destruction more broadly speaking and the corresponding NGO response. The major differences that set the forest story apart from other cases of responses to environmental crises are (1) the rapid pace and global reach of the collaborative approach undertaken by NGOs and private industry and (2) the extent and depth to which NGOs and businesses have collaborated. This collaboration has become fully institutionalized today in the form of a global voluntary governance system overseen by the Forest Stewardship Council. In terms of its global reach, as well as the breadth and depth of commitments from NGOs, businesses, and communities around the world, it is clear that the FSC system is the most significant endeavor ever undertaken as a partnership between nongovernmental organizations and private industry.

DEFORESTATION AND RESPONSES:
THE EARLY STAGES (1970s–1980s)

Deforestation Emerging as a Global Crisis

In the mid-1980s, rates of deforestation worldwide, particularly in the tropics, were reaching new heights and making front-page headlines in all of the world's major newspapers. Approximately 500 million acres of tropical forests, an area equivalent to 7 to 8 percent of the world total or roughly the size of Mexico, were lost just in the 1980 to 1995 time period (FAO, 1993, 2001). The rate averaged around 22 to 30 million acres—the size of Ohio—lost each year, or the loss of one acre per second of every minute of every day.

In the 1990s, the rate of deforestation in the tropics had actually increased, then averaging 35.1 million acres per year or 1 percent of global tropical forest loss each year. What is even more striking is that of the 36.1 million acres of total global forest loss, a full 97 percent (35.1 million acres) of this loss has taken place in the tropics alone (FAO, 2001). Altogether, approximately one-fifth of the world's tropical forests have been erased from the face of the earth since the 1960s. To those concerned with the earth's biological diversity, these are especially alarming statistics given the fact that tropical forests, which cover only about 6 percent of the earth's surface, hold 50 to 80 percent of the world's biological diversity.

Prior to the 1980s, deforestation was certainly a problem in many countries around the world, but there were no reliable assessments available on the extent of the problem at the global level. This is partially due to the fact that deforestation was not in fact a major problem in most tropical countries in the earlier half of the 1900s and for the most part not until the late 1970s and thereafter. By the 1980s, population growth, increasing consumption patterns in Northern countries, increasing technological capacity, improved infrastructure (roads and ports), and an increasingly globalized market for forest products all contributed to unprecedented rates of deforestation in the great majority of the world's tropical regions. Previous country-specific alarms heard in the 1970s added up to a global crisis in the 1980s.

Roles and Impacts of NGOs in the Early Stages (1980s)

In order to better understand the unique case of NGO–business collaboration on forests, one must first understand the historical context through which the collaboration evolved. This section provides an overview of the early NGO responses to deforestation, the impacts they made, and how the new approaches initially began to evolve. During the early stages of global deforestation reactions (primarily the 1980s), NGOs played a largely reactive and antagonistic role in their efforts to confront the crisis. Their responses generally fell into one of two categories: raising awareness and pressuring key actors (primarily through boycotts).

Raising awareness is done at many levels by NGOs. Fortunately for the NGO community, much of the work of calculating forest areas and deforestation rates was already being carried out by national governments and the U.N. Food and Agriculture Organization (FAO) through its Forest Resources Assessments, which were regularly published beginning in 1982. More and more information was processed and disseminated through the FAO and other organizations in the early 1980s, and NGOs also began to acquire greater research capacity and assumed a greater presence in the field of data collection and the use of remote sensing and satellite data. Equipped with greater capacities and growing sets of data, NGOs began sharing the undisputable evidence that the earth was undergoing the rapid loss of major chunks of its remaining tropical forest coverage.

The studies, reports, press releases, public service announcements, and other forms of communication had variable degrees of exposure over the years, but it became rapidly evident to the general public in the United States, Europe, and other industrialized countries that tropical deforestation was directly responsible for dramatic increases in species extinctions, and the loss of indigenous peoples' lands and livelihoods, and was an increasingly important factor in global climate change. Moreover, NGOs helped generate a better understanding that consumption of tropical forest products in the North was one of the most important factors contributing to deforestation.

Antagonistic Approach: Pressuring Key Actors

Pressure by NGOs during the 1980s was primarily aimed at national governments (of industrialized countries), multilateral development banks, private industry, and, to a far lesser degree, the governments of developing countries (where most of the deforestation was taking place). A few examples from Europe and the United States illustrate the NGO tactics well (Bendell, 2000).

In Europe and to a lesser degree in the United States, potent campaigns were launched to promote consumer boycotts and municipal government bans on the use of tropical forest products during the mid- to late-1980s. In the United Kingdom, Germany, the Netherlands, and the United States a significant number of municipal governments considered the NGO arguments and did place bans on the use of tropical timber for government-funded projects. In Germany alone, about 400 municipalities, under pressure from NGOs and the public at large, issued their own guidelines prohibiting the use of tropical timber in government-funded projects.

Moving beyond the level of municipal government actions, the Austrian parliament passed a national law in 1992 requiring that tropical forest product imports be labeled and that a "sustainable sources" certification system be enacted for tropical forest products. Under the threat of a GATT case, the Austrian law was loosened the following year and the mandatory labeling requirement was dropped. The Netherlands, for its part, developed a similar piece of legislation, the Netherlands Framework Agreement on Tropical Timber (NFATT), in 1994. The agreement was signed by the government, timber industry representatives, labor unions, and NGOs, and all parties agreed to stop using noncertified tropical timber by the end of 1995, though this date was later extended to 2000. Both of these national-level legislative acts proved to be highly controversial and evoked strong reactions from tropical exporting countries, which successfully argued that these types of restrictions violated agreements made under the GATT.

In the United States, the general public was less aware and less active, but legislation was enacted in several municipalities (in New Jersey, Pennsylvania, Massachusetts, New York, Arizona, and California) and even introduced, though quickly defeated, in the U.S. House of Representatives. Several NGOs, including Greenpeace and Rainforest Action Network (RAN), initiated rather effective campaigns targeting the private sector, and specifically large corporations. RAN was probably the most active and most focused NGO in the United States with regard to fighting tropical deforestation through boycotts and other antagonistic tactics. The hamburger and Mitsubishi campaigns were the best known and most effective in the United States.

In the 1970s and 1980s, the link had been made between the burning of tropical forests in Central and South America for cattle pasture and the demand for cheap beef in the United States. RAN, which led one of the high profile fast food campaigns, described its success as follows: "Burger King was importing cheap beef from tropical countries where rainforests are denuded to provide pasture for cattle. This campaign succeeded in several ways. After sales dropped 12 percent during the boycott in 1987, Burger King cancelled $35 million worth of beef contracts in Central America and announced that they had stopped importing rainforest beef" (RAN, 2001a).

Among other high-profile efforts, RAN led an eight-year consumer boycott against Mitsubishi Motor Sales of America and Mitsubishi Electric America for its purchasing of large quantities of tropical wood products in the 1980s and 1990s. After eight years of constant antagonism, RAN and the two Mitsubishi entities came to an agreement and signed a memorandum of understanding in 1998 (World Rainforest Movement, 1998). RAN ended its campaign in exchange for a number of significant changes in Mitsubishi's activities in the tropics.

The government bans and private-sector boycotts were effective in significantly reducing the imports of tropical wood, and they were also effective in significantly damaging the public image of many major retailers of tropical woods. However, for a number of reasons the boycotts failed to have any significant impact on the rates and extent of tropical deforestation. In fact, the boycotts led to a devaluation of the standing timber in tropical forests around the world, which in many cases actually led to increases in deforestation as the forests were cleared for other uses, such as subsistence farming, commercial crops, grazing land, and related activities. Despite the success in raising awareness and winning specific commitments from multinational corporations, it became increasingly apparent that NGOs had to move beyond raising awareness and pushing boycotts.

Going Beyond Boycotts:
New NGO Strategies and Progress along the Way

Boycotts, as mentioned, had reached certain limits to what they could accomplish on their own. They continued to pressure specific retailers and continued to restrain, at least to some extent, the level of tropical wood imports to Europe and tropical beef imports into the United States, but deforestation rates in the tropics continued to increase as a result of domestic development programs, land tenure legislation, agricultural subsidies, and the like (FAO, 1993, 2001). While some NGOs continued to push corporate and government boycotts of tropical forest products or temperate old growth products, most NGOs pursued a number of different tactics in the late 1980s and into the 1990s. Most NGOs selectively pursued one or two of these approaches, while some larger ones often chose a broader spectrum of activities. The most commonly seen approaches included the following:

- The Tropical Forestry Action Plan (TFAP)
- New focus on multilateral development bank projects
- Domestic and national legislation focus
- Working toward the establishment of a global forest convention
- Promoting the creation of new protected areas and implementing in-country conservation and development projects
- Pushing forestry standards and certification through the International Tropical Timber Organization (ITTO)
- Beginning initial dialogue on a nongovernmental certification system

Each of these approaches and their relative successes are addressed briefly here. The Tropical Forestry Action Plan of 1985 was one of the first major international initiatives to tackle tropical deforestation. The FAO, the World Resources Institute (WRI, a leading environmental think tank), the World Bank, and the United Nations Development Programme jointly launched the TFAP with the premise that more national government involvement in tropical forest management (and specifically national forestry action plans) was necessary to combat the rampant levels of deforestation. Ultimately the TFAP accomplished very little in terms of fighting deforestation and came under criticism from various circles, including some of its original supporters. Apart from WRI, NGOs were not significant players in the TFAP initiatives, which primarily remained government-led programs.

Another area in which NGOs played almost no part was in the design and implementation of major infrastructure projects in the tropics, but they did eventually play a very significant role in campaigning against such projects and against specific loans through the multilateral development banks (MDBs), the most important of which is the World Bank. The MDBs clearly had been important contributors to the design and financing of major infrastructure projects in the heart of tropical forests, projects such as highways and hydroelectric dams, thus allowing for waves of new settlements and profound losses of forests in some countries (Rich, 1985, 1994; Domask, 1997).

These campaigns, through direct pressure and indirectly through the U.S. Congress and its new environmental restrictions on disbursing money to the MDBs, proved to be highly effective and set into motion a vast array of changes within the World Bank and Inter-American Development Bank in particular. The World Bank, for example, established a new policy in 1991 that prohibited it from financing any forestry-sector projects in moist tropical forest areas. Other changes involved altering the institutional organization of the MDBs by creating environmental departments and new operational procedures and guidelines, while other changes came in the form of restrictions on lending for infrastructure projects in forest regions or in the form of new lending or grants to support "environmental projects."

With regard to the impact of NGOs on producer–exporter country government legislation, most NGOs did not lobby developing country governments directly, but worked indirectly through other actors and processes. In a great number of tropical countries, governments did dramatically alter their past policies, subsidies, development programs, and so on. that were primary drivers of deforestation since the 1950s and 1960s. Governments changed these policies and introduced more environmentally friendly policies for a number of reasons, both internal and external.

Engaging producer country governments (especially Malaysia, Indonesia, Brazil, and several other tropical country governments) through the International Tropical Timber Organization, an intergovernmental commodities organization created in 1986, appeared promising at first, but it soon became apparent that there were clear limits as to how far governments would go in terms of collaboration. In 1990 ITTO members did agree to a "Target 2000" goal, whereby all trade in tropical timber was to be supplied from sustainably managed forests (Congressional Research Service, 1992). The challenge was how to define "sustainable forest management" and whether or not a system of certification could be agreed to by governments, and whether such a system could be implemented without contradicting GATT and later WTO agreements on barriers to trade.

There had been extensive amounts of international dialogue on "criteria and indicators" for sustainable forest management at the intergovernmental level, but there had been very few advances made in terms of ascertaining whether these criteria were being met on the ground and in the forestlands. It was through this dialogue, however, that the idea of forest management standards and certifiable sustainable forestry first emerged. Although governments were unable to come to an agreement on an international certification system, some smaller private initiatives had begun to sprout up in different parts of the world (the first and most important being the 1989 SmartWood certification system, which now falls under the umbrella of the FSC system). The problem with many of these systems is that they lacked credibility and were often "greenwashing" schemes (SmartWood not among these), thus providing a clear need for a global system of accreditation of forest certification systems.

With regard to promoting the creation of protected areas, NGO initiatives were quite successful. With prodding from NGOs, governments around the world increased the global amount of protected areas from about 500 million acres in 1960 to about 3.2 billion acres in the year 2000; that is an area about the size of India and China combined which includes about 10 percent of the world's forests areas. While the numbers and areas of protected lands grew exponentially, the actual implementation of protected areas lagged far behind.

This lack of implementation caught the attention of many NGOs, who in response increasingly became involved in assisting government agencies to design and manage parks and to implement a variety of other on-the-ground projects. Since the 1980s, in-country projects by Northern NGOs began to flourish in number as the capacities and budgets of Northern NGOs grew. Nevertheless, the projects were generally rather small in scale and had little impact on the broader picture of deforestation. It was clear that broader changes were needed in order to make a real impact on global deforestation trends. One of the most obvious initiatives on such a broad scale was the creation of a global forest convention.

As the 1992 Earth Summit (U.N. Conference on Environment and Development; UNCED) drew nearer, most NGOs were focused on influencing government and intergovernmental policy. Most NGOs, in fact, were pushing for a global treaty on forests akin to the global conventions on climate change and on biological diversity (both in 1992). The efforts to establish a global convention on forests also appeared promising at first, but NGOs ran into the same problems and the same governments in opposition as they did in their efforts to strengthen the ITTO. Any treaty likely to be accepted by the world's governments, it was clear, would be heavily biased toward industry interests and actually against the interests of those hoping to slow deforestation. In the end, the Earth Summit produced some major environmental agreements, but in the realm of forests, the modest result was a nonbinding "Forest Principles" document, which ultimately had very little impact.

In looking back over the 1980s and early 1990s, many significant gains were achieved in NGO efforts to curb deforestation. The most notable achievements over this time were (1) the changes in behavior of specifically targeted importer government policies and importing corporations, (2) major changes in World Bank and other MDB lending policies and institutional structures, (3) the tremendous growth in (nominally) protected areas worldwide, (4) the reversal in many developing country development programs, policies, and subsidies, and (5) the generally increased level of dialogue that was taking place among a good number of the most critical actors. Of course, these advances all took place under the context of a very broad consensus, at least rhetorically, concerning the concept of "sustainable development."

One common feature to all of these roles and impacts of NGOs was that they were based on the extent to which NGOs could influence other actors to change behavior. With the exception of research and in-country projects, NGOs generally were not actively implementing initiatives themselves and were not collaborating with governments or with the private sector. This situation changed in the 1990s when NGOs came to the realization that the strategy of targeting governments and intergovernmental organizations, along with select corporations, would make progress only up to a certain point, but not to the level that was needed to better address the global forest crisis. Hence, NGOs sought out progressive businesses to establish a voluntary and nongovernmental system of promoting better forestry practices on a global scale.

CHANGES IN THE GLOBAL CONTEXT

Despite all of the achievements discussed already, deforestation in the tropics by the end of the 1980s and into the early 1990s was at the worst levels in history, and the world was becoming more aware of this problem than ever before. If so much progress had been made on so many different fronts in the war against deforestation, then one must ask why deforestation (primarily in the tropics) continues to be such critical problem. There is no easy answer to this question, but there are some broader factors at play that provide some insight.

Today there are many drivers of deforestation in the tropics, including forestry operations (legal and illegal), conversion of forests to agricultural land, continued government incentives to deforest in many countries, leftover effects of past highway projects that have opened access to the forests, lack of government financing to protect forests, and several others. Some very broad shifts at the global level have also opened up a new set of pressures on forests.

At a very broad level—and certainly this is not the case for a number of specific countries—there is a notable positive trend in terms of the role that developing country government policies play and in terms of the role that MDB forest policies and projects play. The governments, MDBs, and bilateral development plans are generally no longer the primary drivers of tropical deforestation. The promotion of "development"—often in the name of fighting the spread of communism—has given way to "sustainable development," and governments and intergovernmental organizations are going beyond rhetoric to begin to implement more ecofriendly development programs and projects (Domask, 1997).

All of these positive trends in governmental policies, however, are apparently being offset by other national and global trends. The most notable of these trends include the adoption of liberal market economic policies at the national level (i.e., neoliberalism, Washington Consensus policies, structural adjustment policies [SAPs] of the World Bank, or related variations), economic globalization (in terms of interconnectedness of economies), and greater technological capacities to facilitate economic globalization and access to remote forests (Rice, Ozinga, Marijnissen, Gregory, 2001; WWF, 2000).

While in some cases deforestation continues to progress as a result of past infrastructure projects (especially roads), new pressures are being placed on forests around the world as corporations and other private-sector entities encounter

- fewer barriers in gaining access to the forests themselves (with fewer government restrictions on foreign companies operating within national boundaries).
- fewer regulations and other barriers during the exporting and importing processes.
- new incentives for foreign direct investment in emerging markets around the world.
- new markets for exports of wood products as more and more countries dropped tariffs and other nontariff protections.

Beyond the forestry sector itself, it is becoming increasingly evident that trends in liberalizing macroeconomic policies are rapidly undermining other forest conservation efforts by further encouraging rapid resource extraction, expansion of export agriculture, and other export-oriented policies that in one way or another contribute to encroachment of the world's forests. According to the World Bank's recently published forest policy review, structural adjustment policies that have been pushed by the World Bank and IMF over the last fifteen years or so,. which include measures such as devaluation, export incentives, and removal of price controls, "tend to boost production of tradable goods, including agricultural and forestry products. In doing so, and without mitigatory measures, they encourage forest conversion [i.e., deforestation]" (World Bank, 2000, p. 13). Another major report (Rice et al., 2001, p. 6) on the relationship between economic liberalization and deforestation comes to a similar conclusion: The macroeconomic policy shifts in various countries throughout the world constitute an "underlying cause of forest loss and degradation."

In basic terms, the global economy has become increasingly integrated and seamless, thus allowing for the easier flow of goods and services between countries, and relatively weak domestic demand for wood products in the past has been replaced by greater international market pressures on forests (and export agricultural products) and fewer government regulations on these external pressures. Figure 8.1 depicts these broad changes over time.

Under this changed global context, many NGOs consciously or subconsciously have shifted their focus from governmental and intergovernmental policy domains to the domain of markets, trade, and the private sector. In some respects (e.g., ITTO, Global Forest Convention, TFAPs), NGOs reached the limit in terms of how much more progress could be made, and thus they moved into new terri-

Figure 8.1
Broad Changes in Drivers of Deforestation and Responses over Time

Time Period	Primary Drivers of Deforestation	NGO Focus or Strategy	
1960s to 1980s	Government policies, subsidies, land tenure legislation, etc. (all promoting "development")	Government policies, national legislation, intergovernmental organizations	Antagonistic, reactive, focusing on changing behaviors of other actors
	Over Time: (1) NGOs were successful in making many critical policy changes (2) Governmental and intergovernmental organizations and policies became decreasingly relevant (as they voluntarily began to retract from their roles in national economies) (3) Markets, capitalism, economic globalization, and corporations became increasingly relevant in domestic economies (4) Barriers to trade, investment, financing, and other economic activity had gradually been removed (5) Export-oriented economic policies flourished		
1990s to present	Market pressures on forests: trade in forest products, export agriculture expansion, greater foreign investment and access to natural resources, greater domestic industry access to capital, markets, technology, etc.	Shifting focus more on markets, trade, corporations, investment, and economic factors	More sophisticated approach: combining elements of the past with proactive collaborative initiatives, developing a private, voluntary governance system outside of governmental arenas

tory and adopted more sophisticated approaches. The Forest Stewardship Council and its voluntary certification system epitomize this broad shift in NGO approaches to the problem of deforestation.

THE FOREST STEWARDSHIP COUNCIL:
A VOLUNTARY, MARKET-DRIVEN, PRIVATE
GOVERNANCE SYSTEM

The World Wide Fund for Nature (also known as World Wildlife Fund in North America) and several other major NGOs began exploring the possibility of setting up a voluntary global certification and accreditation system that could be used to verify whether or not wood products were harvested in a socially and environmentally sound manner. The great challenge was to develop a system that would be acceptable to environmental and social groups, as well as to the timber industry. The idea of developing such a system was also a response to the growing public perception, based in large part on what has been described here, that forestry in any form was environmentally destructive. Proponents of forest certification sought to show that one can manage a forest that is viable economically to the landowner without compromising the ecological and social benefits that it provides.

NGOs were able to find willing partners among retailers of forest products in Europe and among some progressive timber companies. The progressive companies realized that tropical timber and forest products in general were gaining a bad reputation, and this was seriously beginning to threaten their profitability and even their survival. Substitute materials (everything from plastics to aluminum to cement) were becoming more appealing to manufacturers and to end-of-the-line producers and retailers.

The Forest Stewardship Council

Through years of negotiation among foresters, NGOs, social scientists, and industry, the Forest Stewardship Council was finally established in 1993. During the course of these negotiations, the overwhelming majority of timber companies and a great number of environmental groups opted not to join in this effort, while other groups and companies dropped out because of their disappointment with the way things were developing (namely, because the criteria were becoming too stringent for some companies or too weak for some NGOs to accept).

The FSC serves many different functions and is itself many different things at once, including

- an international nonprofit organization made up of NGOs and business-sector entities.
- a global system of standards, accreditation, and certification.
- a dialogue and standard-setting forum for NGOs, businesses, and other stakeholders at the global level, with North and South in equal representation, and at the local level.

With all these functions and responsibilities, some researchers have come to refer to the FSC more as a privately run "governance system" or a system of "civil regulation." In simple terms, the FSC is an international nonprofit institution through which a global set of forestry standards has been established and under whose oversight (primarily through the accreditation of independent certifying entities) assessments of forestry practices according to these standards are carried out. The end results are (1) certified forest areas and (2) certified forest products in the marketplace. The new approach is unique not only in that it relies on cooperation between NGOs and businesses, but even more important that it is driven by consumption and international trade, two key components behind the original problem of deforestation.

The FSC itself, however, does not go out and monitor forest management practices, nor does it certify forests, companies, or products. Instead, its primary responsibilities are to

- establish and refine the ten principles and criteria: the forest management standards.
- accredit other organizations (certifying bodies) that are to conduct assessments of the forest areas and the "chain-of-custody" for products that enter the market place.
- endorse or reject national and subnational principles and criteria.
- monitor existing standards and existing certifying bodies.
- provide chain-of-custody guidelines for end-product certification and labeling.
- provide various types of assistance to standard setting efforts around the world.

In order to gain buy-in from industry, as well as environmental and social groups, the FSC founders opened up membership to all interested groups, companies, and individuals, but not to governments. The founders formulated a highly democratic and carefully balanced membership and voting system, based on one-third "economic interests," one-third "environmental," and one-third "social," with equal voting power between groups from the North and from the South (industrialized countries with 50 percent and nonindustrialized countries with 50 percent). The board of directors is composed of nine elected members: Two members come from the economic interests (one from the North and one from the South); the remaining seven come from environmental and social interests (with three-year rotating shifts of three or four members from North and South and three or four members rotating from environmental and social interests).

Once the global standards had been agreed upon and once the other basic institutional foundations had been established, including the accreditation of "certifying bodies" that would actually conduct the forest assessments, the process of establishing national and subnational standards could begin. It is in these national and subnational standard-setting processes that some of the most important and intensive NGO–business interactions take place. Within the current system, national and subnational working groups are encouraged to take shape. In the United States, for example, there are nine different regional standard-setting groups according to different forest types and different regionally specific conditions (social, ecological, economic). Each of these working groups must be approved by the FSC, and each group must be governed in the same democratic manner as the FSC, with equal representation among the three chambers: economic, environmental, and social.

The FSC secretariat, which is headquartered in Oaxaca, Mexico, in some ways acts as a national government would: that is, by setting down the ground rules and the broader framework within which the various nongovernmental entities (both for-profit and nonprofit) are to interact. However, unlike traditional governance systems, the FSC does not establish the local, regional, or national standards and regulations. Instead, the FSC only provides the broader "principles and criteria" under which local NGOs and companies negotiate the country-specific or subnationally specific "indicators and verifiers" by which they and others in their region or country will be assessed. Once these national or subnational groups develop and approve of final set of indicators, they may submit these to the FSC for final approval or rejection. Once accepted by the FSC, all subsequent certification assessments must be done according to the nationally and subnationally specific set of standards. Certification assessments conducted prior to the completion of local or national standards are done according to the specific criteria set by and used by the FSC-accredited certifying bodies, in accordance with the global standards.

This framework not only lays out the ground rules for the collaboration between very large and powerful NGOs (e.g., WWF) and corporations (e.g., Home Depot) but also sets the ground rules for local-level dialogue between smaller NGOs, civic organizations, and small forestry operations. In many cases these different interest groups never previously exchanged dialogue. Not only are these various stakeholders often coming together to talk for the first time but they are also, often for the first time, in the position to formulate for themselves the specific criteria by which their local forests will be managed (assuming FSC certification). As a report by the German aid agency, GTZ, describes it, "Forest certification is about sharing power: stakeholders define what is their view of good forest management and owners who want to be certified have to abide by this vision. Certification has opened spaces for participation on forest policy making to groups of interest that did not have it before: indigenous and local communities, NGOs etc." (Vallejo & Hauselmann, 2000, p. 1).

Figure 8.2 presents a summary of the institutional structure and related key actors of the FSC. This is a novel and powerful set of processes and interactions that are just beginning to take shape in such places as Russia, Guatemala, Malaysia, Zambia, Latvia, and many other countries.

FSC IMPACTS AND PROLIFERATION

In less than six years of operational existence (established in 1993, but not operational in terms of certifications until 1996), the FSC has spanned the globe in its reach, covering over 58 million acres in more than fifty countries. In Europe, areas certified under the FSC system account for nearly 30 percent of the forest area, in the United States the figure is closer to 7 percent, and worldwide approximately 4 percent of the total forest area under forest management is certified. Currently in the United States alone there are 8.3 million acres certified in more than 90 forest areas and approximately 400 companies and retailers are included. The range of committed entities include some of the world's largest multinational corporations— Home Depot, Nike, 84 Lumber, Starbucks Coffee, and Gibson Guitar Corporation—as well as a variety of large and small environmental and civic organizations, such as Greenpeace, WWF, the United Methodist Church, and the Hoopa Valley Tribe (FSC–US, 2001).

The following list provides a sampling of some of the major corporate commitments to the FSC system in recent years in North America and internationally. It should be noted that the actual level of commitment varies by each company. All these companies have committed to increasing their buying and selling of "certified" environmentally friendly forest products. Some are FSC members, some are members of the North American Forest and Trade Network (called

Figure 8.2
FSC Institutional Structure and Related Key Actors

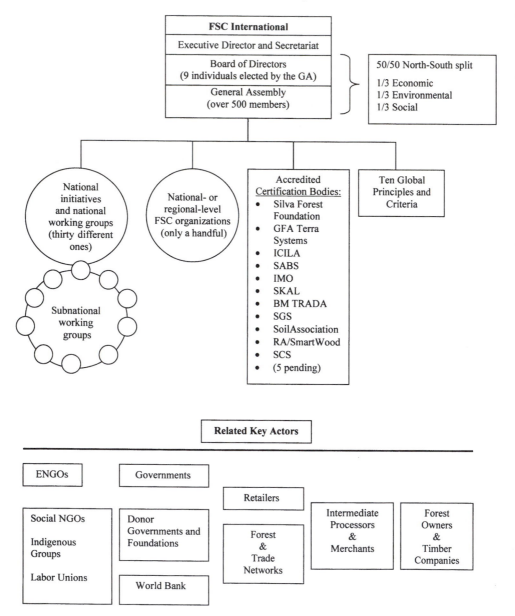

the Certified Forest Products Council; CFPC), and some are not members of either but have made public commitments to certified forest products. Together, these and other FSC commitments represent over 20 percent of all wood sold in the U.S. home-remodeling market and even greater percentages in the European market (FSC–US, 2001).

Company	Commitment
North America	
Home Depot	World's largest timber retailer, declared preference for FSC-certified products (1999), FSC–US member, $38 billion in sales
Lowe's Home Centers	World's second-largest home improvement store and second-largest retailer of timber in the United States, preference for FSC (2000), $16 billion in sales
84 Lumber Company	One of the largest suppliers of building materials, FSC preference (2000)
Turner Construction	The largest construction company in the United States, member of the Certified Forest Products Council (the U.S. Buyer's Group)
Anderson Corporation	Number one window manufacturer in the United States, FSC preference (2000)
Columbia Forest Products	The largest hardwood and plywood producer in North America, FSC certified products for sale
Nike, Inc.	Preference for FSC-certified products, member CFPC
State of Pennsylvania	All state forest lands were FSC certified in 2000
International	
B&Q	The United Kingdom's largest home improvement store, target to purchase and sell only products certified under the FSC system
AssiDomän	The world's largest private land owner, all its forests are FSC certified
IKEA	Largest retail catalog distribution in the world, specifies FSC
J Sainsbury/Homebase	Homebase has about 10 percent of the Do-It-Yourself (DIY) retail stores in the United Kingdom, preference for FSC products
Klabin	The oldest and one of the largest pulp and paper mills in South America, now processing large quantities of FSC-certified wood

The demand by retailers for products certified under the FSC system is likely to grow even more rapidly in the coming years as the ripple effects of these commitments begin to take shape. According to the World Resources Institute (Sizer & Plouvier, 2000, p. 81), "Certification may eventually become a cost of doing business for suppliers of the tropical timber market."

While this commitment and the great number of other major corporate commitments to FSC products has been phenomenal, the actual share of FSC products on the shelves or in the stores of these corporations is far less impressive. There are a number of reasons for this, but the primary reason is that there simply is not enough supply of FSC-certified products in the marketplace because of the short period of time that the FSC system has been in place. It has taken a while for companies to get their lands certified, but it takes even longer for the trees in these forests to make it to the sawmills and through any secondary and tertiary processing before arriving on store shelves.

Improving Forest Management and Promoting Social Interests

Beyond corporate commitments, the FSC has also had on-the-ground achievements in terms of increasing forest management, decreasing deforestation in certain areas, and promoting social interests.

One of the FSC's most basic goals is to promote improvement in forest management practices, and although it can be difficult to quantify, there is no question that the FSC has made great progress in improving forest management practices around the world (Simula & Bass, 1999). Principle 1, for example, requires that the forest manager "shall respect all applicable laws of the country in which they occur, and international treaties and agreements to which the country is a signatory," and that they all have a management plan in place (written, implemented, and kept up to date, with long-term goals and means of achieving them clearly stated). Other general and specific requirements include stipulations to minimize environmental impact (e.g., restrictions on chemical use), harvesting only small percentages of a total forest area per year, strict protection for high conservation value forest areas, avoiding logging near rivers or other particularly vulnerable parts of the landscape, as well as respecting land tenure rights, indigenous rights, workers' rights, and so forth. The Precautionary Principle is also very important in the FSC Principles. As written into Principle 9, "to comply with the precautionary approach, interventions in forests must be extremely cautious if the systems are poorly understood scientifically and unusually susceptible."

One must keep in mind that these and other stipulations are all part of the global principles and criteria, but that the certifying bodies generally have an even more strict set of standards and criteria that apply to one or more specific regions or countries. The majority of operations getting certified are making real changes in the way they conduct their operations in order to pass the field assessments and gain certification. While no studies have amassed a comprehensive report of changes in forestry practices around the world as a result of FSC certification, significant evidence exists in the form of public summaries of on-site certification audits. As required in the FSC system, summaries of each of the certification assessments must be made available to the general public, and it is in the details of these assessments that one can see what specific improvements in practices have been made on the ground and, often, what specific measures still need to be implemented in order to attain certification.

Impacts on Governments, Regulation, and Enforcement

It is ironic that one of the most important impacts of the emergence of the FSC system has been something that its creators were not necessarily trying to accomplish—the impact of the FSC on government policies and legislation. Indeed, it was largely out of frustration at not being able to improve government policies that NGOs decided to create a voluntary system of governance that did not depend on governments but instead on markets and consumer preferences.

The FSC system is having an impact on governmental forestry policy in many ways. It should be remembered that governments are not permitted to be members of the FSC itself, and governments would not be permitted to establish and operate a system of performance-based certification under WTO rules. Apart from these clear exclusionary aspects between governments and the FSC system, national and subnational governments from all regions of the world are directly and indirectly impacted by the FSC system; likewise, governments have various direct and indirect influences on the FSC system.

The most important and most obvious impacts of the FSC system on governments is the impact that FSC standards and the certification have in (1) serving as a model for national forestry legislation and (2) serving as a monitoring and enforcement mechanism for existing legislation, or serving in place of existing legislation. In 1999 the world's largest gathering of experts on certification to date came to the conclusion that two of the most important impacts of certification were "fast-tracking the development of forest policy frameworks at the national level [and] playing a complimentary role to regulatory processes to ensure legal compliance" (Domask, 1999).

The FSC system is in some cases even having more of an impact on national forest policies than many of the previous, high-profile direct efforts (through the ITTO, the TFAPs, World Bank leverage, direct NGO pressure, and the like). According to one leading industry representative, Bill Howe of Collins Pine, "We have long argued against stifling governmental regulations. But certification may provide the internal desire for industry to voluntarily achieve results that regulations . . . rarely accomplish" (WWF, 2000a).

A few examples help illustrate the relationships between national forestry legislation and forest certification. Bolivia is one of the best examples of a case where forest certification standards and the new national forestry law in 1996 have been exceptionally mutually reinforcing. The 1996 legislation and the national FSC standards that had been established by stakeholders in Bolivia are very similar in most respects (Jack, 1998). Thus, in order for commercial or community forestry operations to obtain FSC certification in Bolivia, all they have to do for the most part is abide by the 1996 forest legislation. The Bolivian government has even begun to offer exemptions to the mandatory government inspections for all forestry operations that have achieved FSC certification.

In the case of Guatemala, the government in the Petén region recently began allotting forest concessions to community groups for a period of twenty-five years, but with the requirement that the forests be managed to meet certification standards under the FSC system. Instead of relying on forestry laws set by the government, the government is employing the "voluntary" certification to mandate better forest management on state lands; those failing to obtain FSC certification by a certain date will lose their concessions altogether.

The Indonesian government has also used FSC certification as a means of exempting some forestry operations from specific regulation. In early 2001 the Indonesian government banned the sale and export of one of the world's most valuable timber species—ramin—in order to help protect orangutan habitat. However, an exemption was given to one company, Diamond Raya, which has been certified under the FSC system ("Indonesia Halts Trade," 2001).

Beyond traditional forest regulations and national forestry laws, several national governments have also begun the process of establishing government-run and government-mandated forest certification systems. These government-sponsored certification systems are more directly influenced by and, increasingly, developed jointly alongside the FSC system. At the same time, there has been an even greater emergence of industry-led voluntary certification systems, particularly in Europe and in the United States, where the world's forestry industry is concentrated.

Proliferation of Other Certification Systems

A somewhat ironic and unintended outcome of the development of the FSC system has been the widespread proliferation of other certification systems around the world. In fact, the FSC was originally designed to act as an umbrella organization that had as one of its main objectives the accreditation (or rejection) of the emerging certification systems in the early 1990s, thus reducing the confusion over credible versus noncredible labels. The proliferation of other systems since the beginning of the 1990s has both drawbacks and benefits in terms of improving forest management and reducing deforestation.

Currently, there are approximately fifty different forest certification systems in the world. However, the FSC is clearly recognized around the world as the benchmark system because (1) its rigorous standards requiring on-the-ground performance criteria, (2) the requirement of "independent, third party certification," (3) the multistakeholder and democratic standard-setting process, (4) the transparency of the entire system; (5) the inclusion of social standards such as workers' rights and indigenous peoples' rights, (6) the inclusion of chain-of-custody certification resulting in certified consumer products, and (7) the global nature of the system.[1]

The other three major certification systems in existence today are not global, but they are to some degree performance based and to different degrees in direct competition with the FSC system. These include the U.S. industry–sponsored Sustainable Forestry Initiative (SFI), the Pan European Forest Certification Scheme (PEFC), and the Canadian Standards Association (CSA). While all of these different systems and the whole gamut of national-level systems are constantly evolving, none of these systems come particularly close to including all of the elements that define the FSC system as the benchmark. Recent exceptions to this observation include the ecolabeling scheme in Indonesia and the Malaysian National Timber Certification Council (MTCC), both of which are working directly with the FSC and its certification bodies to synchronize their standards, processes, and methods of certifications. A great number of other countries and industry representatives are watching this ongoing collaboration and experimentation very carefully.

The proliferation of other certification systems is problematic for the FSC in the sense that they act as competitors trying to gain greater buy-in from industry, retailers, consumers, and other stakeholders, and the presence of so many different certifications causes confusion among consumers, who generally do not know the differences among them nor how to ascertain their credibility. However, in terms of improving forest management around the world, most observers would agree that the proliferation of different systems has a positive impact. The FSC is raising the global standards for forest management, both directly and indirectly. Even if the other systems generally are less vigorous than the FSC, at least they provide definitively positive steps in the right direction. They do require at least some of the minimal criteria necessary for improved forest management, and most systems are gradually evolving in a manner that brings them closer to what is required under the FSC system. The SFI in the United States, for example, has moved from what many saw as greenwashing to a system that now incorporates stronger environmental standards, third-party auditing, chain-of-custody certification, and a nonprofit status for the overseeing body, all in the last couple of years. Representatives from the many different systems in existence are nearly all now looking to explore the possibility of "mutual recognition"—whereby two or more different systems and standards recognize and accept each others as equal to their own—with the FSC. FSC proponents do not rule out the possibility of mutual recognition under the right conditions; but they are not likely to undermine the credibility and legitimacy of the FSC system by accepting weaker standards and self-auditing schemes as worthy of the FSC label. The President of Home Depot Canada, Annette Verschuren, for instance, comments that "FSC is the only group that doesn't audit itself. The problem we have with some of the certification schemes is that they audit themselves. . . . The source of supply is key here, and we need to be confident and comfortable that the products the industry can stamp as FSC come from woodlands that are well managed" (WWF, 2000).

Even firms that have been certified under a non-FSC system are often beginning to adopt practices that bring them closer to FSC requirements in anticipation of an even more rapid expansion of demand for FSC products, especially when they hear words like those quoted here from the world's largest retailer of wood products. Based on off-the-record conversations, it is quite apparent that even firms that denounce the FSC system for one reason or another are taking precautionary steps in order to keep from falling too far behind in their operations and one day realizing that there is simply no longer a strong market for wood products not certified under the FSC system, or at least under one of the weaker systems. These changes are major accomplishments that were for the most part not taking place during the 1980s under the former NGO tactics (antagonism, awareness raising, boycotting, and image tarnishing, without providing alternatives).

STAKEHOLDER INTERESTS AND RATIONALES

The Retailers

Before examining specific rationales for retailer buy-in to the FSC system, it is necessary to examine what options are available to them. In the 1980s the only options were (1) to keep doing what they had been doing or (2) to stop purchasing timber from tropical sources, old growth forests, or other endangered forests. Today the options are greater and so too is the system of carrots and sticks employed by NGOs. Current options for retailers include the former two plus agreeing to commit to certified ecofriendly sources of forest products; and a range of different levels of commitments within the three broader options (e.g., phased-in time periods for suppliers, different percentage-based requirements in the final products, etc.).

If anything has driven the growth of forest certification, and the FSC system in particular, it is these buyers groups or associations of retailers who have committed to sourcing and selling FSC-certified wood products in their stores. WWF sponsored the first Buyer's Group in the United Kingdom in 1991 and has since expanded into eighteen different countries around the world (mostly in Europe and North America, but most recently in Brazil and Russia), with more than 600 members. These groups, now called forest and trade networks (FTNs), include forest owners, timber processors, retailers of timber and paper products, and an increasing number of timber specifiers such as architects, local authorities, and construction companies.

Companies have various reasons for joining FTNs, but for the most part they seek to take advantage of the green image they gain and the competitive advantage they can gain in the growing marketplace for ecofriendly products. The forest and trade networks not only demand certified wood from timber-harvesting companies but also raise awareness about certified wood among the general public, who are for the most part unfamiliar with the FSC. Currently, FTNs represent 7 percent of the global commercial forest-products market, and their growth since 1995 has been tremendous (WWF, 2000).

The second major driver of forest certification worldwide has been the pressure by some of the more radical environmental groups placed on retailers of wood products in the United States and Europe. Apart from the 1980s boycotts of tropical wood that helped catalyze certification in the first place, there have been ongoing campaigns by groups such as Greenpeace, Friends of the Earth, Rainforest Action Network, and numerous local NGOs to raise awareness about wood from endangered forests being sold in the local Home Depot store or Lowe's. The bad press and public image damage for many of these companies reached such a level that they had little alternative but to turn to FSC-certified products as a means of getting relief from the persistent bad-mouthing campaigns and to actually gain consumer credibility. Once Home Depot, the mammoth of all do-it-yourself stores, publicly declared its intentions to change its practices, its competitors quickly followed suit. More recently, Greenpeace and others have been going after U.S. furniture manufacturers, who have become the leading importers of tropical hardwoods.

Indeed, the radical NGOs are astutely aware of the powers that they hold and their most effective means of pressuring "noncompliant" corporations. They know, for example, that over one in five consumers report either rewarding or punishing companies in the past year based on their perceived social performance, and almost as many again have considered doing so (Price Waterhouse Coopers, 2000). RAN, probably the most strategic "radical" NGO working on forest issues, is using the recent environmental commitments of key corporations to pressure the noncompliant entities. One of RAN's latest targets is Boise Cascade, which RAN describes as "a dinosaur of the logging industry." RAN (2001b) is currently informing consumers and other stakeholders that

Americans recognize that destroying thousand-year-old trees to make plywood and office paper is barbaric and unnecessary. And hundreds of leading companies—including Kinko's, Home Depot, and Lowe's—have listened and pledged to stop selling products made from endangered forests. But not Boise Cascade. Boise Cascade sells wood products from endangered forests in South America, Southeast Asia, and around the world.

These campaigns and consumer demands are not something that corporations simply shrug off. According to a recent *Financial Times/ Price Waterhouse Coopers* "Most Respected Companies" survey, 750 chief executives were asked their views on the most important business challenges for companies in 2000. Of the challenges listed, "increased pressure from stakeholder groups" was ranked the second most important and "increased environmental demands" was ranked the third most important ("World's Most Respected Companies," 1999).

Forest Managers and Owners

Forest managers and owners have been far less eager to buy into the FSC system for a number of reasons. The first and most obvious reason is that they themselves, and not the retailers or NGOs, are the ones who have to undergo the audits, make on-the-ground changes in their practices, and pay the certifying bodies to conduct these audits. Second, these companies are further removed from consumers and thus usually not as easily or directly targeted through boycotts and protests. Third, there are simply a great number of small forest operators out there in the industry who often do not have the capacity or financial resources to meet FSC standards or pay for the audits. This is clearly one of the FSC's biggest challenges; and while some advances have been made under "umbrella certifications" through which multiple small owners can join together and jointly apply for audits, the small landowner issue is likely to persist for some time.

Despite the reasons that owners and managers have for not going with the FSC, the new commitments by the world's largest retailers of forest products to purchase and sell wood from certified sources— with the FSC as the benchmark certification system—has begun to turn the forest products market on its head. There is currently not nearly enough wood certified under the FSC system in the marketplace to supply Home Depot, let alone Lowe's, 84 Lumber, Turner Construction, and others who recently joined the wave of FSC-related commitments. Many forest operators and large timber companies recognize this imbalance in supply and demand and are seeking to fulfill the new market demands. With these new commitments, the industry has come to recognize that the FSC has climbed out of a niche market and into the mainstream of the forests products industry market, including everything from paper and pulp to precious hardwoods or cheaper plywood sectors.

Business Rationale after Original Buy-In

Once the forest owners, timber companies, retailers, and other private-sector entities have decided to take part in the FSC system in one way or another (becoming and FSC member, joining a FTN, certifying one's operations, etc.), there are a number of compelling reasons for staying with the system and continuing to support it. The most basic compelling reason for companies to continue their support and allegiance to the FSC system is the fact that their commitments become institutionalized in one way or another. Some businesses, for example, become members of the FSC or members of the national or subnational working groups and invest time and money into codeveloping standards, criteria, and the future directions of the system that they have opted into. They form formal and informal relationships with NGOs at various levels and often resolve past conflicts (with radical NGOs, for example) through the confidence-building measures inherent in the FSC dialogue process. Finally, once a company has elected to partake in the FSC system, it shares a stake with supporting NGOs and in competing against nonpartner businesses and competing certification systems and labels. Ultimately, businesses and NGOs in the FSC system begin to share a wide range of mutual interests—shared strategies, shared successes, shared futures, shared goals, and shared problems—and damage to one partner is damage to the others. The reality of the situation is not a utopia, but these shared interests are prevalent and are forceful incentives for continued NGO–business collaboration.

NGO Benefits and Drawbacks

There has never been any overarching, jointly agreed upon strategy by the main NGO proponents of credible certification under the FSC system, but there were certainly major efforts undertaken and significant resources used to help initiate and fortify the FSC system. The World Wide Fund for Nature, the world's largest environmental network with nearly five million members worldwide, has without question been the leading force behind the FSC. It has provided strategic assistance in a number of different ways. Aside from providing funding resources, institutional capacity-building assistance, market promotion, scientific research, and the like, WWF has helped to establish the powerful network of "buyers groups" of certified products around the world (now called FTNs), and has worked directly with corporations, community groups, donors, local government bodies, and the like to build the foundations of support for the FSC system.

In a high-profile move in 1998, WWF joined forces with the World Bank in a formal partnership on forests with the main targets of (1) the creation of 124 million acres (50 million hectares) of new forest protected areas, (2) placing a comparable area (124 million acres) of existing but highly threatened forest protected areas under effective management, and (3) 500 million acres of production forests under independently certified sustainable management. This initiative between the world's largest environmental organization and the world's largest development institution, known as the World Bank/ WWF Forest Alliance, has without doubt brought a great deal of attention and a great deal of pressure on companies and governments to begin thinking more seriously about independent forest certification.

While no other NGO has embraced or championed the FSC system to the extent that WWF has, other supporting NGOs share similar rationales for championing this approach. Ultimately, the key

rationale for supporting such a system is the logic that by supporting certified sustainable forestry the incidence of irresponsible forestry will be greatly diminished, and deforestation and forest
degradation in general will thus be dramatically reduced as more
and more companies and communities adopt this approach. The
utility of NGO support for this approach stems from the increasingly important role that markets play vis-à-vis governments and
their regulations in this era of economic globalization.

While the benefits to NGOs of such an approach are pretty
straightforward, NGOs face a lot of risks and incur a great deal of
costs in championing this cause. The time and resources invested in
a new initiative of this sort in the first place was great for those NGOs
originally involved, and the outcomes were, and to some degree still
are, uncertain. By dedicating resources to sustainable forestry and
certification, NGOs have less time and money for projects such as
panda habitat protection that often more easily win over contributions from the general public than forestry does. Forestry is not glam-
orous to the public, who generally buy in more quickly to the "soft
and fuzzy." The other major risk involved in this type of endeavor
for NGOs is that they are putting their reputations on the line, and if
some forestry operations become certified but later prove to be hurt-
ing the environment or the local peoples, then not only does the
FSC come under fire but so do the supporting organizations. The
other reputational risk is that of associating with big business or
with other entities that have notoriously destructive environmental
histories (e.g., the World Bank).

Continued Challenges

Despite tremendous success and growth, especially in the past
two or three years, the NGO–business partnership behind the FSC
system of forest certification is a constant struggle between uncom-
mon partners. There are occasions for basking in the glories of success, but more often there are hiccups and even all-out battles
between industry groups, private forest owners, and social and environmental NGOs. Maintaining the right balance of rigorous standards and credibility, on one hand, and industry acceptability and
market penetration, on the other, has always been the main challenge facing the FSC system. As one FSC staff member notes, "It is
this middle ground—FSC being pulled by the right and the left—
which leads us to believe that we are doing the right thing and covering the most ground" (Addlestone, 2002). However, it is not the
only challenge in this partnership. There are also significant challenges in the representation and success of the FSC with regard to

the North–South divide. The key to the FSC's success so far, however, lies in its equitable and well-balanced structure of representation and its overall democratic and voluntary nature. This private, voluntary system is still in its infancy, but with such dramatic growth and worldwide reach, it promises to be one that is here to stay and that in very real terms has already begun to transform the global forest products market.

NOTE

1. The only other certification system in existence at the global level is the International Standards Organization ISO 14000 environmental systems certification, which is applicable to all economic sectors and not just forestry. However, the ISO 14000 system is not a performance-based system but a "process-based system" that does not include specific forest management performance criteria. In addition, it does not include any product labeling. The ISO system thus falls into a separate category of certification and largely does not compete directly with the FSC system.

REFERENCES

Addlestone, B. (2002, February 1). FSC News & Views. Retrieved January 11, 2003, from http://www.conservetn.com/Forestry%20and%20 Forests/020102_FSCNews.pdf

Bendell, J. (2000). Civil regulation: A new form of democratic governance for the global economy? In J. Bendell (Ed.), *Terms for endearment: Business, NGOs and sustainable development.* London: Greenleaf and the New Academy of Business.

Congressional Research Service (CRS). (1992). *Deforestation: An overview of global programs and agreements* (CRS Report No. 92-764 ENR). Washington, DC: CRS.

Domask, J. (1997). *A holistic systems approach to international environmental politics and IR theory: A case study of Brazil and Amazonia.* Unpublished doctoral dissertation, University of Miami.

Domask, J. (1999, November 9-10). *WWF/World Bank Alliance Forest Certification/Verification Workshop* (write-up of proceedings). Washington, DC: World Bank.

Food and Agriculture Organization of the United Nations (FAO). (1993). *1990 forest resources assessment: Tropical countries.* Rome: Food and Agriculture Organization of the United Nations.

Food and Agriculture Organization of the United Nations (FAO). (2001). *Forest resources assessment 2000.* Rome: Food and Agriculture Organization of the United Nations.

Forest Stewardship Council (FC-US). (2001). *Status of FSC-endorsed certification in the United States.* Washington, DC: FSC-US.

Indonesia halts trade in valuable hardwood: Exemption given for FSC-certified company. (2001, July 24). *Forest World News Service,* p 1.

Jack, D. (1998). *Of markets and forests: Certification and sustainable forestry in Bolivia* (independent report funded by the Thomas J. Watson Foundation), Providence, RI.

The non-governmental order: Will NGOs democratise, or merely disrupt global governance? (1999, December 1). *The Economist*, pp. 11–17.

PriceWaterhouse Coopers. (2000). *The millennium poll on corporate social responsibility* (commissioned by Environics International Ltd., Toronto, Ontario).

Rainforest Action Network (RAN). (2001a). *RAN mission and history*. Retrieved November 18, 2001, from http://www.ran.org

RAN. (2001b). Stop Boise Cascade campaign. Retrieved November 20, 2001, from http://www.ran.org/ran-campaigns/old-growth/

Rice, T., Ozinga, S., Marijnissen, C., & Gregory, M. (2001). *Trade liberalisation and its impact on forests*. Utrecht: Fern.

Rich, B. M. (1985). The multilateral development banks, environmental policy, and the United States. *Ecology Law Quarterly, 4*, 681–745.

Rich, B. M. (1994). *Mortgaging the earth: The World Bank, environmental impoverishment, and the crisis of development*. Boston: Beacon Press.

Simula, M., & Bass, S. (1999, November 9–10). *Independent certification/ verification of forest management*. Background paper for the World Bank/WWF Alliance Workshop, Washington, DC.

Sizer, N., & Plouvier, D. (2000). *Increased investment and trade by transnational logging companies in Africa, the Caribbean, and the Pacific: Implications for the sustainable management and conservation of tropical forests*, p. 81. Joint report by WWF, WRI, and European Commission, Brussels. Retrieved April 17, 2000, from http://www.pdf.wri/org/transnational-logging.pdf

Vallejo, N., & Hauselmann, P. (2000, June). *Institutional requirements for forest certification: A manual for stakeholders* (working paper no. 2). Deutsche Gesellschaft für Technische Zusammenarbeit (GTZ) GmbH, Forest Certification Project.

World Bank. (2000). *A review of the World Bank's 1991 forest policy strategy and its implementation*. Washington, DC: World Bank.

World Rainforest Movement (WRM). (1998, March). *End of boycott: "Eco-agreement" between RAN and Mitsubishi* (WRM Bulletin no. 9). Madison, WI: Forests.org, Inc.

World's most respected companies. (1999, December). *Financial Times*, Survey Section.

World Wide Fund for Nature. (2000). *The forest industry in the 21st century*. Retrieved November 17, 2001, from http://www.panda.org/down loads/forests/gftn-pr-21stcentury.doc

Corporate Social Responsibility and NGOs: Observations from a Global Power Company

Gregory Adams

> AES's purpose is to supply safe, clean, reliable and reasonably priced electricity globally. The primary way we put this principle into practice is by operating our businesses in a safe manner, improving system reliability, maintaining environmental emissions below permitted levels, and providing electricity at reasonable prices to our customers. In this way, we strive to meet the world's electricity needs in a socially responsible way. (AES 2001a)

AES is a leading global power company. Its mission is to help serve the world's need for electricity. Its activities and operations include competitive provision of generation, distribution, and retail power supply in Argentina, Australia, Bangladesh, Brazil, Cameroon, Canada, Chile, China, Colombia, the Czech Republic, the Dominican Republic, El Salvador, Georgia, Hungary, India, Italy, Kazakhstan, The Netherlands, Nigeria, Mexico, Oman, Pakistan, Panama, Qatar, Sri Lanka, Tanzania, Uganda, the Ukraine, the United Kingdom, the United States, and Venezuela.

AES is dedicated to providing electricity worldwide in a socially responsible way. This commitment results in a range of interactions with governments and NGOs. These interactions have been both cooperative and, at times, challenging. Some of the contention stems from different views about what social responsibility means and how a private corporation can maintain a commitment to social responsibility while serving a diverse range of stakeholder interests—those of customers, suppliers, employees, investors, local communities, and governments.

In this chapter I review AES's commitment to social responsibility and discuss how it has resulted in innovative arrangements with governments and NGOs to develop specific projects and agreements to mitigate some of the negative environmental effects of power generation and to extend economic and social opportunity wherever AES operates. I also address some fundamental tensions between corporations such as AES and NGOs, notwithstanding AES's pursuit of being socially responsible, and how AES has worked to resolve these tensions and to foster enhanced cooperation with NGOs. I will close with some suggestions for future directions for corporate–NGO cooperation.

COMPANY BACKGROUND

AES is one of the largest independent global power companies. The company's generating assets include interests in 182 plants totaling over 63,000 megawatts of capacity in thirty-one countries. AES also distributes electricity in eleven countries through twenty-two distribution businesses that together command a distribution network of over 920,000 km of conductor and associated rights of way and sells over 126,000 gigawatt hours per year to over 17 million end-use customers. In addition, through its various retail electricity supply businesses, the company sells electricity to over 154,000 end-use customers. The two people who started AES in 1981 launched their venture with a modest-sounding goal. They simply wanted to build an enterprise they could be proud of. They were clear about that even before they knew exactly what the company would do. The founders wanted a company that valued people and acted responsibly, a company that was fair and honest in its approach, not only to customers, suppliers, and employees but also to the greater society in which we live (AES, 2001b; Wetlaufer, 1998). AES is a company that is committed to improve the lives of the communities in which we work. To that end, as AES' CEO Dennis Bakke says, "We'll go anywhere we are wanted, needed, and where we believe we can make a difference."

Shared Principles and Empowerment at AES

One of the only centrally controlled aspects of AES is its commitment to four "shared" principles: to act with integrity, to be fair, to have fun, and to be socially responsible. These principles are goals and aspirations to guide the efforts of the people of AES as it carries out the mission of the company (AES, 2001a). AES requires that all of its prospective employees fully embrace these principles.

These principles are facilitated and enabled by the company's approach to its people. AES views its people not as "resources" to be exploited but as human beings who have a shared interest in the success of the company and its contribution to humanity (Wetlaufer, 1998). By treating its people with respect and requiring them (where appropriate) to make decisions and to take responsibility, AES increases the likelihood that the principles that it expects its people to adhere to are honored consistently and without exception (Wetlaufer, 1998). How does AES operationalize these principles? The following brief descriptions show what AES means by integrity, fairness, fun, and social responsibility.

Integrity

AES people try to act with integrity, or "wholeness." This means that they honor the Company's commitments. AES's goal is that the things AES people say and do in all parts of the company should reflect truth and consistency and should honor commitments made by others.

Fairness

It is AES's desire to treat fairly all of its stakeholders: its people, customers, suppliers, shareholders, governments, and the communities in which it operates. In this context fairness means justice; that is, each person or shareholder receiving a just portion or outcome given the situation or circumstance. It does not mean that everyone gets treated equally, but instead treated fairly or justly given the appropriate situation.

Fun

AES wants all its people and those people with whom it interacts to have fun in their work. AES's goal is to create the most fun workplace since the industrial revolution. This "fun" goal does not come from a party atmosphere, but rather from a workplace where AES people can use their gifts and skills to make informed decisions and take responsibility (and be accountable). The leaders at AES know that fun is closely linked with decision making in a workplace, so in order to maximize fun, its important to have as many people as possible making meaningful decisions and not just taking orders.

Decision making for all major business functions, including financing, hiring decisions, and capital expenditures, are therefore the responsibility of the people at each business location. Criteria for hiring new AES people include a person's willingness to accept responsibility and AES's values, as well as a person's experience and expertise.

Social Responsibility

AES believes that it has a responsibility to be involved in projects that provide social benefits such as lower costs to customers, a high degree of safety and reliability, and a cleaner environment. Social responsibility is one of AES's four corporate principles. That said, how does one define the term "social responsibility"? AES believes that the projects with which it is associated are merely extensions of its principles, and thus, by developing these projects in the "AES way" the company is lowering the cost of power in the markets it serves and doing so in a socially responsible manner. 'How can we best love our neighbor?' is a key question in AES peoples' minds as they pursue the company's mission. This perspective suggests that the most important aspect of being socially responsible is to do business well (i.e., provide safe, clean, reliable, low-cost electricity).

AES resists making a direct connection between values and profitability. In fact, it constantly emphasizes that trade-offs between values and profits should always favor values. In AES's view, the values are permanent, coming before profits. These values are the "rules" for AES to do business, while profits are the "score." This point is supported by the fact that the Securities and Exchange Commission (SEC) requires for filings in the United States that AES reveals its dedication to the company's values at the expense of profit maximization to be a "risk factor" to investors (i.e., the "score").

AES is, however, a corporation that needs to ensure its own sustainability, which requires that the projects as a whole produce sufficient returns to fund the company's business operations and, in keeping with AES's fairness principle, adequate returns for its investors. At times this reality prompts critics within the NGO community to question AES's true dedication to socially responsible values. NGOs that dedicate their efforts to promoting a single issue may find fault in a given project without full consideration of all the economic and social impacts of the project in the context of the host country, as well as within the context of the company's project portfolio. In some instances, these differences have resulted in delays, design changes, or, more frequently and more satisfactorily, the codevelopment of programs that try to balance the desires of the NGOs with the goals of the AES project. These projects can enhance the company's positive impact on the world in which it operates.

AES's goal in terms of social responsibility projects is to provide 5 percent of after-tax profits to charities. In 2000, more than 250 charitable organizations were the recipients of more than $21 million through AES social responsibility projects. The portfolio of social responsibility projects chosen by AES's different businesses is quite diverse, ranging from education, to ecology, to health and human services, to civic and community enrichment. AES is involved in a range of projects directly benefiting the natural environment. These projects include forest and wildlife preservation, tree planting, and land trusts and preserves. In fact, there is a great disparity between the average cost of different types of social responsibility projects and environmental ones. The monies allocated for the environmental projects are more than three times greater than other projects, such as education.

AES is also involved in education projects through partnerships with schools, student scholarships, and internship programs. Sports and recreation are supported through programs with the Boy Scouts, the YMCA, sporting events, and toy donations. AES assists in providing public services through projects that involve electrical installations and repairs, fire and police stations, disaster relief, Habitat for Humanity, energy efficiency programs, and donations of construction and office materials in economic enhancement projects. AES is active in projects including hospitals, first-aid clinics, low-income food programs, safety training, health organizations such as the March of Dimes, and more.

SOCIAL RESPONSIBILITY PROJECTS IN ACTION

The following are some specific projects around the world where AES has made a difference in the communities where it operates.

AES Irtish Power (Kazakstan)

In Kazakstan, AES Irtish Power built a 1-kilometer heating pipeline network to supply heat to a community of blind people. This provided heat to approximately 300 apartments that had been without heat and hot water for several years (no one wanted or had the resources to help them, city government included). In an ongoing effort to help disabled children of low-income families, as well as retired and disabled parents who cannot afford prosthetics, AES will send these children to the Prosthetics Center, where they will have their prosthetic limbs made free of charge. AES also assists the Prosthetics Center by paying for its heating and hot water supply.

AES Clesa (El Salvador)

Although providing a power line was not economically attractive for AES Clesa, it would boost the development of the community, and in the view of AES managers, this justified the cost. The power line provided energy for 400 farming families located in remote areas in El Salvador. Among other benefits, this power line enables the locals to install much needed water pumps to irrigate their lands.

In addition to providing power to communities, AES Clesa participates in charitable functions; for example, making sure children in rural areas served by AES Clesa receive entertainment and Christmas gifts. This type of project is carried out by some monetary donations from AES Clesa employees.

An additional project the company is involved in is fighting the ongoing problem of drugs and violence in the community. AES Clesa helps provide recreational areas for youths and adults to spend time, particularly at night. This not only helps the people of El Salvador, but also helps maintain good relations with the municipality.

AES Lal Pir (Pakistan)

AES Lal Pir sponsored a tree plantation and preservation of wildlife and existing forests on 120 acres at two locations in Pakistan, which were donated to World Wide Fund for Nature Pakistan. It also arranged a peoples' awareness program about preservation of wildlife and the environment and is involved in cultivation of semidesert areas, which provides employment. Of this cultivated land, over 550 acres has been planted with more than 400,000 eucalyptus trees.

In addition, AES Lal Pir has engaged in other projects to better communities by helping local communities educate their children. It has done this in several ways. For example, AES Lal Pir constructed and donated a boy's primary school building in Mahmood Kot, a town 4 kilometers from its plant. In addition, 550 girls who previously studied outdoors now have a school building adjacent to the plant. This school was handed over to the education department. This project, together with the sponsorship of 362 poor students from thirteen villages, was done in conjunction with Green Thumbs. It repaired an existing coeducational high school and provided fans, electricity fittings, furniture, sporting goods, and so on. Through donations, AES was able to create scholarships for outstanding students.

AES Warrior Run (Maryland)

AES pledged money to support improvement of classroom technology in Allegheny County, Maryland, a county in which schools had the lowest student-to-computer ratio in the state. The board of education had developed a five-year technology plan, and AES pledged a sum of money to support teacher training and classroom technology improvement. This contribution leveraged a board of education state training grant for teacher training, with more than 300 teachers completing computer training at night. The program has resulted in schools being wired and connected, servers being installed, computers being purchased, and software selections and curriculums being revised to accept this technology (AES, 2001c).

Overarching Project Goals

Although projects span a broad range from education to the environment, the goals of these projects stem from the AES core principles. The "fun" principle is exhibited in the fact that the AES people most closely associated with these projects are the ones who determine what form of social responsibility these programs take. There is no corporate mandate that dictates how the monies must be spent. That decision is left to the team that developed the project. In line with the AES way, those who developed the various projects, whether they are power plants or electric distribution companies, are the ones who have made the decisions, albeit while seeking advice from their colleagues along the way. Ultimately, however, the same team that decides how to target their social responsibility programs makes the decisions that determine the size, price, and location of a new power plant.

AES–NGO INTERACTION: THE BALANCED APPROACH

When building a power plant, especially in a country or region that has heretofore had inadequate service that was unreliable, unsafe, or prohibitively expensive, the question of fairness is paramount and often one with which AES struggles as it tries to balance the interests of all stakeholders involved. The community and the local governments want low-cost power that is safe and reliable. Environmental NGOs are less concerned about project costs and seek power plants that are environmentally friendly. Stockholders want a project that is well designed, under budget, and that succeeds in the marketplace. The lenders want a successful and well-designed project that is financially viable and, in situations where multilateral lenders are involved, a project that also is environmentally friendly.

AES people want to provide reliable, safe, clean, and reasonably priced electricity in the markets the company serves. However, as AES people strive to be fair to its stakeholders, they strive to strike a balance in the interests of these stakeholders, and often these interests are not just diverse, but in direct conflict with one another. For example, one important goal is to provide the lowest cost power. Assuming water is plentiful, one way to achieve this goal is to build a hydroelectric power plant, which involves the construction of dams. Of course, to build a project of this type often involves diverting a river or some habitat, and thus environmental NGOs are likely to object. Some NGOs are so passionate and believe so strongly about green power (i.e., wind and photovoltaic) that they automatically dismiss alternative least-cost power supply options, such as hydroelectric power. However, at present energy prices, the costs of wind and solar projects on a large enough scale to serve more than a small group are prohibitive. AES, as a public company that uses resources provided by bondholders, stockholders, and lenders to develop projects, must yield a return that is fair relative to these stakeholders' investments. Therein lies the dilemma and one that AES works to overcome on every project within every country it operates.

AES–NGO Interaction: Three Illustrative Cases

Over the last twenty years, AES has grown to become a global power company with operations in more than thirty countries, and the company is increasingly interacting with NGOs in many of these regions. AES's experience has generally been a positive one as it has tried to be responsive to NGOs in all its business dealings. AES has successfully worked with NGOs to improve education, feed the hungry, improve medical care, and restore forest land. In many cases, AES's underlying principles, specifically social responsibility, have dovetailed well with the concerns of many NGOs, as the company has sought to protect the environment while illuminating the markets in which it serves. In the following section, three additional AES cases will be illustrated. The first two detail different types of collaborations in which AES has engaged with NGOs to promote social responsibility. In these cases, the company believes that AES and the other parties involved were successful in finding common ground and in working together to produce outcomes favorable to a wide range of concerned stakeholders. The final case provides a broad illustration of an area where there is some conflict between AES and NGOs that has, at times, produced suboptimal outcomes for many stakeholders involved. In spite of its unique corporate culture, as the world's largest independent power producer AES sometimes finds itself at odds, directly or indirectly, with NGOs. AES has demonstrated how it has ultimately bridged differences with some of these NGOs, resulting in projects with significant net benefits for all relevant stakeholders.

Carbon Offsets

In 1987 AES chairman Roger Sant became convinced that the evidence for global warming was compelling enough to warrant action. AES was and remains an independent power producer with a large inventory of coal-fired cogeneration plants, and therefore is a potential contributor to the global warming problem because of the plants' CO_2 emissions (Sturges, 2001). In response to Sant's concerns, AES conducted a research effort to find the least-cost way to reduce AES's net CO_2 emissions. The goal was to make AES part of the solution to global warming instead of part of the problem.

The research concluded that trees (technically "forest enhancement") provided the most practical and effective way to address the CO_2 emissions problem. Trees absorb CO_2 as they grow and convert it to carbon that is locked up (sequestered) in biomass as long as they live. The idea was that if AES could increase the standing stock of trees, the additional trees might be able to absorb enough CO_2 to offset the emissions from an AES cogeneration plant (Sturges, 2001). This is one of many mitigation measures now accepted in the global climate change treaty—the Kyoto Protocol—as a means of achieving legally binding emissions-reduction targets. However, AES was pursuing these initiatives many years prior to the completion of the climate change agreements; legally binding targets were not agreed to until 1997 at Kyoto, and the details of carbon sequestration through forests were not agreed to until 2001 in Marrakech. In this sense, AES was preempting intergovernmental agreements and preempting the likelihood of domestic regulations on the energy sector (which as of 2002 have not been changed).

Once AES decided to implement a CO_2 offset strategy, the company had to address several concerns. In order to address these concerns, AES enlisted the support of the World Resources Institute—one of the most well respected environmental NGOs and a sort of environmental think tank—to find and evaluate appropriate forestry-based offset projects (Sturges, 2001). The team established criteria to select qualifying offset projects. These included requirements that projects (1) be backed by data permitting calculation of the project's carbon offsets that could be collected as part of the project, (2) be supported by organizations capable of successfully managing and monitoring the offset effort, (3) provide significant benefits to local people to ensure project acceptability and long-term sustainability, and (4) include innovative funding mechanisms to allow the achievement of offset goals at the lowest possible cost (Sturges, 2001).

WRI has assisted AES in the evaluation of three offset projects. In 1988 WRI conducted a project solicitation process that yielded eight proposals, and convened a panel of foresters and development experts to evaluate them. Based on this process, WRI first recommended a community agroforestry project in Guatemala. CARE, one of the largest nongovernmental development-assistance organizations, proposed the project. The criteria developed for the selection of this first offset project were then used in screening and evaluating AES's second and third offset projects in 1991 and 1993, respectively. WRI also assisted AES in developing forest biomass estimation protocols for the second project as a basis for estimating carbon sequestration. In addition, WRI managed the project solicitation and evaluation process for the third project, convening an expert panel for proposal evaluation as for the Guatemala project (Sturges, 2001).

Through these and similar projects over the past ten years, AES has committed over $12 million to seven different carbon offset projects. These projects are projected to offset a total of about 67 million tons of carbon (or 250 million metric tons of CO_2) over the next thirty to forty years, the equivalent of the emissions from a typical 1,000 MW coal facility over its lifetime. As mentioned, these projects have included agroforestry (an agricultural practice that incorporates tree planting among crops), forest preservation, and methane reduction through livestock projects located in South America, India, and Pakistan. AES carefully chooses projects that have measurable CO_2 offsets and are supported by organizations capable of successfully managing and monitoring emissions reductions (such as CARE or the Nature Conservancy).

AES-Granite Ridge in New Hampshire

AES is building a 750 MW natural gas–fired combined-cyle electric generation facility in Londonderry, New Hampshire. This plant has SO_2 and NOx emissions (both of which are global-warming greenhouse gasses and contributors to acid rain) as much as 225 times lower than current coal and oil plants. The project created 200 to 250 construction jobs and 30 to 35 permanent professional positions in plant operations. Approximately 120 acres of permanent conservation land will be created. AES is the anchor tenant in the 100-acre Londonderry Ecological Industrial Park, an area dedicated to sustainable, environmentally compatible industrial development.

In keeping with the goals of the ecoindustrial park, AES will recycle approximately 4 million gallons of water per day from the Manchester Wastewater Treatment Facility for cooling purposes. NGOs were involved with the project every step along the way. They helped identify environmental problems and develop workable solutions. AES is also grateful to many NGOs for their contributions to

Granite Ridge, including the American Lung Association of New Hampshire, the Audubon Society of New Hampshire, the Londonderry Economic Development Committee, and the Londonderry Conservation Commission

In this example, where AES originally only sought to provide the least-cost power supply alternative, the ultimate outcome reflected close coordination with a range of NGOs. AES ended up extending its original proposal to include activities in the ecoindustrial park. AES's view was directly influenced by NGOs that had proposed an idea that was, at the time, a deviation from AES's traditional thinking. This was an example of NGOs working with AES to find common ground, and ultimately it enabled AES to deploy its mission of providing low-cost power in New England. AES concedes that it does not have all the ideas or answers. This example illustrates that through a collaborative process with NGOs that have a sense of ownership and shared values, AES's goals can be realized.

AES, NGOs, and Multilateral Lending

AES has gone from a company that began by developing its one facility in Texas in 1983 to a global corporation serving markets in more than thirty countries. To fuel this growth, AES actively pursues aggressive and creative financing strategies that provide the ability to leverage the value of individual projects assets. As a result, AES has been successful in securing over $16 billion in project financing. This growth and scale has drawn attention from a number of quarters, including the NGO community.

Much of AES's growth has occurred, and will continue to occur, in developing markets, such as Africa, Asia, the Middle East, and Latin America. Although AES accesses significant private-sector project funding, the company continues to look to multilateral development banks, such as the International Finance Corporation (the private-sector lending arm of the World Bank) or the Inter-American Development Bank to provide financing which would be unavailable or too expensive from most commercial banks. Commercial banks, if available, will take commercial risks but are less willing to take political risks. Moreover, AES's interest in these markets is often well aligned with the developmental directives of these multilateral lending institutions, providing a good fit for all concerned. Some NGOs that may have maintained fundamental differences with certain types of projects that AES proposed (which realize AES's need to access this type of capital) have, in some instances, approached the multilaterals and sought to block their financing of AES's projects entirely. Some NGOs simply disagree with the power-supply option AES is pursuing. However, in the desire to fulfill AES's ultimate goal of providing low-cost power in the markets in which it serves and cognizant of the economic realties it faces, compromises are often made.

Because AES is an organization that deals with many stakeholders, the company finds itself working with groups without which it would not necessarily be able to serve these markets at all, let alone as the low-cost supplier. The end result is often a project that, while ultimately fulfilling its goal of low-cost power (albeit not the lowest possible), is a collaborative effort, taking into consideration the thoughts and concerns of the community, NGOs, and lenders. AES's projects complement the mandates of these organizations, and together they are helping to bring electricity to the 40 percent of the planet (roughly two billion people) that today does not enjoy such a luxury. However, as development banks come under greater scrutiny from NGOs, the potential exists for these banks to limit financing and support fewer energy projects, thereby limiting AES's ability to undertake projects in areas where they are needed most.

NGOS AND AES: REALITIES AND IMPLICATIONS

AES has had a range of experiences working with NGOs. With many positive collaborations and partnerships, AES's experience suggests NGOs are very committed to their respective causes, often representing a single interest or perspective, and most often concerning the environmental impact of projects. Some NGOs are concerned about the socioeconomic impact of the company's projects as well.

Some NGOs have sought to protest certain AES projects with which they did not agree to the IMF and World Bank. Such activities may inhibit or delay the securing of needed long-term project financing that would result in AES having to access a more costly financing structure, and thus a less competitive price for energy to the end consumer. In some instances, the activities may result in the denial of service to thousands of individuals when projects are blocked or deemed infeasible. Such activities may cause delays in permitting or design changes that affect scheduling or costs negatively, resulting in higher prices to the end consumer.

AES is a company committed to fulfilling its mission in accordance with its core values. To the extent the AES and NGOs share common interests and goals, or at least NGOs understand or appreciate the balanced approach that AES tries to achieve, interactions tend to be constructive and a generally positive outcome is likely. In cases where AES is faced with more narrowly focused NGOs, AES finds it difficult to achieve its goals to serve the range of stakeholder interests to which it feels accountable. Notwithstanding these challenges, AES is committed to continuing communication, cooperation, and collaboration with NGOs as it seeks to improve the lives of large populations and environments around the world.

Lessons Learned

AES's experiences with NGOs have generally been positive. The company believes it is in its own best interest to be open to constructive comments and, when practicable, to incorporate these comments into its project planning. AES also strives to ensure that NGOs have access to the facts. This commitment is facilitated by the unique practice within AES to make project information available to all employees and stakeholders, including the general public. Through proper communication, it is possible to avoid misunderstanding and to create an environment in which AES and the NGOs are on the same page and hopefully find a way in which they can work together. AES's ultimate goal is to provide low-cost electricity in a socially responsible manner.

Some NGOs have disagreed with the company and its role in energy production and will continue to do so. Some NGOs may contend that AES's values are espoused for convenience's sake and lack any true altruistic motives. Some contend that AES is just like any large corporation, focused solely on the bottom line of profit making. AES is a public company that has shareholders and lenders, and as such has an obligation to provide those investors with returns commensurate with the risk of their investments. AES would simply not exist if it did not recognize this obligation. AES depends on the capital markets to provide it with the resources by which it can achieve its long-term, sustainable goal of providing low-cost power. AES cannot fulfill its mission if it does not simultaneously seek to be competitive. Some NGOs suggest that AES should focus solely on certain types of power-supply options, such as windmills and photovoltaic cells. This contention is inconsistent with its focus on the long-term development of society's infrastructure through providing least-cost power in a socially responsible manner.

AES will continue to make every effort to address NGOs' legitimate concerns to the extent this does not inhibit it from achieving its goals. For AES, it is all about finding the right balance among a wide range of stakeholder interests, including those of its customers, employees, investors and the natural environment. While AES is a company built on the strength of over 150 businesses, it is only as strong as the relationships developed within each one of these businesses. AES seeks to be a good neighbor and good corporate citizen. To the extent that it is successful in this regard, AES's track record will provide it with the ability to pursue other opportunities.

CORPORATIONS, NGOs, AND THE FUTURE

Although AES is committed to developing relationships and partnerships with nongovernmental organizations, many at AES have come to believe that the most important thing it can do as a company is to love its neighbors and to do a great job achieving its corporate purpose or mission. That is AES's calling, its reason for existing as a corporation.

Underlying this view is the strong belief in the ability of markets and market prices to result in the best decisions for society. That is, such markets themselves contribute to socially responsible decisions. While far from perfect, no other approach or system has proven to produce results that are ultimately as socially responsible. AES acknowledges that markets alone do not always result in the ideal outcome for society as a whole, particularly with regard to transition costs and/or dislocations in implementing market-based solutions to societal problems. That is why AES has engaged the NGO community, as well as other key stakeholders, including governments, in crafting solutions to energy and development problems throughout the world.

In conclusion, for corporations and NGOs to work together cooperatively there needs to be a respect and understanding of the role of corporations in society in providing basic goods and services, and an appreciation that this contribution can, in itself, be a socially-responsible one. Those within AES believe that it has proven that a company can do well by doing good. It has been successful financially by being successful in its efforts to provide the world with safe, clean, reliable, and reasonably priced electricity. AES continues to focus on long-term development of the markets it serves and must take into account the interests of all the parties with whom it interacts, including NGOs. AES will continue to work with these NGOs in an effort to find a balanced approach while fulfilling its mission. At the same time, corporations must appreciate that NGOs and other representative groups reflect important interests that may result in improvements in the economic and business strategies of firms. Indeed, cooperation and collaboration among governments, corporations, and NGOs is emerging as a model for economic and social development around the world. AES will strive to be a leader in these efforts.

REFERENCES

AES. (2001a). *AES values and principles.* Retrieved December 13, 2001, from http://www.aesc.com/culture/index.html

AES. (2001b). *The energy to make a difference.* Retrieved December 13, 2001, from http://www.aesc.com

AES. (2001c). *Social responsibility.* Retrieved December 13, 2001, from www.aesc.com/culture/responsibility.html

Sturges, S. D. (2001). *Greenhouse gas emissions offsets: A global warming insurance policy.* Retrieved December 15, 2001, from http://www.aesc.com/print/culture/responsibility/electricity_full.html

Wetlaufer, S. (1998, January–February). Organizing for empowerment: An interview with AES's Roger Sant and Dennis Bakke. *Harvard Business Review*, pp. 111–123.

CHAPTER 10

Conclusion: Globalization and the Future of NGO Influence

Hildy Teegen and Jonathan P. Doh

A range of perspectives has been advanced in this volume regarding the increasingly important influence of nongovernmental organizations in influencing, guiding, and at times supplanting the roles of governments and corporations in an era of increasing globalization. These contributions make clear that NGOs are having a profound impact on governments and corporations separately, and shaping and altering the historical interactions between these two sectors. Our volume title points to a challenge posed by NGOs. Our contributors have detailed not only how NGOs challenge the dominance and legitimacy of governments and firms in society, but also point up the challenges that academics and practitioners in all three sectors (government, business, NGO) face in understanding this emerging NGO role. In particular, these authors challenge the reader to consider how NGOs can work with governments and businesses for the good of various constituencies. Although the chapters have presented arguments and examples that demonstrate both opportunities and challenges associated with the emergence of NGOs, in this concluding chapter we provide some integrating comments so that our readers will be better armed for this NGO challenge, and thus be better able to recognize, leverage, and respond constructively to the power and unique resources that these third sector players contribute in society at large.

We begin our synthesis of these chapters by introducing a trichotomy of roles and impacts seen in the examples of contemporary

NGOs. We frame this synthesis through extension of a well-known strategic management paradigm of stakeholder analysis (Freeman, 1984). We use this extension to consider the roles of NGOs as stakeholders, stakegivers, and staketakers, a simple but useful typology to capture the various ways in which NGOs engage in society. This typology will be referred to throughout this conclusion, where we will highlight the predominant and cross-cutting themes of the chapters:

- What are NGOs?
- Why and how do NGOs differ from each other and from the other organizations?
- How do NGOs operate and interact with other NGOs and other public and private organizations in an increasingly integrated global economy?
- How do NGOs fit within the operating milieu of societies?
- How do NGOs influence others in their environments?

In this discussion we pay particular attention to broad themes, concerns, and issues regarding the role of NGOs in major contemporary global debates related to globalization: North–South issues and arguments regarding local empowerment versus global integration. Throughout the discussion of the cross-cutting themes presented in these chapters we draw linkages to relevant theory and offer current examples to demonstrate how these chapters contribute to research and theory building as well as to practical application. We conclude this chapter by acknowledging questions that remain unanswered from our original research objectives, as well as identifying new questions raised by the contributors to this volume (references to chapters in this volume are given by chapter authors' names in parentheses).

NGOs AS STAKEHOLDERS, STAKEGIVERS, AND STAKETAKERS

According to Freeman (1984) and the many others who have followed in this research tradition of stakeholder analysis, the well-advised manager will craft strategies that respond appropriately to the needs and demands of a wide range of interested parties. Increasing the scope of stakeholders accounted for by strategies will promote those parties' support for management actions or minimize the fallout from their being closed out but impacted by management choices.

In moving beyond the traditionally addressed shareholder–employee–customer–government parties to include parties such as community residents, citizens who could benefit from a firm's products but for some reason are denied access, and those who argue for protection of global environmental resources, firms as well as public sector managers are explicitly and implicitly noting an increasingly important stakeholder role for nongovernmental organizations of all stripes: Advocacy, operational, and hybrid types (Parker) are all arguably relevant stakeholders for various private sector and public sector strategy and policy decisions. Thus we conclude that in myriad cases NGOs should be considered legitimate stakeholders.

NGOs as Stakeholders

Furthermore, our evidence indicates that they are indeed increasingly viewed as legitimate stakeholders by a variety of decision makers, including those in multilateral institutions such as the WTO and FTAA (Deslauriers & Kotschwar), national governments (Keim; Teegen), private sector business managers (Parker; Domask; Adams), and other NGO decision makers (Doh, Newburry, & Teegen; Teegen). Their incorporation as legitimate stakeholders has produced benefits for the focal organization, and, in many cases, for the NGO itself, although both Parker and Soule point to cases in which inclusion of NGOs in organizational decision making may not yield positive outcomes from the perspective of the other organizations with which they interact. From the contributions to this volume we can conclude that due to increased activism, greater reach in operational activities, and heightened awareness by society at large about the important functions performed by NGOs that they are stakeholders that firms and governments must and do increasingly value in the formulation of their strategies and policies.

NGOs as Stakegivers and Staketakers

We extend Freeman's (1984) framework to include two additional characterizations in our overlay typology: stakegivers and staketakers. Stakegivers refers to those parties who can provide benefits to others with which they interact. In the case of NGOs, we see their roles as stakegivers in the form of their resource contributions (Parker; Doh, Newburry, & Teegen), lending prestige, legitimacy, and perceptions of neutrality or moral authority (Domask) to other organizations. In addition, NGOs provide information (Deslauriers & Kotschwar; Keim; Adams) and serve as mediators of potential conflicts among other parties (Teegen; Soule). Their presence in organizational interactions and in broader societal decisions can improve net outcomes of activities in which they participate by increasing efficiency, reducing transaction costs, and creating or facilitating otherwise overlooked opportunities.

Further, NGOs can play negative roles as staketakers, at least as perceived by governments, businesses, other NGOs, and potentially society at large (Teegen, 2002). As perceived holders of the moral high ground, NGOs have wreaked havoc with private sector business interests that pursue wealth creation and maximization for shareholders potentially at the expense of others (animate and otherwise). Soule's discussion of how NGOs dominated the initial framing of the issue of introduction of genetically modified organisms as a threat to society, as opposed to viewing the introduction as solving a societal problem (such as in the case of genetic modifications to combat dietary vitamin deficiency), resulted in a contentious and intractable situation. Soule proposes an alternate framing that considers the social benefits and proprietary rights of private firms as a means to counter the counterproductive and opportunistic NGO actions in similar situations.

Adams details the mission of AES corporation in promoting societal well-being, and working in consort with NGOs, even when those NGOs are unnecessarily obstructionist (in AES's view), as another method for countering the more typical inimical relationship between NGOs that demand firm accountability beyond profits. Governments, too, are taken to task by NGOs (Parker; Keim), particularly where the public good is not protected and promoted by governmental bodies. NGOs themselves can wield their power in detrimental ways. Parker discusses NGO unwillingness to credit or acknowledge the accomplishments of private sector interests. She argues that this intransigence denies the public the opportunity to differentiate among companies and reward socially responsible firms through their consumer purchases and investment decisions. Societal welfare is reduced as the incentive for other firms to "do the right thing" in the face of a record of retribution by NGOs is hampered.

Throughout this conclusion we detail various themes relevant to the NGO challenge. These themes generally identify NGOs as stakeholders, stakegivers, or staketakers. These roles and actions vary, depending on the other parties with which NGOs interact and the environments within which they are engaged. As Doh points out in Chapter 1, NGOs assume multiple and often overlapping roles, and this is not less true in our discussion here.

CROSS-CUTTING THEMES

What are NGOs?

NGOs take many forms. Broadly, they include organizations of individuals and donors committed to the promotion of a particular (set of) issue(s) through advocacy work and/or through operational activities whereby services are delivered (Parker; Doh; Keim; Deslauriers & Kotschwar). The public perceives the members of a given NGO to be "on the same page" concerning the fulfillment of the organization's mission. Although unified by a common mission, the members of a given NGO may not be monolithic, that is, they may represent differing perspectives or be pursuing distinct and at times incompatible agendas (Doh, Newburry, & Teegen). Keim notes that a principal–agent problem may ensue as a result of a lack of monolithicism among members of an NGO; NGO managers may be thwarting the pursuit of members' interests in order to promote their own status within the organization or a larger community within which they seek an enhanced reputation. Where an NGO is not monolithic, there is opportunity for the development of collaboration and cooperation, both within the NGO and among various NGOs, on issues, campaigns, and initiatives, and these relationships may result in one organization or segment becoming coopted by other interests outside the organization (Doh, Newburry, & Teegen). Similarly, more extreme factions of an NGO can effectively alienate moderate members or donors, as is highlighted in the chapter by Soule. He uses the example of a former director of Greenpeace publicly breaking ranks with the organization. In negotiation parlance, monolithicism provides an organization with negotiating leverage because it is unresponsive to opponents' efforts to divide and conquer. Hence, a given coalition represented by a monolithic NGO is more able to powerfully and effectively advocate because of the credibility and legitimacy that accompanies such unified and stable sets of positions (Keim).

On the other hand, there are increasing numbers of NGOs whose members consist not only of individuals but also of other organizations and even for-profit enterprises. While they lack the monolithic and unified set of members, their credibility and legitimacy may actually stem from having such a diversified collection of members with widely divergent core interests. The Forest Stewardship Council, whose membership consists of environmental NGOs (both radical and conservative), church groups, tribal groups, academics, and a great number of corporate members, provides one of the best examples of an NGO whose credibility and legitimacy are largely based on this diverse set of members. This is one of the obvious cases where the NGO, the FSC, acts more like a government entity (or as an overseer of a governance system) than as the better-known types of advocacy or operational NGOs.

Not all NGOs are created equal. Some NGOs are more successful than others (in terms of fundraising, influence, and efficient operations) due to differences in composition, resource base, mission, geographic scope, operating experience, or strategic focus. Keim also highlights a temporal dimension to NGO hierarchies: "first mover" status in an issue area provides an NGO with the ability to set the agenda that later entrants must adapt to—effectively raising entry barriers to newcomers because the issue is inextricably linked with the NGO first to enter that issue arena. Although we discuss the relative power of NGOs in a later section, it is useful here to note that hierarchies exist among NGOs that partly define their images, reputations, and roles in a given policy environment. These hierarchies give rise to competition among the players within a geographically defined or issue-specific context. The competition among these players includes efforts by NGOs to acquire the best managerial and technical talent, often "poaching" from other NGOs, to gain access to key donors to enhance fundraising, or to establish relationships with key decision makers in their advocacy efforts (Domask; Keim; Teegen; Parker). Deslauriers and Kotschwar point to a particularly obvious hierarchy in status among NGOs seeking to influence Organization of American States trade negotiations: Only certain NGOs are accredited to provide input into OAS deliberations.

That important differences exist among these NGOs provides opportunities for collaboration that transcend the often more immediate competitive pressures (Doh, Newburry, & Teegen). As is well founded in the strategic alliance literature, by sharing novel resources and expertise, partnering organizations can improve the outcomes for the group through specialization and rationalization gains and by reducing the costly competitive battles that otherwise might ensue between NGOs engaged in the same context. By linking fates, transactions costs for engagement with other NGOs is lessened (Teegen) as the risks of opportunistic behavior are minimized.

Part of the challenge in understanding NGOs, then, is recognizing their immense diversity in focus, size, structure, and internal consistency and their relations with other NGOs working in their immediate and related issue areas. The authors in this volume have provided important insights into how differences among NGOs can be usefully leveraged by firms, governments, and other NGOs in their efforts to promote their own interests in society.

Why and How Are NGOs Different?

When we highlight the differences presented by NGOs, an obvious question is begged: "different from whom or what?" The contributions in this volume point to two sorts of differences: those between and among NGOs themselves and those between NGOs and firms or between NGOs and governments (i.e., intersectoral differences). We addressed differences between and among NGOs in the preceding discussion of hierarchies among NGOs. Here we focus on the important ways in which "third sector" organizations are unique constructions vis-à-vis their private sector and public sector counterparts in society.

Public sector entities are created and principally operate for the benefit of the public at large. Public authorities raise funds and access other resources through fiscal and other regimes to fund the provision of important public services. From the standpoint of standard economic theory, the public sector—government—serves an important function in society to provide services for which there are no incentives for the private sector to furnish (i.e., where market failure occurs). Although subject to budget constraints and political pressures, public sector organizations are not constrained by expectations of financial returns under temporal pressure, as is common in the private sector. In private markets, scarce funds are provided by investors by choice instead of by fiat. The wave of privatizations and other movements toward economic liberalization that have occurred throughout the developed and developing world over the past two decades provide evidence that the universal effectiveness of the public sector in providing critical services to a demanding public has been called into question. Furthermore, in many nations a crisis of confidence has taken place owing to corruption and self-interest on the part of government officials at the dire expense of a needy public. Finally, in the developing world in particular, a basic lack of needed resources, at times compounded by high population growth rates, has taxed the ability of public sector organizations to provide the necessary public services. Hence, NGOs often play an important role in assuming some of these responsibilities previously vested in governments.

Accountability for public sector officials is managed largely through the rights of citizens in democratic societies to replace government officials at the ballot box. These rights are expressed through multiparty systems, wherein opposing parties monitor the opposition (often for their own political gain and not for the protection and preservation of the public good). These rights are also expressed via institutional systems of checks and balances, as captured in the United States between the executive, legislative, and judicial branches at the national level, complemented by a federal system that grants significant rights and powers to the states vis-à-vis the federal government. All these accountability measures are somewhat sluggish in ensuring effective public leadership; often bureaucratic pressures and inertia prevail, limiting retribution for individual leaders. Thus, for many activities, either due to bureaucratic inefficiencies in operating public sector enterprises, public mistrust of corrupt government officials, and the lack of required resources, public sector entities have been supplanted by private sector or NGO interests in providing valuable public services.

Private sector interests—firms—are organizations committed to maximizing wealth creation through investing in business opportunities that will enhance the returns to the owners of funds or resources invested in the firm, the shareholders. As discussed, a stakeholder perspective on firm management argues for incorporation of other interested parties beyond shareholders. Ultimately, however, management is responsible to the owners of the firm. Since firms are creatures of the market, they seek out the best opportunities for growing the investment of their shareholders. The provision of some goods and services will not be deemed profitable by any firm if the expected returns on investments in providing those goods and services, when adjusted for risk and for opportunity costs of investing elsewhere, will be insufficient. This describes the situation of market failure. A classic example of market failure concerns public goods. These are goods that provide benefits that are shared by all, but the costs for their provision are borne unequally. An example of such a public good concerns clean air. While a private sector firm may be called upon to invest in cleaner emissions technology at great expense, its investments provide benefits to society at large, a society that does not pay the full cost on a pro rata basis (Teegen, 2002). Without a regulatory obligation to install this technology, the firm may deem the rewards of such an investment insufficient to justify the costs. Thus, the primordial value for firms is to maximize shareholder wealth, and they seek situations that provide a profit incentive for their actions.

Firms are believers in markets. Markets provide profit incentives to allocate scarce resources to their highest and best use in society, in terms of wealth creation. Thus, by entering markets, firms can enjoy access to investor funds to allow them to grow beyond the confines of reinvested capital earned from operations. Investors in firms expect fairly speedy returns on their capital and tend to be uncommitted to a given firm as an investment vehicle. When operated as publicly traded companies, firms have special legal requirements for disclosure and financial reporting, such that investors can make informed choices about where to lodge their investment capital. Honesty and clarity in reporting are minimum standards to which publicly traded firms are held. Thus, managers of firms are ultimately accountable to the whims of typically fickle investors. Where profits are not earned, or are earned at levels inferior to those available elsewhere, the managers of firms can expect capital to flow away from their firms. Retribution for miscalculations on the part of a firm's management is swift and powerful in these liquid equity markets. Given the heavy demands placed on firm management by investors for profitable operations and maximization of wealth, it is difficult for firms to enter to provide services of a public nature. Historically, governments provided these services; but as described already, governments also frequently encounter difficulties in providing basic public goods and services.

NGOs, as third sector organizations, often bridge the gap between private sector firms and public sector governments. They are motivated by their issue area(s), including, for example, poverty reduction, environmental protection, promotion of the rights of persecuted or alienated groups, and disaster relief, among many others. Many of these issue areas may present profitable opportunities for engagement and will attract private sector interests. Most of these issue areas, however, are of the public good variety, where insufficient profit motive exists for firms to enter the market. In these cases, public sector entities have traditionally been relied upon to provide these services. Recent experience has suggested, though, that governments face increasing challenges for the effective provision of these services. A particular class of the public good problem concerns benefits that extend beyond national borders (e.g., clean air) but that require local investments for protection. National governments may be unwilling to provide resources for goods benefiting citizens beyond their borders (Teegen, 2002).

Given their inherently nonprofit focus, NGOs claim the moral high ground concerning their issue area(s), often leading to seemingly intractable conflict versus private sector "profiteers," who put shareholder wealth above other considerations. That is not to say that market-based incentives do not function well for NGOs. NGO reliance on an internationally recognized accreditation system, such as in the forest-products industry (Domask), on the creation of a global carbon credits trading mechanism (Teegen; Adams), and in official recognition and labeling of fairly traded products such as coffee (Parker), demonstrate how the third sector embraces market mechanisms to promote and advance its interests. The growing use of market mechanisms by NGOs is consistent with economic liberalization efforts globally (Deslauriers & Kotschwar; Domask). So, although NGOs are not motivated by profits per se, they, like their private sector counterparts, can use the market to help to achieve their goals.

Since NGOs can use the market in achieving their goals yet pursue the fulfillment of public-good type goals, they may be well positioned for identifying ways to align incentives between public sector and private sector organizations (Teegen; Parker; Soule; Adams). In this way, these organizations may improve the efficiency of transactions globally through their sector's natural "in-between" status.

NGOs are not subject to the same degree of accountability as private sector firms or even public sector entities. Although they ultimately must answer to their donors or members, few legal requirements exist to constrain their activities (other than use of funds for nonprofit purposes), and few checks exist to require their claims' validity (Soule; Keim; Parker). Furthermore, there are almost no watchdog groups to monitor or keep in check the activities of NGOs. Occasionally the media uncover stories of corruption, misuse of funds, or false claims by NGOs; but compared to governments and private sector firms, nonprofit NGOs are left to operate without much institutional oversight. Although some high profile cases exist (such as public outrage upon discovery of the American Red Cross's planned use of funds donated for September 11 disaster relief for other program requirements [Strom, 2002]), there is little retribution for NGO ineptness or irresponsibility in a manner analogous to market or political disciplines exerted on the private or public sectors (Soule; Parker).

Gauging NGO performance has presented a particular difficulty. Obtuse or questionable measures such as individuals "touched" by an NGO program or species "saved" provide little information to potential donors or partnering organizations (Parker). Financial measures capturing notions such as proportion of donated funds used for administration, future fundraising, or operations, try to impose private sector–like performance standards to measure the operating efficiencies and strategic purpose of NGOs. Even these "objective" measures are subject to significant manipulation. Like their public sector counterparts, which ultimately are subject to the whims of voters in democratic societies, and not unlike their private sector counterparts, which continue to seek investment funds from outside the firm, NGOs must continually acquire donated funds (or create market-driven revenue sources for sustaining programs internally). Those funding sources provide the ultimate accountability insurance for NGOs.

NGOs are third sector participants that share important values, incentives, and interests with both the private sector firms and the public sector governmental entities that they engage. Yet we have shown them to be unique organizations in terms of values, incentives, use of market mechanisms, accountability and retribution, and performance measures. We now turn our attention to a discussion of how NGOs work and interact within society.

How Do NGOs Operate in a Global Economy?

This book has demonstrated a wide range of ways for NGOs to organize, mobilize, and operate. In particular, we note that NGOs leverage their attachment to single or similar issues to engage other organizations: public, private, and not-for-profit. A primary tool used is prowess in communication. This prowess includes two elements: the message crafted and the modes of communication employed. Finally, we see NGOs using data and information in novel ways to promote their interests, and in so doing, to help society at large as well as counterparts in the public and private sectors.

NGOs tend to organize around single issues (or a grouping of tightly linked multiple issues). Thus, the World Wide Fund for Nature and the Nature Conservancy are known for environmental protection (Doh, Newburry, & Teegen; Teegen); Save the Children is known for promoting the interests of children (Parker), and the Forest Stewardship Council promotes protection and sustainability of forests (Domask). As Keim notes, NGOs can be effective advocates for issues at key places along an issue's lifecycle. NGOs can serve in a catalytic role in focusing initial attention on an issue, or can "keep an issue alive" and maintain attention when the profile would have otherwise dissipated. The simplicity of a single or narrowly constrained set of issues gives an NGO credibility and eases the creation and presentation of relevant message content (Soule). Firms and governments do not enjoy similar luxuries. They are invariably faced with myriad interests that they pursue (as captured by the influence of various stakeholders on managerial decision making and "logrolling" and other political maneuvering to attempt to satisfy varied constituents' interests). The case of AES is instructive. As a publicly traded firm committed to social welfare, the firm is in a daily struggle to craft strategies that reconcile what at times may represent seemingly incompatible issues: profits and social welfare. The firm's management must expend resources across a much more diverse set of issues than an NGO counterpart (Adams).

Both advocacy and operationally oriented NGOs (Parker) must communicate effectively to achieve their goals. One important NGO contribution is the apparent role of NGOs in engaging broader groups in major public policy issues, thus countering traditions of public apathy or disengagement from issues that affect them (Deslauriers & Kotschwar). Given their "purity" of intent and single-issue focus, NGOs can readily frame messages in popular terms to engage citizens and mobilize support (Parker; Soule; Teegen). Due to limitations on accountability of NGOs, though, this framing often comes in the form of posturing that may be unverified, distorted, exaggerated, or false (Soule; Keim).

The advent of cheap and instant communications afforded through the global spread of Web-based communication modes has drastically altered the ways in which NGOs can operate. Global mobilization of support and dissemination of information is now possible without the great investments in technology, long-distance fees, travel, and so on that were required to support similar levels of outreach in the past (Keim; Deslauriers, & Kotschwar). NGOs have become so effective at getting the word out about issues, and in particular about the actions of private sector firms, that firms find joining these organizations for access to up-to-date information to be a critical component of business intelligence (Keim). Public opinion is increasingly shaped by the efforts of NGO communications, potentially to the benefit of governments and firms, but often to their detriment (Parker; Doh).

NGOs' successes in communication have created a special function for NGOs in society, that of data mediator and information broker (Parker; Domask). By joining the ranks of an NGO, an individual (or firm, or public agency) wishing to become engaged in an issue can reduce the cost of accessing information that is relevant to their purposes (Keim). For an individual working alone to tap into the myriad streams of relevant information is difficult at best, but membership in informational networks facilitated by NGOs allows quick and inexpensive access for individuals (Doh, Newburry, & Teegen). NGOs also enter the global decision-making fray by leveraging technical expertise and membership clout, leverage that gains them access to important decision-making institutions and fora. The filing of amicus briefs for global trading regime deliberations is one example of information brokering facilitated by NGOs (Deslauriers & Kotschwar). Given their "in-between" character, NGOs can also perform important data mediation roles between disputants in the private and public sectors (Teegen). In this capacity the NGO uses its knowledge and expertise in promoting the public interest (along the narrow confines of its particular issues) to gain the trust and understanding of public sector organizations, and subsequently in utilizing market mechanisms to more efficiently and effectively allocate and employ scarce resources to gain the trust and understanding of private sector organizations. By working closely with entities from the other two sectors, NGOs can perform critical bridging functions between the sectors (Teegen; Doh).

NGOs do their work on single or closely aligned multiple issues by effectively communicating messages through framing, posturing, and utilization of Internet communications to mobilize support for their issues. In the following section we discuss how NGOs fit within their operating context, as and with institutions outside the formal institutional framework, through political bargaining and negotiation.

How Do NGOs Fit within Societies?

As third sector organizations, joining the ranks of private sector firms and public sector governmental organizations, NGOs can be considered legitimate institutions in their own right. Following seminal work by North (1991, 1994), Keim notes that organizations are themselves important institutions alongside formal and informal societal institutions. Keim notes the incorporation of NGOs into policy making in some countries through required umbrella-group participation in political processes. Even where such participation is not legislated, NGOs are seen to influence party agendas through political support they give to candidates (Keim). Deslauriers and Kotschwar describe the formal role for NGOs as information-providing institutions in trade deliberations. Domask describes the creation of a new institution for governing forestry products and standards composed of NGOs in conjunction with private sector and public sector interests. In these ways NGOs can use their status as institutional insiders to play important policy roles and to gain access to resources that can facilitate the achievement of their goals.

The protests common at global policy gatherings such as the World Economic Forum and the WTO negotiation sessions exemplify NGOs that choose not to become institutions per se, but rather to take advantage of outsider status to promote their purposes. These outsiders are likely banking on their "antiestablishment" credentials to win public support (opinions and financial support). All NGOs utilize their potential independence as a credibility-enhancing mechanism. Given recent scandals and accountability challenges in the private and public sectors, such a role may be particularly important to the viability of NGOs in the future. However, NGOs are increasingly gaining status as organizational institutions whose contributions are inextricably linked to public and private organizational processes, as opposed to "outsiders" providing alternatives to those processes (Doh & Teegen, 2002). Recent trends would seem to indicate that NGOs are increasingly operating as institutional "insiders" in both their advocacy and operation roles (Deslauriers & Kotschwar) as they interact with private sector and public sector counterparts. Taken to its extreme, NGOs may supplant the efforts of governments (Parker; Doh; Domask). This role can result from the emergence of NGOs as viable alternatives to public sector service provision, but also a result of the outsourcing behavior of governments, which increasingly view NGOs as a viable service-delivery option that is more connected to the civil societal groups that represent those receiving such services (Parker).

NGOs compete among themselves. One way in which this competition has manifested is the process of setting various types of standards (Teegen; Parker). By creating standards that are adopted by others, NGOs take on an important institutional role. Here, the Forest Stewardship Council is instructive (Domask): Competing accreditation organizations exist, but the FSC appears to have jumped way out ahead in the standards game in forestry products and management practices. While competition from the emergence of other standards systems is threatening in some ways, it is ultimately a positive trend in that weaker, industry-set standards and requirements are better than a complete lack of standards that used to exist prior to the FSC.

As Doh notes in the first chapter in this volume, NGOs are clearly changing the traditional business–government bargaining relationship. For instance, international NGOs are emerging as an increasingly viable counterpoint to the activities of multinational corporations and intergovernmental organizations (IGOs). The nature of international NGO pressure is a powerful force in corporate policy and governance. NGOs have become increasingly active in pursuing boycotts, developing public-relations initiatives, and sponsoring shareholder resolutions in order to press for changes in corporate behavior. Recently, Friends of the Earth (FOE) sponsored a resolution at the May 30, 2001, Exxon Mobil shareholder meeting that would require the company to move away from fossil fuels toward clean energy, one of hundreds of such resolutions organized by NGOs during 2001 ("Firm Resolutions," 2001). Although most of these proposals are unlikely to win significant support in the short term, such shareholder activism, bolstered by public relations and broader advocacy, will have an increasingly powerful impact on MNCs, especially those involved in politically and socially sensitive industries.

Parker describes how governments often set nonnegotiable performance requirements on funds allocated to operational NGOs involved in poverty-relief issues. Soule shows how ineffective negotiation with one NGO—Greenpeace—created potentially devastating results in the consideration of Monsanto's regulatory petitions. We described earlier the insider role given to many NGOs today in global deliberations. Given their operational and technical expertise, access to unique resources, effectiveness in communication, and perceived legitimacy in citizens' minds, private sector and public sector interests are increasingly realizing that negotiating with

NGOs is imperative: Treat them as stakeholders and they can become stakegivers (Adams); ignore them as stakeholders and run the risk of their becoming dangerous staketakers (Soule). By linking private sector and public sector interests, they can become instrumental in forging self-sustaining negotiated settlements, creating value for all concerned (Teegen).

NGOs work in society as institutions in their own right and through negotiation with other institutional actors to achieve their interests. Their success in working in society depends to a great extent on their ability to influence others in their environments, which we address next.

How Do NGOs Influence Other Organizations?

In the chapter by Doh, Newburry, and Teegen, special attention is paid to how NGOs use the rules of influence to network successfully with other NGOs, including leveraging reciprocity and affinities and liking among individuals and organizations. Perceived moral high ground, discussed earlier, also lets NGOs influence others who do not enjoy that status. By recognizing these influential methods, NGOs can become powerful in achieving their goals.

The resource-based view of the firm (Barney, 1991) can be extended readily to apply to NGOs. According to this view, those organizations that have access to valuable, rare, or inimitable resources will be successful over time. Although NGOs possess varied resources that can afford them this success, the resource of identity, akin to the branding concept in the private sector, is one that has been shown to be particularly powerful in propelling NGOs ahead (Parker). Another important resource used by NGOs is that of size, enabling the larger NGOs to more readily access relevant constituencies and to present a more formidable force to potential opposition (Keim; Domask). When an NGO sets the standard for practice in an issue area due to esteemed identity, size, or other valuable resources, other NGOs, firms, governments, and citizens may become dependent upon the NGO to provide the service. This works to the advantage of the standard-setting NGO, but potentially at the cost of lack of choice and stale responses to societal needs.

In terms of network benefits, a given NGO's position within a network or degree of centrality (closeness to others in the network) will allow that NGO to be influential (Doh, Newburry, & Teegen). By filling structural holes (Burt, 1997), the NGO can provide valuable linkages between otherwise separated entities and gain value for itself in the role of broker (Teegen; Doh, Newburry, & Teegen). In this way

NGOs can mediate or moderate the relationships between others to their advantage (Doh).

NGOs influence others, relying on valuable resources and leveraging network effects. Their influence is particularly germane in several areas that the authors in this volume have identified: jurisdictional, geographical, and development issues, and the inclusion of various stakeholders relevant to NGO issue contexts, which we address next.

NGOs, GLOBALIZATION, AND THE FUTURE: A RESEARCH AND PRACTICE AGENDA

In this section we offer some final observations regarding the contribution of this volume to research and practice related to NGOs. We first identify some concerns that are (and are not) addressed by our discussion of NGOs, and then describe just a few of the many remaining questions we suggest for future research efforts and practice agendas.

Concerns Addressed (and Not Addressed) by NGOs

Public sector organizations have well-bounded constituencies. Such constituencies are clearly defined by national, state, or municipal boundaries and contain those citizens to whom the organizations must provide for and answer to. Private sector organizations are not similarly constrained, although for practical purposes most firms operating across the globe have areas or regions within which they concentrate their activities. NGOs may have similar concentrations in terms of activities (perhaps because of their issue context definition) or donor members, but they are not otherwise constrained by geographic borders. As argued previously, many issues relevant to NGOs are global issues, such as disease prevention, poverty relief, clean air, and the like. NGOs can use their significant experience in local venues (Parker) or partner with other NGOs with that experience (Teegen) to be effective players on the ground, but they also can leverage their global scope, when relevant, to advocate and access widely dispersed resources. For public goods that transcend national boundaries, NGOs may be the best organizations/institutions for addressing those pressing needs (Teegen).

Keim notes that the supranational experience of many NGOs positions them well for involvement in multilateral negotiations, a role specifically described by Deslauriers and Kotschwar. International NGOs will increasingly shape the terms of global trade regimes. NGOs were largely responsible for the defeat of the Multilateral Agreement on Investment. More recently, NGOs have challenged the efficacy of trade-related intellectual property protection within the Uruguay Round of trade negotiations, the so-called TRIPS agreement. In May 2000, five of the world's largest pharmaceutical companies agreed to slash prices on HIV drugs for people living in certain poor nations in response to widespread, officially sanctioned counterfeiting and public outrage as voiced through the work of influential NGOs such as Doctors Without Borders, which decried the human rights impact of denying such treatments (Waldholz, 2000). While most would agree that this new pricing policy is appropriate and necessary, it could set a precedent for companies to reduce prices on other drugs (or high-demand proprietary technology) or face government-sanctioned or NGO-promoted patent infringement, forcing the multilateral trading community to reconsider basic assumptions about trade law and intellectual property rights enforcement.

North–South issues concerning the debates over inequities between the industrialized and developing worlds are most often taken up by NGOs globally (Deslauriers & Kotschwar; Teegen). Given their resource base and communication skills, NGOs have become effective advocates for developing-nation citizens and their interests in global venues. In this way, NGOs actually ensure that otherwise "missed" stakeholders are given a voice in matters affecting them locally, regionally, nationally, or globally (Adams). NGOs are effectively changing the game for firms and businesses by bringing more viable parties into the negotiation fray (Teegen), inclusions that can produce benefits as well as harm for private sector and public sector parties (Soule).

NGOs in the Future: Remaining Questions

We are pleased with the answers that the contributors to this volume have provided in answer to the NGO challenge. Some questions remain, and these we leave for future work by the growing group of scholars and practitioners who have recognized the importance of NGOs in society.

One issue that faces private sector firms and public sector organizations concerns how to identify which NGOs matter; that is, which are true stakeholders or able to present viable partnering options to firms and governments. Given the difficulties identified with measuring NGO performance, identifying and selecting appropriate NGOs reduces to reliance on less-than-perfect measures of quality, such as size. A more fully developed effort to operationalize stakeholder management practice in a manner to measure and value NGO efficacy could help guide this valuation. Significant work remains on creating valuable and actionable performance measures for NGOs, an activity that NGOs themselves should be, and are, embracing. Like private sector firms that disclose information to potential investors in exchange for invested funds, so too can NGOs expect to reap rewards from greater transparency and meaning in performance reporting.

A related question is how firms and governments should best engage NGOs. NGO independence from these sectors seems critical for NGOs to retain their perceived high ground; avoiding cooptation is key to effectiveness. A diverse array of partnering arrangements with long-term consequences for all involved have been undertaken by NGOs, including cobranding, technical training exchanges, sharing membership lists, and so on. With time and systematic examination, we will begin to understand the most effective ways for governments and firms to work with NGOs and for NGOs to work among themselves in achieving their objectives.

By understanding models for successful interaction across the sectors and within the third sector, we will begin to be more conclusive about the future shape of political economy. Will the third sector ultimately replace significant portions of either the private sector and/or the public sector? Is there a natural evolution in NGO involvement in society that may wax and wane over time? If so, what precipitates the inflection points in NGO involvement and impact?

Finally, the lingering and pressing concerns presented by the tension between local and global issues advancement is a central concern that will in many ways define the future trajectory of NGOs. In many nations, global considerations take a back seat to more politically salient and palatable local issues. Bridging this gulf is one challenge for which NGOs appear to be ideally suited. How might NGOs play a more definitive role in global political economy, particularly in terms of supranational issues that private sector and (national) public sector interests have seemingly failed to address?

We are grateful to our contributors for sharing their extensive knowledge and experience working within and with NGOs. We hope that upon reading this volume you recognize the challenges posed by NGOs and are better equipped as practitioners and researchers to integrate NGOs into your thinking and practice.

REFERENCES

Barney, J. (1991). Firm resources and sustained competitive advantage. *Journal of Management, 17*, 99–120.

Burt, R S. (1997). The contingent values of social capital. *Administrative Science Quarterly, 42*, 339–365.

Doh, J., & Teegen, H. (2002). Nongovernmental organizations as institutional actors in international business: Theory and implications. *International Business Review, 11*, 665–684.

Firm resolutions. (2001, May 12). *The Economist*, p. 64.

Freeman, R. E. (1984). *Strategic management: A stakeholder approach.* Boston: Pittman.

North, D. (1991). *Institutions, institutional change and economic performance.* Cambridge: Cambridge University Press.

North, D. (1994). Economic performance through time. *American Economic Review, 84*, 359–368.

Strum, S. (2002, June 23). Families fret as charities hold a bilion dollars in 9/11 aid. *New York Times*, p. 29.

Teegen, H. (2002, March 23). *NGOs as global institutions: Their impact on MNEs and governments.* Presentation to the third annual International Business Research Forum, Institute for Global Management Studies, Temple University, Philadelphia, PA.

Waldholz, M. (2000, May 11). Makers of AIDS drugs agree to slash prices in Third World. *Wall Street Journal*, p. 1.

Index

Accountability, NGOs, 98, 209, 212
"Activities Implemented Jointly"
   (AIJ), 111
Adams, Gregory, 61, 206
Advocacy NGOs (ANGOs), 85–87,
   101
Advocacy organizations and
   institutional settings, 23–25
AES global power company,
   corporate social responsibility,
   187–188, 213; AES–Granite
   Ridge in New Hampshire, 196–
   197; AES–NGO interaction, the
   balanced approach, 193–198;
   carbon offsets, 195–196; company background, 188–191;
   corporations, NGOs, and the
   future, 200; lessons learned,
   199–200; multilateral lending,
   197–198; NGOs and AES,
   realities and implications, 198–
   200; shared principles and
   empowerment, 188–191; social
   responsibility projects in action,
   191–193
Agency theory (principal–agent
   theory), 7–8

Agle, B. R., 5, 14
Agriculture (agricultural). *See*
   Genetically modified (GM) crops
Agroforestry, 196
Alba, Carlos, 60
Allegheny County, Maryland, 192–
   193
Alliances, 11, 12
Americans in Europe, GM crops,
   140–141. *See also* United States,
   GM crops
Antagonistic approach, deforesta-
   tion, 159–161
Appellate Body, 47
Arctic National Wildlife Refuge, 76
Argentina, 74
Arrogance, 92
Associations, United States, 1
Austrian (parliament, law), 160

Bakke, Dennis, 188
Bangladesh Garment Manufactur-
   ers Association, 100
Bargaining, 35. *See also* Clean
   Development Mechanism
BATNA (Best Alternative To a
   Negotiated Agreement), 114

Belize, 115, 117–118, 121, 122, 123, 124
Ben and Jerry's Ice Cream, 99
Bernhard, Prince of The Netherlands, 72
Beyer, Peter, 151
Biodiversity (biological diversity), 121, 158
Biodiversity Support Program (BSP), 76–77
Biotechnology. *See* Genetically modified (GM) crops
Blackhurst, Richard, 47
Blalock, H. M., 69–70
The Body Shop, 99
Boise Cascade, 180
Bolivia, 176
Bontempo, R. N., 136
Bovine somatotropin (BST, Posilac), 129, 130, 150–151
Boycotts, 6
Boycotts to global partnership, protecting the world's forests, 157–158; antagonistic approach, 159–161; business rationale after original buy-in, 181–182; changes in the global context, 165–168; continued challenges, 183–184; deforestation emerging as global crisis, 157, 158–159; deforestation and responses, early stages, 158–165; forest managers and owners, 180–181; Forest Stewardship Council (FSC), 168–171; FSC impacts and proliferation, 171–178; going beyond boycotts, 161–165; impact on governments, regulation, and enforcement, 175–176; improving forest management and promoting social interests, 174–175; NGO benefits and drawbacks, 182–183; proliferation of other certification systems, 177–178; roles and impact of NGOs in early stages, 159; stakeholders interests and rationales, and FSC, 179–184

Braithwaite, J., 83, 99–100
British. *See* Great Britain
Buchanan, James, 20
Burger King, 161
Business (model, approach, perspective), NGOs, 96–97
Business, Rio Bravo CDM project, 116–117
Business Coordinating Council (CCE), 60
Businesses, 91
Business–government interface, 1–2, 4–12
Business–government–NGO bargaining. *See* Clean Development Mechanism
Business–government relations and NGOs, the importance of institutions, 19–20, 25–27, 27–32, 32–33; collaborations and coalitions, 30–32; collective actions, 28–29; information acquisition, 20–21; institutional settings, NGO activities, and advocacy organizations, 23–25; issues advocacy and life cycles, 26–27, 28; national and supranational institutional settings, 30; organizational affiliations, 22–23; organized interests and public policy process, 20–23; political and legislative action, 29–30
Business Partners for Development, 83
Business rationale, FSC, 181–182
Business social responsibility, 98–102
Buzzard, Shirley, 91–92, 102
Byrne, David, 135

Canada, 43; consultation process, 57–58
Canada Gazette, 58
Canada–United States Free Trade Agreement (CUFTA), 57
Carbon credits (offsets), 111–112, 116, 125–126; AES, 195–196
Carbon dioxide (CO_2) emissions, 108–110, 111–112, 116, 195

Carbon sequestration, 195, 196
Carbon (forest) sinks, 109
CARE, 88
Catalysts of business social responsibility, 100
Certification, (certified) forest, 170–174, 175–176, 179, 181; other than FSC, 177–178, 184 n.1
Challenges, 89–98
Championing, 70
Chandler, A., 5
Charities, 191
Charles, D., 133, 138
Chemical, 8
Children, 88, 100, 191, 192
Chile, consultation process, 58–60
Chocolate Manufacturers Association, 87
Civil society, 35; accreditation, 51–53; Canada, 57; and WB, 49, 50
Clean Development Mechanism (CDM) projects, business–government–NGO bargaining, 107–108, 126; CDM, 111–113; critical roles of INGOs, 123–125; differences create joint value, 125–126; Kyoto Protocol, 107, 108–111, 116, 123; negotiation context, 108–113; negotiation framework, 113–115; negotiation result, 122–123; parties to negotiation, 115–122; Rio Bravo CDM project, 115–126
Clesa, 192
Climate change, 107, 108
Clinton, Bill, 24
Coalitions and collaborations, 30–32
Cognitive heuristic approach, 135–136
Collaboration with MNEs. *See* Multinational enterprises
Collaborations and coalitions, 30–32
Collective actions, 28–29
Commercialization, GM crops, 131–132
Committee of Government Representatives on the Participation of Civil Society, FTAA, 53–55

Communication(s), 38, 40, 213, 214
Competitions, NGOs, 216
Complexity theory, 14
Conservation Foundation (CF), 72, 73
Consultation processes (mechanisms), national practices, 56–60
Contingency model, NGO cooperation, 67–68
Coolants, 32
Cooperative strategies, 11, 12
Cooperative strategies, environmental NGOs (ENGOs), 65–67, 77–79; contingency model, 67–68; framework for understanding, 67–72; internal positioning cooperation, 68–70, 73–75; multiple front cooperation, 71–72, 76–77; outside champion cooperation, 70, 75; united front cooperation, 70–71, 76; WWF, 72–77
Coordinated Regulatory Framework for the Regulation of Biotechnology, 133–134
Coordinating Body of Foreign Trade Business Organizations (COECE), 60
Corporate commitments to FSC system, 171–174
Corporate Community Investment Services, 91–92
Corporate social responsibility. *See* AES
Corporate strategy and public policy, 1–2, 12–15; business–government interface, 4–12; emergence of NGOs, 2–5; future research directions, 13–15; interactive stakeholder roles, 8–10; rise of NGOs, 2–4

Daele, Wolfgang, van den, 138–139
Dairy production industry, 150–151
Dams, 74–75
Debt relief, 30
Deforestation. *See* Boycotts to global partnership

Department of Foreign Affairs and
International Trade (DFAIT), 57,
58
Deslauriers, Jacqueline, 82, 208,
215, 218
Developed and developing coun-
tries, 56
Developing nations, 110
Disputes, 39
Dispute-settlement mechanism, 47
Doh, Jonathan P., 5, 216, 217
Domask, Joseph, 28
Downs, Anthony, 20, 21
Drahos, P., 83, 99–100
Duchin, Ron, 138

Earth Island Institute, 8–9
Earth Summit, 164
Economy (economic), 118; and
forests, 165–167; and NGOs,
213–215
Education (projects), 191, 193
Edwards, M., 93, 94
Eisenhower, Dwight D., 73
El Salvador, 192
Electricity (power). *See* AES
Ely, R., 95
Emergence of NGOs and trade
negotiations, 41–42
Enforcement and FSC, 175–176
Englander, E. J., 5
Environmental (issues, protection,
degradation, etc.), 42, 48–49,
119, 121; and GM crops, 137–
138, 142. *See also* Boycotts to
global partnership
Environmental Defense Fund, 28
Environmental NGOs (ENGOs),
138, 142. *See also* Cooperative
strategies
Eugenics, 143
Europe, protecting forests, 160
European Union (EU), 25, 108;
GM crops, 140–141, 148, 150;
Monsanto, 137, 138; regulation,
132–135; risk assessment, 141–
142
Exxon Mobil, 216

Factions, 19
Fairness, 189
Farmers, organic, 149–150
Finance. *See* Global trade and
finance agenda
Financial pressures, 94–98
Firms, 210–211, 213, 220
Five-Point Plan to Save the World's
Water, 74–75
Food (markets), 143–146
Food and Agriculture Organization
(FAO), U. N., 159
Food industry, organic, 149–150
Ford Foundation, 75
Forest and trade networks (FTNs),
179
Forest certification, 170–174, 175–
176, 179, 181; other than FSC,
177–178, 184 n.1
"Forest enhancement," 195–196
Forests, 7, 28. *See also* Boycotts to
global partnership
Forest (carbon) sinks, 109
Forest Stewardship Council (FSC),
7, 207, 216. *See also* Boycotts to
global partnership
Formal institutions, 23, 23–24
Fowler, Alan, 89–90, 100
Frames, 135–136
Framing, 135–136; and gain–loss
(loss–gain) framing, 136; and
reframing, 146–152; and win–
loss framing, 146–147
Freeman, R. E., 204, 205
Free Trade Area of the Americas
(FTAA), 53–55, 56–57; Chile, 59
Friends of the Earth (FOE), 216
Fun (principle, goal), 189–190, 193
Funding, 91–92, 93–96

General Agreement on Tariffs and
Trade (GATT), 39, 45, 46, 160
Genetically modified (GM) crops,
129–130, 152–153; Americans in
Europe, 140–141; backdrop to
controversy, 130–136; commercialization of GM crops, 131–
132; controversy, framing and

reframing, 146–152; controversy, NGO aversion to GM technology, Monsanto 137–146; framing of disputes, theoretical underpinnings, 135–136; GM technology and risk assessment, 141–143; Monsanto and its entry into life sciences, 130–131; regulation and NGO involvement in Europe and the United States, 132–135; stakeholder management, 137–140; strategy options for Monsanto, 148–152; structure of food markets, 143–146

Genetically modified (GM) material, 9

Genome (genomic, genomics), 131, 143; rice, 151, 152

Gerber, 144–145

Germany, 24, 138, 160

Giunta, Ken, 92

Global and local issues, 220

Global climate change coalition, 12

Global Exchange, 86–87

Globalization and the future of NGO influence, 203–204; concerns addressed and not addressed, 218–219; how NGOs fit within societies, 215–217; how NGOs influence other organizations, 217–218; how NGOs operate in global economy, 213–215; NGOs as stakeholders, stakegivers, and staketakers, 204–206; remaining questions, 219–220; research and practice agenda, 218–220; what are NGOs, 206–208; why and how are NGOs different, 208–212

Global partnership. *See* Boycotts to global partnership

Global trade and finance agenda, after Seattle, 35–37, 61; Canada, 57–58; Chile, 58–60; changing face of trade policy, 37–42; consultation processes with NGOs, national practices, 56–60; empowerment of international NGO community, 40–41; FTAA, civil society, and transparency, 53–55; IMF, 50; insiders and outsiders, 43–44; institutional steps to accommodate NGO views, 44–55; MAI negotiations, 42–43, 44; Mexico, 60; multilateral financial institutions, 48; NGOs, trade, and the road to Seattle, 42–44; OAS, 51–53; World Bank, 48–50; WTO, 45–48

Global 2000, 75

Golden rice, 151

Government(s), 41, 209, 211, 213, 215–216, 220; and FSC, 175–176. *See also* Business–government interface; Business–government relations; Clean Development Mechanism project

Governmental funding, 94, 95–96

Graham, E. M., 43

Granite Ridge, 196–197

Great Britain (British), 29, 30

Greenhouse gases (gas emissions), 112

Greenpeace, 32, 138, 139–140, 144

Guatemala, 176, 196

Guidelines for the Participation of Civil Society Organizations in OAS Activities, 51–52

Härlin, Benedikt (Benny), 138

Havana Charter, ITO, 45

Herbicides, 131

Hierarchies, 208

Hillman, A., 4–5

Hitt, M. A., 5

HIV drugs, 219

Hoekman, B. M., 36–37

Holmer, Majia, 135–136

Home Depot, 28, 178, 180

Howe, Bill, 176

Hudon, Jean, 143

Hybrid NGOs (HNGOs), 87–89

Indonesia (Indonesian), 176, 177

Influence, 217, 218

Informal institutions, 23

Information (acquisition, sources)/ informed, 20–21, 22, 28–29, 214; framing, 136; GM technology, 147; IMF, 50

Insiders (and outsiders), 43–44, 215, 216

Institutional steps to accommodate NGO views, 44–55

Institutions (institutional), 215–216, 217. *See also* Business–government relations

Integrity, 189

InterAction, 92

Interests, 114

Internal positioning cooperation, 68–70, 73–75, 77

International Center for Trade and Sustainable Development (ICTSD), 46

International Chamber of Commerce, 45–46

International Federation of Inspection Agencies (IFIA), 45–46

International Monetary Fund (IMF), 48, 50

International NGO community, empowerment of, 40–41

International NGOs, 216

International NGOs (INGOs), CDM projects, 119–126

International NGO Training and Research Centre (INTRAC), 93

International organizations, 44

International Standards Organization ISO 14000 environmental systems certification, 184 n.1

International Trade Organization (ITO), 45, 46

International Tropical Timber Organization (ITTO), 162, 163

International Union for Conservation of Nature and Natural Resources (IUCN), 72, 73

Internet, 21, 22, 27, 28; Canada, 57

Investor firm government, 119

Investors, 210

Irtish Power, 191

Isolation effect, 147–148

Issue development, 136

Issues (advocacy, life cycles), 26–27, 28, 213; local and global, 220

Kaufman, A. M., 5

Kazakstan, 191

Keim, Gerald, 207, 207–208, 215, 218

Kenya Agricultural Research Institute (KARI), 152

Kobrin, S. J., 82

Korzeniewicz, P. R., 36, 43

Kostecki, M. M., 36–37

Kostova, T., 14

Kotschwar, Barbara, 82, 208, 215, 218

Kyoto Protocol, 107, 108–111, 116, 123, 195

Lal Pir, 192

Lambrecht, B., 144

Larsen, Fleming, 50

Legislative and political action, 29–30

Liew, J., 139, 143

Life sciences, 129, 130–131

Liking, 69–70

Local and global issues, 220

Local environmental NGOs (LNGOs), 120, 121–122, 124

Local government, Rio Bravo CDM project, 117–118

Londonderry, New Hampshire, 196–197

Macroeconomic policies, 166–167

Mad cow disease, 147

Madison, James, 19

Malaysian National Timber Certification Council (MTCC), 177

Management, forest, FSC, 174–175

Managers and owners, forests, 180–181

Marcus, A. A., 5

Marine Mammal Protection Act, 42

Market(s), 210, 211

Market failure, 210

Martens, Klaas, 149

Maryland, 192–193
McDonald's, 7, 144
McHugen, A., 133
Mechanisms, 35–36, 39; consulting, 56–57. *See also* Clean Development Mechanism
Mecklenburg, Sue, 100
Media, 26, 27
Melchett, Lord, 139–140
Memorandum of understanding (MOU), WWF, 73
Mexico, 42; consultation process, 60
Meznar, M., 5
Milk, 150–151
Mitchell, R. K., 5, 14
Mitsubishi, 160, 161
Monocultural organizations, 95
Monolithicism (monolithic), 207
Monsanto, 9. *See also* Genetically modified (GM) crops
Moral high ground, 91, 211
Multilateral Agreement on Investment (MAI), 42–43, 44
Multilateral development banks (MDBs), 162, 197–198
Multilateral financial institutions, 48
Multilateral negotiations (trading), 218–219
Multinational enterprises (MNEs), collaboration with, 81–83, 102–103; business social responsibility due to pressure, 101–102; catalysts of business social responsibility, 100; challenges faced by NGOs, 89–98; experience of collaboration, 98–102; experience of partnerships, 91–94; financial pressures, 94–98; NGO types, 83–89; socially responsible MNE, 98–100
Multiple front cooperation, 71–72, 76–77, 78
Myerson, D., 95

National and supranational institutional settings, 30

National Geographic, 75
National practices, consultation processes, 56–60
The Nature Conservancy (TNC), 119–121, 123–124, 125
Neale, M. A., 136
Negotiation. *See* Clean Development Mechanism
The Netherlands, 160
Network benefits, 217–218
Network theory, 10–11
Neural network theory, 14
Newburry, William E., 217
Newhall, Sarah, 88–89
NGOs, 206–208; how they are different from public and private sector, 208–212
Nigeria, 101
Nigh, D., 5
Nongreenhouse gas impacts, 113
North, 119, 169–170; North–South issues, 219
North, Douglas, 23
North American Free Trade Agreement (NAFTA), 42, 57; Mexico, 60
Northcraft, G. B., 136
Northern NGOs (NNGOs), 93–94
Novartis, 130–131, 140–141, 144–145

Odell, John, 41
Office of International Economic Relations (DIRECON), 59
Office of the United States Trade Representative (USTR), 56–57
Offsets. *See* Carbon credits
Olson, Mancur, 20, 21
Open Invitation to Civil Society, FTAA, 54
Operational NGOs (ONGOs), 84–85, 89, 90, 94, 95, 101–102, 103
Organic food industry (farmers), 149–150
Organizational affiliations, 22–23
Organization for Economic Cooperation and Development (OECD), 3, 43, 94

Organization of American States (OAS), 51–53, 208
Organizations, 23, 25; international, 44; monocultural, 95
Organized interests and public policy, 20–23
Ostry, Silvia, 37
Outside champion cooperation, 70, 75, 78
Outsiders and insiders, 43–44
Overconfidence, 147
Oxfam International, 88

Pact, 88–89
Pakistan, 192
"Paper campaign," 7
Parker, Rani, 205, 206, 216
Parliamentary systems, 32
Parties (party), political, 24, 29
Parties (party) in negotiation, 113–115; Rio Bravo CDM project, 115–126
Partnerships, 91–94
Pasquero, J., 140
Patents, biotech, Monsanto, 151
People, AES, 189
Performance (measures), NGOs, 212, 219–220
Permanent Council's Committee on Civil Society Participation in OAS Activities, 51, 52
Permanent Council's Special Committee on Inter-American Summit Management (CEGGI), OAS, 52–53
Pest (-protected, predation, etc.), 131, 133, 134
Pharmaceutical, 134
Philanthropic relationships, 96
Philip, Duke of Edinburgh, 72
Poland, 73–75
Political and legislative action, 29–30
Political decision makers, 20, 22
Political strategies (actions), 4–5
Poor countries, 45, 81
Posilac® (Bovine somatotropin or BST), 129, 130, 150–151

Potatoes, 144; sweet, 152
Potrykus, Ingo, 151
Power (electricity). *See* AES
Precautionary Principle, FSC, 174
Pressure (pressuring), 101–102, 159–161
Price, Tom, 31
Price Waterhouse Coopers, 87
Principal–agent theory (agency theory), 7–8
Principles, AES, 188–191
Private sector, 206, 209, 210–211, 212, 218; in conjunction with (partnering) NGOs, 215, 216–217, 219–220; global economy, 213, 214
Profit and values, 190
Programme for Belize (PfB), 121
Protected areas (lands), 164
Public goods, 210, 211
Publicity, 31
Public policy, 19, 20–23, 24–25, 26, 30; and trade, 39. *See also* Corporate strategy and public policy
Public sector, 209–210, 211, 211–212; in conjunction with (partnering) NGOs, 215, 216–217, 219–220; constituencies, 218; global economy, 213, 214
Putnam, Linda, 135–136

Rainforest Action Network (RAN), 160–161, 180
Reciprocity, 69, 70
Reframing and framing, 146–152
Regulation: and FSC, 175–176; GM crops, 132–135
Relative valences, 114
Resource(s), 72, 95, 118, 217
Resource-based view, 217
"Responsible Care" Initiative, 8
Retailers, forest certification, 179–189
Rice (genome), 151, 152
Rich countries, 45, 81
Rifkin, Jeremy, 138
Rio Bravo CDM project, 115–126

Risk assessment (risks), GM technology, 141–143, 143–144
Rowley, T. J., 13
Royal Dutch Shell, 29
Rule of liking, 69–70
Rules of influence, 217

Sanders, Bernard, 29
San Jose Ministerial, 53
Santiago Summit of the Americas, 51
Save the Children, 88
Schools, 192–193
Scorecard.org, 28
Seattle. *See* Global trade
Sen, G., 93, 94
Shapiro, Robert, 130, 133
Shareholder(s), 210, 216
Shell in Ogoniland, Nigeria, 101
Shrimp–turtle case, 47
Sinks (carbon, forest), 109
Smith, Benjamin, 31
Smith, W. C., 36, 43
Social interests, FSC, 174–175
Social responsibility, 98–102. *See also* AES
Soule, Edward, 9, 205, 206, 207, 216
South, 119, 170; South–North issues, 219
South Africa, 6
Southern NGOs (SNGOs), 93–95
Soybeans, 141, 149, 150, 151
Stakegivers, 204–206, 217
Stakeholder analysis, 204
Stakeholder interests and rationales, forest certification, 179–184
Stakeholder management, Monsanto, 137–140
Stakeholders, 8–10; AES, 193–194; NGOs as, 204–206, 217, 219
Stakeholder theory, 5–6, 10, 13, 14
Staketakers, 204–206, 217
Standing Committee on Foreign Affairs and International Trade (SCFAIT), 58
Starbucks Coffee Company, 88, 100
"Still Waiting for Nike to Do It," 86–87

Strategy options, Monsanto, 148–152
Structure of food markets, 143–146
Substantial equivalence test (standard), 134
Summit of the Americas (process), 51, 52, 57, 58
Supplementarity, 109, 112
Supranational and national institutional settings, 30
Sustainable forest management (forestry), 163, 183
Sweet potatoes, 152
Symposia, WTO, 48

Technology, 118, 129, 148–149; and trade, 38. *See also* Biotechnology
Teegen, Hildy, 8, 217
Third sector, 212, 215, 220
Timber, 168, 178, 179
Tobacco, 8
Tocqueville, Alexis, de, 1
Toronto Ministerial, 54
Trade (trading), 218–219. *See also* Global trade and finance agenda
Transparency: NGOs, 93–94, 97; WB, 50
Transportation, 38
Trees, 195
Tropical (forests, countries, timber, etc.), 158–163, 165, 168
Tropical Forestry Action Plan (TFAP), 162
Trust, 11
Tullock, Gordon, 20
Tuna–dolphin case, 42
Turcotte, M.-F., 140
Types of NGOs, 83–89

Umbrella associations (organizations, groups), 25, 30
United front cooperation, 70–71, 76, 78
United Nations, 25, 44, 91
United States, 209; associations, 1; CDM projects, 116, 117, 119; GM crops, 132–135, 141–143, 148;

United States (*continued*)
parties, 24; political and legislative action, 29; protecting forests, 160, 171, 178; tuna–dolphin case, 42; utilities, 116; voters, 21. *See also* Americans

U.N. Framework Convention on Climate Change (UNFCCC), 107, 108, 109, 111

U.N. Food and Agriculture Organization (FAO), 159

Uruguay Round, 39, 45, 46

U.S. Agency for International Development (USAID), 76

U.S. government, 123; shrimp–turtle case, 47

Utting, P., 91

Values and profit, 190

Vega, Gustavo, 60

Verschuren, Annette, 178

Virus resistance, 152

Vistula river, 73, 75

Vitamin-A deficiencies (VAD), 151

von Wartburg, W., 139, 143

Voters, 21

Warrior Run, 192–193

Washington, George, 25

Water, 74–75

Web page: economic secretariat,

Mexico, 60; FTAA, 55; USTR, 56–57

Web site, 28; DFAIT, 57, 58; DIRECON, 59, 60; WTO, 47–48

Wloclawek Dam technical expert team, 73–75

Wood (products), 178, 179. *See also* Tropical

Wood, D. J., 5, 14

World Bank, 10, 48–50, 83; and forests, 162, 163, 166

World Bank/WWF Forest Alliance, 182

World Health Organization (WHO), 151

World Resources Institute (WRI), 162, 195–196

World Trade Organization (WTO), 10, 25, 39; and Canada, 57–58; environmental issues, 42; Marrakech to battle in Seattle and beyond, 45–48; symposia, 48; Web site, 47–48

World Wide Fund for Nature/World Wildlife Fund (WWF), 66, 72–77; Pakistan, 192; protecting forests, 168, 179, 182–183

Yeager, Brooks, 76

Zaheer, S., 14

About the Editors and Contributors

Gregory Adams is a project manager at AES Corporation.

Jacqueline Deslauriers is a senior summit specialist at the Organization of American States.

Jonathan P. Doh is assistant professor of management at Villanova University, senior associate at the Center for Strategic and International Studies, and member of the executive faculty at GSBA–Zurich. He is also associate director of Villanova's Center for Responsible Leadership and Governance. Previously, he was on the faculty of American University and Georgetown University. From 1991 to 1995 he served as an international economist and trade official with the U.S. Department of Commerce, first as director for trade policy in the Office of Canada and later as director of the NAFTA Affairs Division during the implementation of the North American Free Trade Agreement. He has published extensively on international economics, global strategy, and business–government relations and has served as a consultant to corporations and governments.

Joseph Domask is assistant professor of international environment and development at American University. He previously worked for the World Wildlife Fund.

Gerald Keim is professor of management at Arizona State University and a government relations consultant. He was previously on the faculties of the Richard Ivey School at the University of Western Ontario and Texas A&M University.

Barbara Kotschwar is senior trade specialist at the Organization of American States and adjunct professor in the Center for Latin American Studies at Georgetown University.

William E. Newburry is assistant professor of international business and business environment at Rutgers University.

A. Rani Parker is a doctoral student in public administration and international business at the George Washington University. Previously, she was with Save the Children.

Jone L. Pearce is interim dean and professor of organization and strategy in the Graduate School of Management, University of California, Irvine. She is also the president of the Academy of Management. Her most recent book is *Organization and Management in the Embrace of Government.*

Edward Soule is assistant professor of management at the McDonough School of Business, Georgetown University. He is a CPA and was previously a senior executive in the financial services industry.

Hildy Teegen is associate professor of international business and international affairs at the George Washington University in Washington, D.C. Previously, she was on the faculty of the College of William and Mary. She participates in executive-training programs on international business and international negotiation sponsored by the University of Texas, Duke University, the Center for Strategic and International Studies, and several prominent universities in Latin America. She has published widely in the areas of cross-border alliances, international negotiations, and international exporting and investment strategy. She received the Governor's Export Award from the state of Virginia for her work assisting small business exporters in that state.